"I Sing for I Cannot Be Silent"

※ ※

Pittsburgh Series in Composition, Literacy, and Culture

David Bartholomae & Jean Ferguson Carr, Editors

"I Sing for I Cannot Be Silent"

The Feminization of American Hymnody,

1870–1920

June Hadden Hobbs

University of Pittsburgh Press

Published by the University of Pittsburgh Press, Pittsburgh, Pa. 15261

10 9 8 7 6 5 4 3 2 1

LIBRARY OF CONGRESS CATALOGING-IN-PUBLICATION DATA

Hobbs, June Hadden, 1948–

   I sing for I cannot be silent : the feminization of American hymnody, 1870–1920 / June Hadden Hobbs.

      p.   cm. — (Pittsburgh series in composition, literacy, and culture)

   Includes bibliographical references and index.

   ISBN 0-8229-3990-8 (alk. paper). — ISBN 0-8229-5638-1 (pbk. : alk. paper)

   1. Hymns, English—United States—History and criticism.

2. Women hymn writers—United States—History—19th century.

3. Women hymn writers—United States—History—20th century.

4. United States—Church history—19th century.   5. United States—Church history—20th century.   I. Title.   II. Series.

BV313.H63   1997

264'.23'0820973—dc21   97-4809

                                        CIP

A CIP catalog record for this book is available from the British Library.

Chapter 3 was first published as "His Religion and Hers in Nineteenth-Century Hymnody," in *Nineteenth-Century Women Learn to Write,* ed. Catherine Hobbs (Charlottesville: University Press of Virginia, 1995). Reprinted by permission of the University Press of Virginia.

This book is dedicated with love to my children:

Kevin Lee Hobbs, Nathaniel Patrick Hobbs, and

Valerie Hadden Hobbs

Contents

Acknowledgments

The book of Hebrews pictures life as a race surrounded by a "great . . . cloud of witnesses." Writing this book would have been impossible without the heartening company of those who cheered me on. I have especially felt the warm presence of the female hymnists whose work I analyzed; I began many writing sessions by invoking the memory of Fanny Crosby, who wrote her first hymn at forty-four, the age at which I began writing what became this book. My title, *"I Sing for I Cannot Be Silent,"* is a line from her hymn "Redeemed."

I also thank those faithful friends and counselors who guided, edited, and encouraged my writing. Joyce Zonana first challenged me to write about hymns in a feminist theory class at the University of Oklahoma. Catherine Hobbs invited me to present that preliminary study as part of a panel at the 1991 Conference on College Communications and Composition and then asked me to revise it for inclusion in *Nineteenth-Century Women Learn to Write*. That essay became the third chapter of this book; it is reprinted here with the kind permission of the University Press of Virginia. David Mair, Gwenn Davis, Lawrence Frank, Henry McDonald, and Judy Lewis generously shared their expertise while I was at the University of Oklahoma. Jean Ferguson Carr, Catherine Marshall, and others at the University of Pittsburgh Press have offered wise counsel and encouragement.

I am deeply grateful to many others for help of various kinds. Judith Drummond, Vicki Roberts, Terry Taylor, Jeanne Rogers, and Susan Cessna loaned and gave me hymnals and other materials I could not have found otherwise. Mary Zimmer helped sharpen my insights about female spirituality, and Scott LaMascus taught me about the Church of Christ tradition. Steve Hobbs and Ted

Vaughan helped with the technical aspects of producing my manuscript. Thoreau scholar Suzanne Rose and I have spent hundreds of hours in conversation about American literature, and her insights and support have been indispensable. She even loaned me her personal copy of *Walden*. Eileen Spears, Donna Shelton, Bobbie Thomason, Mary Ramsey, and my dear colleagues at Gardner-Webb University have been in the forefront of those cheering me on.

A special thanks is due to Nicholas Howe. Many of the ideas in this book came into focus during classes and conversations with him. He has guided my reading, edited my writing with a superb ear for language, and proven himself a true and faithful Barnabas. I am especially grateful for his wise and perceptive insights about a cultural community that must, at times, have seemed very alien to him.

My most basic debt of gratitude is to my parents, Robert G. and Mary L. Hadden, who raised me in a community of singing people. I also thank Dan Hobbs for scholarly conversation and Betty Hobbs for feeding me. Finally, I thank Kevin, Nathan, and Valerie Hobbs, who put up with a lot. Their love and belief in me have been sustaining.

"I Sing for I Cannot Be Silent"

Words and Women in
the Evangelical Community

"Let me make the hymns of the people, and I care not who makes their creeds."
—PIERRE JEAN DE BÉRANGER

"Something in its favor . . . is the influence that every ritualized faith has with women. . . . Women must have form. They don't care for freedom."
—WILLIAM DEAN HOWELLS, *Indian Summer*, 1886

The Invented Tradition of Gospel Hymns

Looking back at her southern childhood in the early decades of the twentieth century, Eudora Welty describes what it was like to grow up in "a religious-minded society." Many of her memories organize themselves around hymns: her mother singing Fanny Crosby's "Blessed Assurance" as she washed the dishes, the evangelist Gypsy Smith luring sinners to the altar with Will Thompson's "Softly and Tenderly Jesus Is Calling," and children belting out gospel songs in the Methodist Episcopal Sunday school (55, 34–36). Welty pokes gentle fun at the hymns she learned in Sunday school, but she notes with approval their venerability:

> Those favorite Methodist hymns all sounded happy and pleased with the world, even though the words ran quite the other way. "Throw out the lifeline! Throw out the lifeline! Someone is sinking today!" went to a cheering tune. "I was sinking deep in sin, Far from the peaceful

shore, Very deeply stained within, Sinking to rise no more" made you want to dance, and the chorus—"Love lifted me! Love lifted me! When nothing else would help, Love lifted me!" would send you leaping. Those hymns set your feet moving like the march played on the piano for us to enter Davis School—"Dorothy, an Old English Dance" was the name of that, and of course so many of the Protestant hymns reached down to us from the same place; they *were* old English rounds and dance tunes, and Charles Wesley and the rest had—no wonder—taken them over. (34–35)

Welty's memories illustrate the importance of hymns in a community where children learn to sing them before they can read them. And although Welty describes herself as someone whose "reverence . . . for the holiness of life is not ever likely to be entirely at home in organized religion" (36–37), remembering hymns allows her to write about the religion of her childhood with affection and respect.

The only problem is that she has the dates all wrong. The hymns she assumes were written by Charles Wesley and other eighteenth-century fathers of the church and set to Old English dance tunes were, in fact, composed in the late nineteenth or early twentieth century. "Love Lifted Me" is not even as old as Welty herself. She was born in 1909, and James Rowe wrote the text in 1912. It was set to music in 1915 (Reynolds 107). When she sang that hymn as a child, in perhaps 1916 or 1917, it was new to Methodist churches. But, typical of people reared in an evangelical community, Welty assumes that gospel hymns are timeless or very old; she invests them with authority they are too young to warrant. Growing up in a small-town Oklahoma Baptist church in the 1950s, I too thought that "Throw Out the Lifeline," "Blessed Assurance," "Softly and Tenderly," and "Love Lifted Me" were almost as old as the Bible even though they are all products of the late nineteenth or early twentieth centuries. As an evangelical, I learned no catechism, no creed, and no liturgy. Yet my religion was a religion of words because, by the time I entered first grade, I knew many hymns from the 1940 *Broadman Hymnal* by heart. We sang them on Sunday mornings and evenings and at Wednesday night prayer meetings. We sang them with renewed fervor at the spring and fall revivals, one planned in that farming community to mark the end of planting and the other to celebrate the harvest. Like most evangelical children, I learned hymns by rote and often with amusing variations in their words. Robert Lowry's Easter hymn "Low in the Grave He Lay, Jesus My Saviour!" sounded to me like "Low in the gravy lay Jesus my Saviour." And it seemed perfectly logical to a five-year-old to begin the chorus, not with "Up from the grave He arose," but with "Up from the gravy, a rose."

Every person reared in an evangelical church has a similar story to tell. And we were all learning the same hymns. The Methodists a block away were singing their Robert Lowrys and Fanny Crosbys from the 1938 *Cokesbury Worship Hymnal;* people worshiping in the Church of Christ across town took theirs from the 1937 *Great Songs of the Church*. But they were the same songs, most of them—aside from some eighteenth-century hymns by Isaac Watts, John Newton, and Charles Wesley—written between 1820 and 1920 and a large majority of those between 1870 and 1920. (Here, as elsewhere, I use the term *hymn* to refer to the words rather than to what would more properly be called the hymn tune.) Perhaps because of the complex associations of childhood, these hymns are the ones still most likely to prompt protective emotional responses in evangelicals of the late twentieth century. A recent, rather cranky letter to the editor of a weekly Oklahoma paper called the *Baptist Messenger,* for example, objected to another writer's notion that using contemporary Christian music instead of gospel hymns in church is a good way to attract young people. The letter writer states that denominational success for Baptists requires resisting "the shaping of our church music by a wicked pop culture" and argues that "church music, like all church institutions, should go untouched by the times" (Howard). The writer's assumption, of course, is that hymns he learned as a child were produced somewhere back in the mists of Christian antiquity, not as part of the popular culture of the late nineteenth and early twentieth centuries. Observing the same attitudes toward "traditional hymns," contemporary Baptist pastor Nancy Hastings Sehested remarks dryly that her congregation, admittedly "liberal," still divides into those "who like new hymns" and "those who want to stick to the old hymns, the ones Jesus sang when he was a boy" (244). Apparently, gospel hymnists even perceived themselves as preservers of a venerable tradition. As one late-nineteenth-century gospel hymn puts it, that "old time religion" was good enough for "the Hebrew Children," "Paul and Silas," "our mothers," and "our fathers," and "it's good enough for me."[1] The truth, though, is that old time religion is not all that old.

Coming at the end of centuries of Protestant hymnody, gospel hymns of the late 1800s and early 1900s seem far too young and far too informal to be called "traditional." The distinguishing marks of gospel hymns are their simplicity and concern with, in Donald Hustad's words, the "basic gospel" of sin, redemption, and personal experience; the secular sound of their tunes;[2] and the use of repetition, particularly in the characteristic refrain (Hustad 132). Through these features, gospel hymns differ from the more self-consciously literary hymns of the eighteenth century, which relied on argument rather than simple narrative and on complex figures of speech for their rhetorical power. Such differences made gospel hymns easier for the nineteenth-century working-class people who made up the bulk of evangelical churches to learn and remember. It is not difficult, for example, to see why Isaac Watts's "Alas and Did My Saviour Bleed" (1707) was improved considerably for relatively uneducated people in 1885 when Ralph E. Hudson turned it into a gospel hymn by adding a refrain. The first verse of the original hymn, entitled "Godly sorrow arising from the sorrows of Christ," poses a grave theological question:

> Alas! and did my Saviour bleed?
> And did my Sovereign die?
> Would He devote that sacred head
> For such a worm as I? (BR 112, CWH 27, GS 4)

Watts's response to the overwhelming significance of the crucifixion, "When Christ, the mighty Maker, died / For man the creature's sin," is the decision to "give myself away," thus making a pitiful return for the "debt of love I owe."[3]

To subdue this complicated theological argument about the economy of heavenly love and to change the solemn tone of the hymn, Hudson simply added the refrain that prompted the hymn to be retitled "At the Cross":

At the cross, at the cross where I first saw the light,
And the burden of my heart rolled away,
It was there by faith I received my sight,
And now I am happy all the day! (BR 112, GS 4)

This chorus, repeated four times to every one singing of "such a worm as I" and sometimes simply sung alone, shifts the emphasis from the complexities of soteriology to the immediate joy of perception, receiving sight. It transforms doctrine into narrative because it compares the believer to Bunyan's Christian, who also was filled with joy when he saw the cross and felt his burden fall away.[4] The tune Hudson wrote to accompany his new version of the hymn features a running bass line and a sprightly rhythm, elements that change an eighteenth-century composition into a gospel song suitable for use in a revival service. By the time "At the Cross" appeared in the 1956 *Baptist Hymnal* the year I entered the third grade, hymnal editors had also changed the phrase "such a worm as I" to "sinners such as I," an alteration most exasperating for people who already had "such a worm" in their memory.[5] Some people simply refused to change, and, even today, I can identify old-time Baptists by noticing who slips up on this phrase.

Such resistance to change in a familiar hymn suggests that these gospel hymns serve important social functions, one of which is to create a sense of order for those who sing them. Because these texts have acquired a constructed history and authority they do not deserve, they present a stunning example of what Eric Hobsbawm terms an "invented tradition," that is, "a set of practices, normally governed by overtly or tacitly accepted rules and of a ritual or symbolic nature, which seek to inculcate certain values and norms of behaviour by repetition, which automatically implies continuity with the past" (1). Hobsbawm argues that invented traditions are of particular interest to historians because they represent a response to a world of disorienting changes, "an attempt to structure at least some parts of social life . . . as unchanging and invariant" (2).[6]

Resistance to the Proponents of Modernity

As an invented tradition, gospel hymns were a bulwark against turn-of-the-century liberalism or, as it was also called, "modernism." Theological modernism refers to a movement that attempted, in William E. Hordern's words, to "rethink Christianity in thought forms which the modern world can comprehend" (74). Unlike aesthetic modernism with its sense of breaking with the past and its traditions, theological modernism viewed history (including sacred history) as an evolutionary process through which God was revealed more and more fully. Theological modernism did not engender nostalgia for the past because change was considered crucial to human progress. Science and technology were especially beneficial because they removed limitations on human knowledge of God. "Progressive revelation," as this modernist perspective was called, held that the Old Testament portrayal of a God who would require the total annihilation of the Canaanites was imperfect: God was more accurately portrayed as the loving God of the New Testament. It was not that God had changed, according to modernists, but that human beings had progressed to a fuller understanding of God. Moreover, as a result of continued spiritual progress, human beings at the beginning of the twentieth century could trust themselves as a more fully evolved species of Christian than that described in the New Testament. Optimism countered the sense of alienation and fragmentation characteristic of aesthetic modernism.

The God of modernism was reasonable and immanent, at work in the world just like human beings. In fact, this God was rather like the Wizard of Oz in L. Frank Baum's novel of the same name, which was published in 1900: His reputation as a magician was the illusion of the unenlightened. In truth, God was just "a very good man" (Baum 162), like the Christ of the social gospel. Hordern tells of one liberal who, "having been raised on a grim creed of Calvinistic predestination," was greatly relieved "to find that God was at least as good as some of the elders in his church" (78). Furthermore, the modernist view of humankind was hopeful. One could earn salvation from despair and alienation as Dorothy did in *The Wizard of Oz*, not through faith in a savior, but through faith in oneself and through the hard work that earns self-esteem. One must set one's feet on the path toward enlightenment and accomplish the tasks that lead to success. As the wizard tells her, "In this country everyone must pay for everything he gets" (109).

The world of work, however, was also under assault. In *No Place of Grace: Antimodernism and the Transformation of American Culture, 1880–1920*, T. J. Jackson Lears speaks of a secular version of theological modernism that supported the economic, social, and cultural changes of America in the late nineteenth and early twentieth centuries. Secular modernism promoted the changes necessary to the progress many Americans believed was their providentially designed destiny. It endorsed time clocks and assembly lines, the ethics of capitalism and the veneration of science. However, these agents of modernity created as well as solved problems. Richard Hofstadter observes that the urbanization and industrialization of America brought about the American dream of material progress so rapidly that a sense of moral force and optimism went out of the American people. He argues that in an age when the population of Chicago "more than doubled . . . in the single decade from 1880–1890" and unregulated railroads exploited farmers, Americans had somehow neglected to develop "the means of meeting human needs or controlling or reforming the manifold evils that come with any such rapid physical change" (1–2). Or, as Lears puts it, by the late nineteenth century,

> Europeans and Americans alike began to recognize that the triumph of modern culture had not produced greater autonomy (which was the official claim) but rather had promoted a spreading sense of moral impotence and spiritual sterility—a feeling that life had become not only overcivilized but also curiously unreal. (4–5)

Among Protestants, these problems were exacerbated by modernist theologians' promotion of the higher criticism of the Bible drifting in from Europe and by their support of the social gospel movement with its underpinnings in social Darwinism. These movements further disoriented reality by calling into question the absolute authority of Scripture. And in the postwar South, where gospel hymns became a staple of life, evangelicals badly needed stability.

One possible response to this "world of disorienting changes" was what Lears calls antimodernism, a reaction to the forces of modernity that encouraged social stability by, among other things, inventing traditions to maintain connections with the past.[7] The rhetoric of gospel hymns was an antimodern reaction to philosophies that demystified spirituality and displaced spiritual authority. These demystifying strategies struck at the very heart of a religious style that grew out of the revival movements of the eighteenth and nineteenth centuries instead of within organized churches (Marsden 2) and that depended heavily upon a romantic view of reality.[8] As several writers have argued, theological modernism was a movement designed to rescue Christianity by revising it to fit the assumptions of a modern world (Hyde 116; Szasz 69; Hordern 73; Marsden 32; Lears 23). But it modernized Christianity at the cost of what had made it satisfying to evangelical Christians and by challenging the very principles that defined evangelical Christians.

Standard definitions of evangelicalism usually include what Donald Hustad calls "evangelical distinctives":

1. Evangelicals accept the scriptures as authority rather than tradition or ecclesiastical institutions.

2. Evangelicals believe that salvation is achieved through faith, rather than through the sacraments.

3. Evangelicals emphasize a personal experience of conversion; in this regard they may be called modern pietists.

4. Evangelicals are zealous in outreach, in which (2) and (3) are emphasized, often in the context of evangelistic services.

5. Evangelicals tend to worship in a non-liturgical, "free" tradition. (15)[9]

Another way to say all of this is that, to borrow a phrase from Quaker theologian Richard Foster, evangelicals are "word centered." As I see it, however, *word* does not necessarily mean written words.[10] Evangelicals value the Bible over other authority because it is the "Word of God," the actual spoken words of the divine or, at the least, the result of spiritual rather than rational inspiration of a scribe. They trust themselves to read and interpret the Word—often orally and with the multiplicity of meanings inherent in oral speech.

When Richard Foster pronounced the phrase "word centered," evangelicals can assume he refers to all of the meanings I describe here or to none of them. The point is that interpretation is as important as speaking. Evangelicals assume that reading the Bible and hearing "the Word" preached will inspire interpretation and lead them to a personal relationship with Christ, the incarnate word. They feel compelled to share the gospel—as one gospel hymnist puts it, the "wonderful words of life"—with others. And they do not want to be limited by written creeds or what Hustad calls "the bondage of a required liturgy" (37). Theological modernism challenged all of these assumptions in its attempts to make Christianity, as Ferenc Morton Szasz puts it, "more easily digestible" to modern Americans (69) and to solve the problems that arose when nineteenth-century Christianity butted up against the assumptions of a modern world.[11] However, evangelicals found in gospel hymns a rhetorical solution to the problem. That solution reduced the threat of modernism but only at the cost of changing the social structure of the evangelical community.

The Words of God

The first problem theological modernism addressed was the dilemma of biblical authority: higher criticism of the Bible called into question the truth of biblical history and science and, perhaps more important, the composition narratives of the authors. If three different Isaiahs wrote the book of that name, as some critics were claiming, how could one trust Scripture that claimed to be "the vision of [one, discrete] Isaiah" (Isaiah 1:1, KJV)? Modernists solved the problem by, in George Marsden's phrase, "deifying historical process" (33). In other words, modernists said that God intervened in history, and that, as I describe above, Scripture was not a message from a transcendent god but the historical record of an immanent god's progressive revelation to various people. To evangelicals, of course, this shift in perspective allowed the horrifying vision of a world with no absolute authority. If believers could not trust the words of biblical authors, whom could they trust?

Deified history also solved the problems caused by Darwin and other scientists by assuming that scientific laws simply reveal God's work in nature and will, of course, have to change as human minds grow more sophisticated and become better able to grasp the ways of an immanent God. As the popular nineteenth-century preacher Henry Ward Beecher saw it, science and religion are not in conflict at all because "evolution is God's way of doing things" (Marty and Appleby 54). This modernist solution to the issue immediately made the evangelical belief in the "priesthood of the believer" suspect since the idea of every believer as a priest was based in part on the assumption that every Christian was capable of interpreting Scripture with the aid of human reason.[12] This assumption relied, in turn, on the notion that Scripture is literally true, that God intended it to be readily accessible to all. But if one cannot trust to be literally true the biblical claims that God created the earth in seven days or that Joshua made the sun stand still or that Balaam's ass spoke in a human voice, then how can one trust the theological claims about salvation and eternal life?[13]

Gospel hymns provided an answer to the vexing dilemma of authority by investing it in the hymnists. They also solved the problem of interpreting the Bible by focusing on the hymnists' personal spiritual experiences rather than on the complexities of science and philosophy. These two changes allowed both men and women to compose authoritative texts. Consider the composition narratives of gospel hymnists. Nearly all of them begin after the hymnist has had an overwhelming emotional experience, say, recovery from illness, experiencing the beauty of nature, or hearing a compelling tune. Spiritually elevated, he or she receives a rush of words that seem to come unbidden from God. Acting more as scribe than composer, the writer records the words (and sometimes a tune as well) as quickly as possible. Many hymnists comment that their words required no revision once they were recorded.

Fanny J. Crosby, the most prolific gospel hymnist of all time— she claims to have written eight thousand hymns (*Memories* 169)— gives an example of this scenario in her *Memories of Eighty Years* (1906):

"Blessed Assurance" [1873] was written to a melody composed by my friend, Mrs. Joseph F. Knapp; she played it over once or twice on the piano and then asked me what it said to me. I replied,

> "Blessed assurance, Jesus is mine,
> O what a foretaste of glory divine!
> Heir of salvation, purchase of God,
> Born of His spirit, washed in His blood:
> This is my story, this is my song,
> Praising my Saviour all the day long."

The hymn thus written seemed to express the experience of both Mrs. Knapp and myself. (168)

Composing so rapidly was apparently not unusual for Crosby. She recalls that the words to "The Bright Forever" came very quickly: "all at once, almost in a twinkling, the words came stanza by stanza as fast as I could memorize them" (*Memories* 180).[14] Her reference to memorizing the words indicates that she works in an oral mode; the first step in composition is hearing and learning the words to the hymn. On another occasion, Crosby writes:

> When informed of the death of a dear friend of Mrs. Currier's and mine we sat down and wept together, and these words flowed from my heart,
>
> > "Only a little while pilgrims below,
> > Then to our Fatherland home we shall go."
>
> When I repeated the hymn to Mrs. Currier, she immediately sang it to the music coming from her heart as the words did from mine. Both words and melody were written in less than half an hour. (*Memories* 190)

Male hymnists record versions of the same experience. Sanford F. Bennett explains that a visit from his morose friend Joseph P. Webster triggered "The Sweet By and By" (1868):[15]

> He came into my place of business, walked down to the stove, and turned his back on me without speaking. . . . Turning to him, I said, "Webster, what is the matter now?" "It's no matter," he replied, "it will be all right by and by." The idea of the hymn came to me like a flash of sunlight, and I replied, "The Sweet By and By! Why would not that make a good hymn" [sic] "Maybe it would," said he indifferently. Turning to my desk I penned the words of the hymn as fast as I could

Gospel hymnist Fanny J. Crosby with one of her collaborators, the composer, hymnal editor, and revivalist Ira D. Sankey. From Crosby, *Memories of Eighty Years* (Boston: James H. Earle, 1906).

write. I handed the words to Webster. As he read his eyes kindled, and stepping to the desk he began writing the notes. Taking his violin, he played the melody and then jotted down the notes of the chorus. It was not over thirty minutes from the time I took my pen to write the words before two friends with Webster and myself were singing the hymn. (qtd. in Reynolds 223)

These narratives suggest that hymn composing is a sacred activity for late-nineteenth- and early-twentieth-century gospel hymnists, an occasion on which they become the instruments of God. Their hymns, thus, transcend categorization as mere poetry; they are sacred texts, transcribed in response to divine dictation rather than composed. The notion that they come directly from God parallels the notion of biblical inspiration espoused by conservative evangelicals in nineteenth-century America, when higher criticism of the Bible was introduced into theological circles.[16] Veneration for the Bible in the evangelical community was so pervasive and heartfelt during this period that R. Heber Newton, rector of All Souls' Church in New York City, characterized it as superstitious "Bibliolatry" in a sermon published in 1883 (12). Speaking for the "science of Biblical criticism" (25), Newton compares the conservative evangelical view of biblical composition to the Islamic tradition that the Koran was "uncreated": "that a copy, in one volume, on paper, was, by the hands of the angel Gabriel, sent down to the lowest heaven in the month of Ramadan; from when Gabriel revealed it to Mohammed in instalments [sic]" (40). Newton claims that medieval art aptly expresses what he calls the "traditional"—by definition, the unenlightened—view of biblical inspiration:

Mediaeval illuminations picture the evangelists copying their gospels from heavenly books which angels hold open above them.
A book let down out of the skies, immaculate, infallible, oracular—this is the traditional view of the Bible. (16)

Newton's statement suggests that, until the advent of higher criticism, the Bible—for the nineteenth-century American Protestant, the King James Version of the Bible—could be perceived as words received directly from God and biblical authors could be seen as practicing something closer to automatic writing than to composition of history, poetry, theology, and philosophy. To complicate the issue, though, contemporary theologian Ernest R. Sandeen claims that what Newton regards as the "traditional" view of biblical inspiration is itself an invented tradition: "A systematic theology of biblical authority which defended the common evangelical faith in the infallibility of the Bible had to be created in the midst of the nineteenth-century controversy [over higher criticism]" (106). As Sandeen suggests, competing views of history and human progress could make life uncomfortable for Protestants who wanted an uncomplicated faith.

For those with doubts, gospel hymns provided the reassuring evidence that God's words were received by the chosen in modern times just as they had been in the days described in the Old and New Testament. Composition narratives of gospel hymns imply that many hymnists saw themselves as the counterparts of biblical authors such as Moses and Paul and viewed their hymns as authoritative revelations from God only slightly less important than Scripture. The 1877 biography of Philip P. Bliss, a well-loved and enormously prolific gospel hymnist, claims that he

> never felt that the songs *originated* with him. They seemed to him to come *through* him from God. As he grew in the knowledge of God's word [i.e., the Bible], he would marvel at the truth he had expressed in his songs without knowing it. (Whittle 60)

Similarly, Fanny Crosby wrote that "some of my hymns have been dictated by the blessed Holy Spirit. . . . That the poet has any right to claim special merit for himself is certainly presumptuous" (*Memories* 166–67). Like most testimonies, these statements seemed to have been accepted at face value in the evangelical community.

The Word Incarnate

Modernists also updated Christianity, and thus horrified evangelicals, by emphasizing the humanity and ignoring the divinity of Christ. Instead of focusing on the theological and supernatural significance of the incarnation, they chose to emulate the historical Jesus. According to William E. Hordern, some modernists adopted the slogan "'Not Christ, but Jesus,' signifying that 'Christ' stood for a doctrine while 'Jesus' represented the simple Galilean prophet" (81). While evangelicals certainly believed in a historical Jesus, this new perspective troubled them in two ways. First, it limited Jesus to a particular time and place. For an evangelical such as the novelist and hymnist Elizabeth Prentiss, loss of the transcendent Jesus would have meant loss of the only thing that made life worth living. At the end of Prentiss's novel *Stepping Heavenward* (1869), the heroine, Katy, has endured six difficult pregnancies, the deaths of her beloved brother and oldest child, poor health, and the care of a cranky father-in-law. But she decides that "personal love to Christ" transforms everything (362). This Christ is a constant presence and spiritual guide who invades her consciousness and to whom she prays as easily as she would speak to a familiar houseguest. To the evangelical mind, denying the divinity of Jesus would mean the death of Christ.

The humanization of Christ also made ethics more important than a personal relationship with the Word of God incarnate in Jesus. This shift in perspective made the social gospel movement possible. Charles M. Sheldon's popular social gospel novel *In His Steps* (1896) gives a clear narrative description of what following Jesus as an ethical model would mean. The story begins with a crisis that prompts a minister to challenge his congregation never to act without first asking, "What would Jesus do?" In a sermon at the end of the book, the Rev. Mr. Maxwell predicts that reformed society could result from accepting his challenge:

> The call of this dying century and of the new one soon to be, is a call for a new discipleship, a new following of Jesus, more like the early, simple, apostolic Christianity, when the disciples left all and literally followed the Master. Nothing but a discipleship of this kind can face the destructive selfishness of the age with any hope of overcoming it. . . . What is it to be a Christian? It is to imitate Jesus. It is to do as He would do. It is to walk in His steps. (280–81)

In His Steps has been so popular among evangelicals that it remained a popular graduation gift in small-town Oklahoma through the 1960s. But the social gospel movement itself offended and disturbed many evangelicals and not only at the turn of the century. Its influence lingered well past the midpoint of the twentieth century because it was used to support the civil rights movement.

The evangelical charge was that the social gospel focused too much on this life and not enough on the one to come. Too much emphasis on exemplary behavior could divert attention from oral transmission of the words nonbelievers needed to facilitate their eternal salvation. At the same time, the modernists accused the traditionalists of believing in a religion that offered only fire insurance, a rescue from hell. Modernists suggested that rescuing those damned to misery in a modern world was a nobler goal than persuading people to believe in "pie in the sky by and by." Jane Addams even claimed that Christianity was not a religion at all but a model for social relations (122). One of her contemporaries agreed that "it was not the promise of immunity from individual punishment in another world with which [Jesus] won frightened adherents to his cause. It was by . . . the establishment of a society founded upon service" (Hyde 147). But evangelicals feared the loss of security inherent in a religion that offered no assurance of a better life to come. Perhaps more than that, they feared the loss of language that structured reality.[17] In other words, conservatives resented changing "such a worm as I" to "sinners such as I" on two levels: it made the doctrine of salvation less momentous by reducing the distance between God and human beings, and it challenged a rhetorical pattern that expressed important theological assumptions in an economical and familiar way.

Even more important, the modern Jesus-as-role-model denied the pleasure of mystical experience. So the therapeutic answer of gospel hymns to the sterility of modernism was to tell stories of personal encounters with the divine. Many hymnists describe God and Jesus as family members or close friends, and some of these hymns are clearly antimodern in other ways as well. Ironically, even hymnists such as Maltie D. Babcock, who also wrote theologically modern social gospel hymns, sometimes produced antimodern texts. Babcock's "This Is My Father's World," first published in 1901, according to William J. Reynolds, in *Thoughts for Every-Day Living* (225), for example, holds back the modern age by combining a romantic view of divinity pervading nature with Renaissance cosmology:

This is my Father's world,
And to my list'ning ears,
All nature sings, and round me rings
The music of the spheres. (CWH 106)

His hymn, more consciously literary than most gospel hymns, makes of the world a new Garden of Eden in which the speaker hears God as Adam did: "In the rustling grass I hear him pass, / He speaks to me everywhere." Babcock's hymn is full of references to sound; even the birds "declare their Maker's praise." Singing the hymn becomes a performance in which the participant creates afresh Babcock's testimony. Human words proclaim the intimate knowledge of a creator just as the sounds of birds and grass do. Both are testimony to a personal God, not an ethical ideal.

They also testify to the value of singing as worship. As befits an invented tradition, gospel hymns affirm earlier ideas of hymnody. In particular, they assume that hymns are the "words of God" in both senses of the phrase; they are both words from God and words about God. Writing of Isaac Watts's hymns a century earlier, James Wendall Plett notes that the man known as the father of English hymnody frequently uses a motif of God as speaker in his hymns; thus, "the song of the Christian, a response to God's voice, possesses some qualities of the divine voice; it escapes the bounds of both space and time" (68–69). Plett also observes that "evangelical fervor, even in a highly literate population, is always best conveyed through the spoken word" since speech is the medium of public testimony (80). As the singer—both the Voice of the hymn and the one who sings it—verbalizes the testimony, the experience of God takes on reality as surely as the universe took on material reality when God spoke it into being. When a gospel hymnist speaks of a personal encounter with God, the words give physical presence to the spiritual reality of a transcendent God. Jesus lives in the words because Jesus is the incarnate word.[18] A typical response to hearing such a hymn is to assume that it not only proclaims one person's experience of God but affirms the reality of God for others. As a hearer of Fanny Crosby's hymn "Saved by Grace" (1892) put it, "It seemed that God had spoken to me through the voice of that song" (*Memories* 185).

In many gospel hymns, the idea of singing or having a song is

Fanny J. Crosby, "Queen of the Gospel Hymn." From Crosby, *Memories of Eighty Years.*

proof of genuine spiritual experience. James Rowe writes that God's love "merits my soul's best songs" (B H 1956 212). Luther B. Bridgers titled his hymn about the constant assurance of divine aid "He Keeps Me Singing." Fanny Crosby, whose hymns are full of references to songs, mentions the reassurance of a Savior who provides "songs in the night" (B H 1956 203). Philip P. Bliss encourages his audience to "sing them over again to me, / Wonderful words of Life" (B H 1956 181). And Edwin O. Excell wrote in 1884 "I have a song I love to sing, / Since I have been redeemed" (B H 1956 208). A verse of his hymn that was omitted in later printings gives some idea of the nature of his song because he writes "I have a joy I can't express, / Since I have been redeemed" (qtd. in Reynolds 97). A "song" then becomes his way to articulate spiritual perception, leaving ordinary speech to fill the needs of material reality. Using *song* or *singing* figuratively implies that other forms of oral communication, including perhaps sermons, are somehow less spiritual than singing, the one truly democratic form of testimony. Women and children could participate in congregational singing during the gospel hymn era, but in most evangelical churches only adult males could pray aloud and only an adult male separated from the congregation by ordination and sometimes by education could preach. Many churches today still follow these rules of social separation by age and gender. Though David B. Morris was speaking of an earlier century, he describes the inclusive nature of hymns in later times perfectly when he writes: "Of the three worship forms used in the churches of Watts's day—the sermon, public prayers, and the hymn—only the hymn served as a medium by which the entire congregation could participate in an oral event testifying to inner religious experience" (qtd. in Plett 80). Donald Hustad, a twentieth-century church musician, chides those who think singing is just "for women and children" by emphasizing its necessity: "The truth is, singing is for believers. The relevant question is not 'Do you have a voice?' but 'Do you have a song?'" (75).

In gospel hymns, evangelicals preserve not only the mystical component of religious experience but the doctrine lost in the modernist preoccupation with ethical behavior. A seminary professor recognized the hymnic function of preserving doctrine when he said in 1985 that "'the scripture does not tell us anything about what the church has done for the last two thousand years. . . . The only place we find this is in the hymn book'" (qtd. in "Speaker Says"). And in churches without formal creeds or liturgy, hymns are also the most important and effective way to teach doctrine. Evangelicals are, for example, usually devoted to the general idea that salvation is available to everyone even though various denominations may differ on, say, the question of whether salvation once attained may be lost again. In other words, evangelicals since 1870 have rarely believed in the doctrine of election. Accordingly, the doctrine of free grace or what a Puritan might have called "general election" is a staple of gospel hymns. J. Edwin McConnell's "Whosoever Meaneth Me" and Philip P. Bliss's "Whosoever Will," for example, allow the singers to proclaim that the "whosoever" of John 3:16 refers to any person and, more important, to themselves: "For God so loved the world, that he gave his only begotten Son, that whosoever believeth in him should not perish, but have everlasting life."

Besides preserving doctrine, gospel hymns articulate what Brian Stock calls "procedural knowledge" or social behaviors that enact the understood meaning of a text (146). The many hymns interpreting *The Pilgrim's Progress,* for example, gave evangelicals a script for a religion that would take sinners along the right road. Jessie Brown Pounds's "The Way of the Cross Leads Home" (1906) combines an allusion to Bunyan's allegory with the confluence of heaven and home in domestic novels. The first line challenges modernism's assumption that saving souls for a home in heaven is less important than improving homes for souls on earth: "I must needs go home by the way of the cross, / There's no other way but this" (BH 1956 196). Inherent in this hymn is social behavior that makes proclamation of the gospel more important than good works. It is no accident that evangelical worship services give more time to the sermon than to anything else or that the pulpit is usually the visual center of the church sanctuary. People must be brought to the cross to make sure they are on the road to the Celestial City. More literally, hymns that emphasize forward movement suggest the response of a sinner to the altar call or invitation at the end of a worship service. At this time, people are invited to "come forward" and demonstrate that they are making a profession of faith. The phrase "walk the aisle" is even today synonymous for many evangelicals with professing one's faith. And it is no wonder, since this procedure is described in countless "invitation hymns" that urge nonbelievers, in Will Thompson's words, to "come home, come home, / Ye who are weary come home" (BH 1956 236).

The Bondage of Words

The challenge to evangelical Christianity offered by modernism rested ultimately on a particular view of perception and language. Both modernists and evangelicals emphasized personal experience over doctrine and individual testimony over written communal creeds. However, modernists challenged evangelicals in their use of the notion of personal experience and in their idea of emotion. What an evangelical means by the expression "personal experience" is the romantic notion of spiritual perception that occurs apart from the operation of intellect. Babcock hears God in the rustling grass because he is perceiving spiritually, not because he has scientifically verifiable evidence of God's presence. This personal experience is ostensibly very democratic; it is not related to tradition or to external authority although the Bible or a person with spiritual insight may be helpful in interpreting spiritual perception. It is an answer to Emerson's questions to a "retrospective" age: "Why should not we also enjoy an original relation to the universe? Why should not we have a poetry and philosophy of insight and not of tradition, and a religion by revelation to us, and not the history of theirs?" (3) In contrast, when modernists spoke of personal experience, they meant something like "empirical observation of natural phenomena." Social Darwinist Amory H. Bradford wrote in 1895 that

> the science of sociology has taken its place beside theology, and even disputes its claim to be queen of the sciences; now theology itself is studied inductively. Its teachers no longer form their theories and then endeavour to adjust facts to them; but they study the facts of human nature and divine revelation and from them derive their theories. (vii)

In an example of this inductive theology, William DeWitt Hyde claims that "answer to prayer belongs not to the realm of magic and miracle; but lies clearly within the sphere of causality and law" (129). Among the data from which he derives his notion of prayer is a fairly sophisticated concept of late nineteenth-century germ theory. Hyde argues that the universe is orderly and that certain bacilli will, in an orderly and predictable way, cause disease and death. But God is like the physician who can bring other laws to bear in treating the disease: both are benevolent, sensitive, and powerful, but neither works outside the realm of natural law (122–23).

The relationship between a human being and this modern God is not modeled on human relationships used in the familiar evangelical metaphors. And a god who is not a parent, brother, companion, friend, or lover does not provide the emotional resonance of the outdated evangelical God. Hyde refutes Elizabeth Prentiss's ideas about the overwhelming necessity of emotional love for Christ, ideas expressed in both *Stepping Heavenward* and in her popular hymn "More Love to Thee, O Christ," published in 1869. Instead, he suggests that "feeling" in religion is less important than having noble sentiments and acting upon them:

> The great question, after all, is not, Have I a love for Christ of which I can be conscious all the time? That way lies discouragement, despondency, despair. Faith must lead the way to love. And the question of faith is, rather, Have I Christ? Whether with little emotion or with much, am I resolved that what work I do shall be done in his name; what influence I have shall be cast on his side; however cold and dead my emotions may become, however weak and blundering my efforts may prove, such as I am, I will be his? If we are thus resolved to serve him, we already believe in him; and we shall come to love him in due time. (119)

In other words, salvation is not mysterious at all; it is the reward of everyone who behaves according to Christian principles and who renounces "anti-social [attitudes]" (146), Hyde's modernist euphemism for what the orthodox Christian would call sin. Emotions, clearly, are an unreliable indicator of reality.

Gospel hymns take exactly the opposite view. They assume that feeling is evidence of spiritual perception and that, as Emerson put it, "words are signs of natural facts" and "particular natural facts are symbols of particular spiritual facts" (13). But the words of gospel songs have never been absolutely fixed entities in the evangelical community because hymns are known orally; since about 1870 they have been published in written form mostly as an aid to performance, rather than as devotional material. Academics frequently describe evangelicals as anti-intellectual, and certainly this is true in a sense: evangelicals do tend to be suspicious of what happens in universities and seminaries. It is no accident that Southern Baptists had only one theological seminary until well into the twentieth century (Gaskin 49). But a more subtle and perhaps more accurate view of the matter is that evangelicals are really anti-print.[19]

Historically, this bias is almost inevitable. In her 1913 history of the Woman's Missionary Union, Fanny E. S. Heck describes the association among earlier Baptists of doctrine fixed in ritual or word with persecution under Catholicism: "anything savoring of 'Popery,' 'form' or 'creed' was regarded with unfeigned horror, which their former sufferings fully justified" (21). In contrast, the free church tradition affirms the sense that ostensibly spontaneous oral worship is a true expression of personal faith rather than affirmation of an official position. Many evangelicals cringe, for example, at the notion of a written prayer. Reading someone else's words is not prayer at all but submission to rhetorical enslavement. It is not even acceptable to read one's own words written out beforehand because that would deny God's immediate influence and inspiration. In truth, evangelical prayers tend to be quite formulaic, but the fact that the formula is never articulated allows believers to maintain an illusion of spontaneity.

This attitude toward written words actually affirms two important intellectual functions: memory and spontaneous oral improvisation. Somewhat ironically, evangelicals greatly revere the Bible and study it all their lives. Sunday school is not just for children but for everyone "from the basket to the casket." The emphasis, however, is twofold. First, since the Bible is transcribed speech, it must be memorized to interiorize the voice of God. The words of Psalm 119:11 are commonly believed to refer to the necessity for memorizing Scripture: "Thy words have I hid in mine heart, that I might not sin against thee." Second, evangelicals spend a great deal of time talking about Scripture and listening to preachers' comments on it, and a common method of interpretation is relating personal experience to particular Scripture. Some people quote memorized Scripture in prayers and testimonies. Interpreting and articulating the Bible in these ways thus creates a new text. Gospel hymns simulate the features of language valued in the evangelical community: they are oral and informal; they frequently quote the Bible, but they interpret it in light of personal experience; they aid memory and allow the "voice" of God to speak to the singer or hearer. In short, they articulate the new text that results from the interaction of oral and written language. They also counter the modernist tendency to validate experience only when it can be supported by objective data because Scripture interpretation varies from person to person. And they have great authority because they can be used flexibly in a community that values improvisation. Congregations can leave out verses to a hymn, make one up to fit a pattern already established, or splice two hymns together.

Hymns are associated with play, and they are often the subject of jokes and puns. What is the appropriate hymn to go with a sermon on the girdle of righteousness? "How Firm a Foundation." Did you know that Jesus' name was really Andy? The hymn says "Andy (And he) walks with me, Andy talks with me."[20] The fact that evangelicals can play with hymns suggests that they associate them with freedom, the freedom of a church tradition without "the bondage of liturgy" and the freedom of orality, with its multiplicity of meanings and its dependence on the subjective interpretation of the hearer. Inductive theology treats language as a fixed system for discovering fixed natural laws. Evangelical theology treats language as a way to thwart the establishment of reality that is too predictable.

Evangelicals also joke about hymns because they associate them with the pleasure of fantasy and imagination and ultimately with the pleasure of sexual intimacy. My mother recently gave me the revival hymnal published in 1911 that my grandmother owned when she was sixteen and accompanied congregational singing on the piano at a small church at Sterling, Oklahoma. Throughout the book, I find notes in her handwriting that show her playing with hymns, changing the words to fit her teenaged dreams. She changed the title "'Tis So Sweet to Trust in Jesus" to "'Tis So Sweet to Trust in Rob." To the title "How You Will Love Him!" she adds a wistful "Who?" Her joys seem close to home, for she alters "When We All Get to Heaven" to read "When We All Get to Fletcher," naming the next little town up the road, perhaps the home of the now unidentifiable Rob.

We played a more sophisticated but perhaps less personal version of this game when I was a teenager. It was called "Between the Sheets" and consisted of penciling in (or simply imagining) the words *between the sheets* at the end of a hymn title or line: "The Master Hath Come" (between the sheets), "O Why Not Tonight?" (between the sheets), "Only Trust Him" (between the sheets). It seemed very funny and very naughty to add sexual innuendos to hymns, but the hymns themselves suggested the possibility because erotic references in gospel hymns are very common. Salvation, for example, is often described as submission to sexual authority. These jokes, then, suggest a tacit understanding of the nature of spiritual experience. It is highly individual, totally absorbing, enormously pleasurable, and completely inexplicable in straightforward terms. In short, the only human experience that comes close is sexuality. The desexed modernist God with his dreary ethics and model behavior was just not the God we imagined between the sheets. Gospel hymns kept alive what the new theologians thought was too primitive for a modern age.

Women in the Evangelical Textual Community

The invented tradition of gospel hymns created among evangelicals is what Brian Stock calls a "textual community," that is, "a group in which there is both a script and a spoken enactment and in which social cohesion and meaning result from the interaction of the two" (100). The interaction of written and oral texts produced an interpretation of evangelical doctrine as well in what Stock calls "procedural knowledge," in this case the representation of doctrine in figurative language that prescribes attitudes and behavior. As Stock puts it,

Texts . . . are both physical and mental. The "text" is what a community takes it to be. Texts have propositional content, but they are procedural knowledge. For like meaning in language, the element a society fixes upon is a conventional arrangement among the members. (146)

Both the "propositional content" and the "procedural knowledge" of gospel hymn texts confirmed what evangelicals had always thought about themselves—that they were democratic, ready to credit personal testimony and grant soul equality to all believers; that theirs was true religion unfettered by ecclesiastical corruption; that they listened directly to the voice of God and constructed reality as a community from what they heard.

The truth was, though, that all believers were not equal in evangelical churches. In churches that so highly valued the oral expression of faith, women were forbidden to speak by uncontextualized interpretations of Scriptures such as I Corinthians 14:34: "Let your women keep silence in the churches; for it is not permitted unto them to speak." This proscription seems to have been extended to any public gathering. Catherine B. Allen observes that although women praying aloud with other women was marginally acceptable, evangelical men seemed to fear giving women the power of articulating prayer in any situation. Missionary support societies that sprang up among women in all evangelical denominations during the nineteenth century specifically encouraged verbal prayers for missionaries, but, as Allen reports, "the history of every denomination's women's missions organization seems to contain the same apocryphal story. A man was reputed to rise in a church meeting to complain, 'You never could tell what those women might take to praying for if left alone'" (166).

By the time I was growing up in an evangelical church during the 1950s and 1960s, many women felt comfortable praying at missionary society meetings attended only by women or teaching in Sunday school classes of both boys and girls. Women sometimes gave their testimonies in church services and quoted Scripture in that context. However, prayer and preaching in "mixed" company were suspect because these uses of language required interpretation and risked contamination of the Word (words) of God. I was an adult before I heard a woman pray, teach, or preach in the presence of both adult males and adult females. A Church of Christ friend tells me that in his tradition women still do not pray in mixed company, even if the setting is a Sunday school class for toddlers.

What all of this means is that evangelical women usually could articulate and interpret spiritual experience only in print, a mode inferior to oral expression in the evangelical community. Very often, writing seems to have been an almost secretive activity to give form to religious experience. Many hymn annotators, for example, tell the story of how Elizabeth Prentiss's "More Love to Thee, O Christ" was first scribbled down unfinished around 1856 and shown to no one, "not even to her husband," until many years later, when it was published to the astonishment of the author (Tillett and Nutter 171; McCutchan 382; Reynolds 142). Seen rather than heard, the poem is the idiosyncratic musings of a pious woman. Sung by congregations of hundreds and even thousands, as it is today, it is the expression of vital evangelical doctrine. As this incident shows, women could gain a voice in evangelical churches through hymn writing.[21] But being able to speak in this way depended on dramatic changes in both American hymnology and in the way women viewed themselves.

Lucy Larcom's *A New England Girlhood* (1889) includes a chapter called "The Hymn-Book" that describes typical attitudes toward hymns in the time of Larcom's childhood. Larcom was born in 1824, and she describes herself at three years old memorizing hymns at home and "at meeting":

> Almost the first decided taste in my life was the love of hymns. Committing them to memory was as natural to me as breathing. I followed my mother about with the hymn-book ("Watts' and Select"), reading or repeating them to her, while she was busy with her baking or ironing, and she was always a willing listener. She was fond of devotional reading, but had little time for it, and it pleased her to know that so small a child as I really cared for the hymns she loved. (58)

Like me, Larcom sometimes misunderstood the hymns she learned so young, but it was because she saw them wrong, not because she heard them wrong. She interpreted the line "I'll go to Jesus, though my sin / Hath like a mountain rose," for example, to be about a beautiful flower (59). As these anecdotes show, Larcom—like her contemporaries—regarded hymns as devotional reading. They were sung as well, but she regarded memorizing them from the hymnal as "a pastime" and "a pleasure" (68). The main emphasis was on the printed page because hymns were primarily literary rather than oral expressions of personal faith.

All of this changed around 1870, when hymns became more important for corporate singing than for private use. In *On the Banks of Plum Creek* (1937), an autobiography thinly disguised as fiction, Laura Ingalls Wilder describes the life of a family homesteading in Minnesota during the 1870s. On the way home from the first church service they have attended in some time, the family discusses the congregational singing:

> Pa turned on the seat and asked, "How do you girls like the first time you ever went to church?"
> "They can't sing," said Laura.
> Pa's great laugh rang out. Then he explained, "There was nobody to pitch the hymn with a tuning-fork."
> "Nowadays, Charles," said Ma, "people have hymn books."
> "Well maybe we'll be able to afford some, some day," Pa said. (187–88)

As this conversation suggests, hymn books as aids to congregational worship in church meetings were what Pa might call a "new-fangled" invention in the 1870s.[22] In earlier days, hymn books were less necessary because hymns were lined out or deaconed by a man who sang them one line at a time to the congregation, who then echoed his words. The deacon not only set the pitch, as Pa says; he literally "pitched" the hymn to the singers one line at a time. But with more widespread use of hymnals, the task of leading the singing was assumed more and more by a choir, which typically included both men and women.

This development transformed the way hymns were perceived in the evangelical community: instead of being primarily printed texts for private devotions, hymns became primarily oral texts printed as a memory or teaching aid. By this time, religious or devotional writing was a respectable vocation or avocation for women because it was associated with the private sphere of the home. Through writing a woman could be, in the words of twentieth-century scholar Mary Kelley, a "private woman" with a "public stage." A woman could in this way preserve her anonymity but still "shape society by influencing and controlling men" in their own homes, where woman's literature was read (Kelley 308). But when hymns moved out of the private sphere to become the public proclamation of doctrine and behavioral norms in evangelical churches, women's voices were heard for the first time.

These women had a great deal to say. The nineteenth century has been called the "Woman's Century," and the phrase is apt not only because American society was feminized in some ways during this time but also because the white, middle-class women about whom I write had a new sense of their own identity by the end of the nineteenth century. The idea that women considered themselves to be living in a time of change was implicit in the handwritten dedication I found in a signed copy of Mrs. J. C. Croly's massive *The History of the Woman's Club Movement in America* (1889).[23] On the flyleaf, Croly writes: "This book has been a labor of love; and it is lovingly dedicated to the *Twentieth Century Woman* by one who has seen, and shared in the struggles, hopes, and aspirations of the woman of the nineteenth century." Reaching as it does across a century of American history, Croly's inscription proclaims a kinship with other women and an identity distinct from that of men. In the text of her history, Croly attributes women's new consciousness to romantic notions of the self, especially to those based on Goethe's "unity of structure in organic life," which "brought women and children within the pale of humanity" (9–10). The result was a philosophy that allowed women "to live *with* rather than for others":

> This new view, this great advance of the moral and spiritual forces, addressed itself with signal significance to women. To those who were prepared it came not only as an awakening, but as emancipation— emancipation of the soul, freedom from the tyranny of tradition and prejudice, and the acquisition of an intellectual outlook; a spiritual liberty achieved so quietly as to be unnoticed, except by those who watched the progress of this bloodless revolution and the falling away of the shackles that bind the spirit in its early and often painful effort to reach the light. (11)

In other words, the same romantic worldview that powered evangelical ideas of the self allowed women to see themselves as uniquely valuable.

More often than not, actually, women saw themselves as morally and spiritually superior to men. However, Croly argues, they lacked as isolated individuals the educational opportunities and community structure necessary to change their world (12). The nineteenth-century women's club movement, which her book describes in overwhelming detail, was a solution that brought women together in small groups to read literature, engage in intellectual conversation, and sponsor community projects. This movement began, says Croly, among evangelical women who in the early nineteenth century formed "cent" societies and other missionary support groups (8). Women's missionary societies allowed women to gain control over their monetary and human resources. Cent societies, for example, encouraged women to save a cent a week from their housekeeping money to support missionaries. Women sometimes designated a "mission hen" or the "Sunday eggs" for the cause. More important, women gathered to pray and study the missionary literature that became an important form of women's writing in the nineteenth century (J. Hobbs 1985, 4). These activities united them in a common purpose. By the late nineteenth century, women had formed missionary support societies in almost all Protestant denominations, and many of these groups actually ran the boards that managed missionary affairs such as training and appointment. The behavior of these women challenges the ideal of True Womanhood promoted in domestic novels. Women who organized other women, ran administrative boards, and managed the money from offerings for missionary support seem far from the pure, pious, domestic, and submissive woman of novels such as Susan Warner's *The Wide, Wide World*.[24] But for evangelical women, the domestic ideal could be used to support all of these activities as extensions of what pious Christian women supposedly did in their homes to care for others and to maintain the values of the kitchen as a counter to the corrupting ethics of the marketplace.

Missionary literature became a way of promoting the power of mothers and the home. Patricia Ruth Hill, twentieth-century historian of the woman's missionary society movement, claims that "the very elasticity of the definition of woman's sphere" was crucial to female identity because it allowed women to be mothers not only to their own households but to the world at large (115). Indeed, many early societies were referred to as "Woman's Mission to Woman." As part of a missionary society, a nineteenth-century woman could literally go anywhere in the world through her offerings and prayers.[25] Sandra Sizer sees these societies as an alliance between evangelical ministers and middle-class women, two groups cut off from the corrupting influences of the marketplace but, at the same time, deprived of its economic power (86).

This alliance endured until, by the 1870s, evangelical clergy and evangelical women were writing most of the gospel hymns that now preserve the invented evangelical tradition. However, the women were beginning to envision spirituality in their own terms and to separate their Christianity from that of their fathers, brothers, and sons. When Helen Barrett Montgomery wrote *Western Women in Eastern Lands: An Outline Study of Fifty Years of Woman's Work in Foreign Missions* (1911), which includes statistics on some thirty-six different women's missionary societies in a number of Protestant denominations, she pondered the problem of allowing men into the societies. She dismisses the suggestion by describing the men's chauvinism:

> In the first place, are men ready for [joint societies]? Are they emancipated from the caste of sex so that they can work easily with women, unless they be head and women clearly subordinate? Certain facts seem to indicate that in spite of the rapid strides undoubtedly made in this direction we still have a long stretch of unexplored country to be traversed before the perfect democracy of Jesus is reached. When the Religious Education Association was formed, for example, although for years almost the only really scientific work in the Sunday school had been done by women in the primary department, no woman was asked to speak. (269)

Although women had marked out their territory in the evangelical community, the continuing and urgent need was for a public voice to proclaim a gospel of "perfect democracy" and one that promoted their view of domestic Christianity. Montgomery's use of modernist rhetoric in this passage, especially the references to "the perfect democracy of Jesus" and the "scientific" approach to Sunday schools, suggests that evangelical men may have kept women silent out of fear.[26] Montgomery represents both the acceptable theology of care appropriate to "the primary department," that is, the children's Sunday school classes, and the theology of a New Woman who reinterprets true womanhood as submission to "the caste of sex." She represents both what her Christian brothers most needed to preserve and that which most threatened it. At the same time, she identifies herself both with the object of much foreign missionary work, the pagan woman enclosed in a zenana, and with the liberator who frees the colonized. The only position left in this scheme of things for evangelical men is to see themselves either as oppressors or as the defeated.[27] And to make matters worse, no one doubted that women were crucial to the social maintenance of churches. After the Land Run of 1889 in Oklahoma, for example, it took six months to establish a single Baptist church in the new territory, probably, one writer speculates, because women did not participate in the run with their husbands (D. Hobbs 15). The dilemma, then, was that evangelical men needed both to protect themselves against the evangelical New Woman and to preserve her important functions in the church, while women who were beginning to see themselves as not only uniquely valuable but perhaps as uniquely Christian needed to speak. Gospel hymns provided a compromise to this conflict of interests.

The chapter epigraph from Howells's *Indian Summer* (1886) may seem very odd in a discussion of a religion that prides itself on the free church tradition. Mr. Waters, the Emersonian minister who speaks these lines, is praising the Anglican church for its ritualized worship. He points out that "the other Protestant systems are men's systems. Women must have form. They don't care for freedom" (244). The free church tradition, however, gave freedom of expression only to men. Proscriptions on public speaking for women and fear of the power women could gain if they were allowed to interact with God in the spontaneous improvisation of prayers and sermons made evangelical churches even more restrictive for women than denominations that valued ritual and form. And there was another problem: the language of Christianity was largely the rhetoric of men. Excluded from preaching, women had to find another mode of expression for their spiritual insights.

Gospel hymns provided a solution by giving women a complex rhetorical system of figures and forms that were already associated with women and the cult of domesticity. So, in a sense, Howells was right. Women do sometimes seek form in religion because it allows them to speak. The problem, though, is not that "they don't care for freedom" but that they don't care for a freedom that excludes them from participation or a freedom that requires their silence to maintain order. Gospel hymns did not create perfect equality in churches, but they may have given women more power than some evangelical men could stand. The most ardent fundamentalists—the ones who vehemently oppose the ordination of women and teach that a man is the "head" of his wife—are now moving away from the "traditional hymns." Instead, they favor simplistic choruses that quote Scripture without interpretation or that repeat one very simple, almost hypnotic phrase such as "God is so good" over and over. This behavior suggests that gospel hymns give voice to something that requires suppression in a patriarchal community. Hymns with so much power must be worth examining as a key to the lives of the evangelical women who wrote them.

Hymns as the Cultural Property of Nineteenth-Century Women

"What is there I can do for you?" said he. . . .
"If you would," said Ellen faintly,—"if you *could* be so kind as to read
me a hymn?—I should be so glad. I've had nobody to read to me."
—SUSAN WARNER, *The Wide, Wide World*

Hymns as Devotional Texts for the Private Sphere

Anna Warner's *Wayfaring Hymns, Original and Translated* (1869)
is a tiny hymnal, only 5½ inches long and 3½ inches wide. As Warner explains in the preface, it "is meant to be only the first of a series
of six or eight pocket-books; all small, helpful, easy to carry, fit for a
wayfarer's use" (vi). Significantly, the collection contains twenty-six
hymn texts but no hymn tunes. One can imagine the reader pulling
it out of her pocket for a devotional moment in the privacy of her
home or perhaps during a rest on a solitary walk. The physical features of Warner's hymnal indicate that the hymns were never meant
to be sung. Indeed, the shift in thinking that made hymns primarily
a component of worship services—as we think of them today—began about the time *Wayfaring Hymns* was published. Ann Douglas
associates this movement of hymns from the private to the public
sphere with what she calls the "feminization of American culture,"
the cultural shift that made what had been considered feminine
values the controlling element in the evangelical community. As

Douglas puts it, hymns "were originally conceived as best adapted for domestic and familial rather than communal and ecclesiastical uses. It was only when the church itself had been redefined in domestic terms that hymns could be central to their forms of worship" (217–18).

Before this time, hymns were the subject of some controversy.[1] Until the mid-eighteenth century in America, Protestants primarily sang psalms or versified Scripture rather than hymns. The difference is that psalms and other biblical passages were perceived to be God's words transcribed by human beings while hymns were of "human composure" (Ninde 80–81). Hymns were used in public worship during the Great Awakening, which began in the 1730s (Reynolds 9; Ninde 80–81); however, until after the Civil War, Protestants in general were suspicious of words that could have been formed by human craft. Many of them would have agreed with John Calvin, who had been of the opinion that "only God's Word is worthy to be used in God's praise" (qtd. in Hustad 116). One way to still the controversy raised by the move from psalmody to hymnody was to deny hymns the authorization of inclusion in hymnals published by organized churches. As Warner's hymnal shows, however, hymns were published as devotional material to be used privately, in the sacralized female sphere of the home and the emotions. In other words, as long as hymns were looked upon as private experiences that provided models for Christian meditation and as long as private religious experience was the domain of women, hymns were the cultural property of women.[2]

Owning property requires entitlement, which may come through founding or creation, inheritance, an economic exchange, or some sort of investment. In this case, women did not begin the tradition of hymnody, nor did they inherit hymns from men; instead, hymns became part of an exchange through which women received control of private Christianity and men assumed control of its public promotion and power. This exchange occurred during the late eighteenth and early nineteenth centuries in what Amanda Porterfield calls "the domestication of theology." In this change from the Puritan to the evangelical model, "attention was drawn away from feminine love toward God to the beauty of feminine nature, in and of itself." Put another way, Puritans envisioned Christians as feminine in submission to God, their spiritual husband; nineteenth-century evangelicals celebrated the feminine in God and, accordingly, idealized feminine characteristics (52).

The shift from Puritan to evangelical models of spirituality parallels an economic shift from production in the home to industrialization, which separated American society into the male world of business and the female sphere of the home, the domain of personal religious experience. Puritan poetry also frequently used the home as the locus of God's work of grace and depicted all believers as female. Edward Taylor's "Huswifery," for example, compares the believer to a spinning wheel or loom on which God produces "Holy robes for glory" (467).[3] However, by the nineteenth century the home is a spiritual arena precisely because it is not the place of production. God is likely to be described as having feminine characteristics such as kindness and empathy, and the believer relates to God as a child to a mother or, at times, as a childish husband to a long-suffering wife, rather than as a bride to a bridegroom, the Puritan model for this relationship.[4]

Lydia Maria Child makes the relationship between a woman and her child analogous to the relationship between God and a woman in her advice manual *The Mother's Book* (1831). Her book assumes that the home is the appropriate place for religious training and emphasizes maintaining its atmosphere of quiet and peace because children "come to us from heaven, with their little souls full of innocence and peace; and, as far as possible, a mother's influence should not interfere with the influence of angels" (3). Child suggests that the mother do everything possible to maintain a spirit of "tranquillity and purity" in order to quiet the child; children, she notes, "have died in convulsions, in consequence of nursing a mother, while under the influence of violent passion or emotion" (4). If the mother should have trouble maintaining her own tranquility, she should pray so that God can calm her in the same way she should soothe her child:

> Do you say it is impossible always to govern one's feelings? There is one method, a never-failing one—prayer. It consoles and strengthens the wounded heart, and tranquillizes the most stormy passions. . . .

The inward ejaculation of "Lord, help me to overcome this temptation," may be made in any place and amid any employments; and if uttered in humble sincerity, the voice that said to the raging waters,
"Peace! Be still!" will restore quiet to your troubled soul. (5)

Thus, women who provide a safe haven from the storms of life
nurture the religious sensibilities of their children precisely because
that sort of nurture is a divine attribute. Child also asserts that
"there is no real religion that does not come from the heart" (66);
since emotion is in the province of women, a chapter of her book
teaches mothers how to manage "the affections" of their offspring.
For Child, God is very much like a good mother, and mothers represent God to their families.

Barbara Welter describes the True Woman who, in Child's view,
displays the attributes of God, as the nineteenth-century man's
"hostage in the home." She argues in "The Cult of True Womanhood" that materialistic concerns led him to ignore "the religious
values of his forbears" and that giving religion to women was a way
to "salve his conscience" (151). As Linda Kerber points out, Welter's
essay argues that the ideology of separate spheres is both "encouraging" and "restraining" for women (12). Later feminist historians, emphasizing the victimization of women, reinterpreted the separation
of spheres as a tool of social control that "served the interests of the
dominant class" (Kerber 13–14). However, Kerber suggests a third
and more interactive point of view that emphasizes

> how women's allegedly "separate sphere" was affected by what men
> did, and how activities defined by women in their own sphere influ-
> enced and even set constraints and limitations on what men might
> choose to do—how, in short, that sphere was socially constructed both
> *for* and *by* women. (18)

Kerber's articulation of the "third stage in the development of the
metaphor of separate spheres" (18) describes the view I take toward
evangelical women's relationship to hymns. I argue that pious, sin-
cere Protestant women were able to treat notions of gender that
were in circulation and shared by others as a medium of cultural exchange. They invested the currency of their special value as women
when they collected hymns, used them in their novels, and, especially later in the century, wrote hymns. In this process, women gained

the power to challenge the organizing myths and androcentric models of Protestantism: the idea of the Christian life as a journey in time toward a heavenly reward rather than as a Christian "walk," important for its own sake; the superiority of reason and thought to emotion and experience; the scheme in which life became a battle between the church and the world rather than an interior fight to submit the self to God's will; the model for salvation that required separation of the believer rather than absorption into a community; and a soteriology that focused on acceptance of doctrine rather than on behavior as the way to be saved.

The Walk of Faith

Collecting hymns, weaving them into their fiction, and analyzing hymn texts allowed women to develop scripts for a specifically feminine model of spiritual formation and to gain acceptance for these scripts in the evangelical community. Revising the journey model for salvation was crucial to this endeavor. Carol Ochs's *Women and Spirituality* (1983) describes the traditional model of spirituality as "male-centered" because it makes spiritual growth "an extension of the male maturational process that emphasizes individuation—coming into selfhood" (2). In this scheme, "traditional spirituality has . . . been characterized as a solitary journey to achieve salvation" (23). Ochs describes this journey as having a specific length and following a marked path. It is accomplished in stages that may be marked on a linear time line. The point of the journey is to bring the traveler to "a clearly defined destination." In contrast to this journey is what Ochs calls a "walk," characterized by "indeterminate" length, an unmarked or poorly marked path, and "no clearly defined destination." A walk is not linear; because it has no specific goal, its time scheme is cyclical. The point of the walk is the walk itself (117). Ochs uses the walk as a model for female spirituality, which values individual experience, relationships, and a nontraditional approach to space and time, and it is this female version of the spiritual journey that Anna B. Warner associates with hymns used as devotional aids. She justifies her interpretation of the journey with references to the most familiar and resonant texts of nineteenth-century

Protestantism, the King James Bible, and *The Pilgrim's Progress*.

As the title of her hymnal suggests, Anna Warner's *Wayfaring Hymns* is for travelers. Her dedication compares these wayfarers to nomads in the time of the Jewish patriarchs:

> I am asked for a dedication,—and to whom should it be, but to those who in every place, of every colour, of every age; owning "not so much as a foot," as yet, of the Promised Land; are "dwelling in the tabernacles with Isaac and Jacob."
>
> For they look for a "city which hath foundations."

The destination of the travelers in the passage is somewhat unclear; they are tent dwellers looking for a "city which hath foundations." This description of the wayfarers refers to a time before the communal exodus led by Moses, and each traveler, supported perhaps by a family, has an individual experience of the journey. Landmarks are less important than they would be if the journey were on a well-marked road because every small group of nomads may take a slightly different path. The length of the journey is also insignificant; the dedication is to people "of every age." Or, perhaps "of every age" means "of every era in history," a reference that makes no single historical experience of Christianity a monolithic standard. Further, Warner's reference to people "of every colour" implies that even the experience of those with little status in society is worth encouraging. Above all, with a promise but no clear path to "the Promised Land," the journey of faith itself is more important than reaching the goal. The biblical allusion in Warner's dedication is to Hebrews 11:8–10:

> By faith Abraham, when he was called to go out into a place which he should after receive for an inheritance obeyed; and he went out, not knowing whither he went. By faith he sojourned in the land of promise, as in a strange country, dwelling in tabernacles with Isaac and Jacob, the heirs with him of the same promise: For he looked for a city which hath foundations, whose builder and maker is God.

This passage names Abraham as one of the faithful who illustrate the definition of *faith* in Hebrews 11:1: "faith is the substance of things hoped for, the evidence of things not seen." Abraham, like others in the list (Abel, Noah, Sarah, etc.), gets "a good report" (v.2) because he travels without knowing exactly where he is going. Salvation lies in faithful behavior, i.e., in undertaking the journey, not in reaching the destination.

Similarly, the preface to Warner's 1859 collection called *Hymns of the Church Militant* emphasizes the value of making a personal pilgrimage over the accomplishment of reaching a goal. The preface to this hymnal states that it is "simply a book of hymns for private use" (iii); and the scriptural epigraph preceding the first hymn refers to the Exodus:

> Thou shalt remember all the way which the Lord thy God led thee these forty years in the wilderness, to humble thee and to probe thee, to know what was in thine heart, whether thou wouldest keep his commandments, or no. (Deut. viii. 2)

The context for this quotation is Moses' farewell address in Deuteronomy, delivered as the Israelites are encamped, ready to begin their assault on the inhabitants of their promised land. Moses directs their attention, not to the destination that lies ahead, but to the value of the journey they have just finished. As he tells them, it was a time of testing to determine if they were ready to reach the destination. In her preface, of course, Warner speaks to other Christians, for whom the Jewish people provide a typological analogy. Like the children of Israel at the beginning of Deuteronomy, the "church militant" is ready for battle—in contrast to the "church triumphant," the believers in heaven after the final victory. As warriors, their strength results from the demands of the journey just completed. The journey itself is a crucial experience, and hymns are an important aid on the journey.

In her preface, Warner removes the journey from the bounds of time and space when she separates genuine Christian experience (i.e., an individual and personal journey) from the doctrine of a particular sect, place, or period in history adopted as a universal model by every Christian. In short, she claims, the hymns in her collection are not "hymns written to order" but "living words of deep Christian experience" that prove "the Church is one" (iv). She explains, for example, that the hymns in her book are by hymnists who include Martin Luther, Charles Wesley, and an "old Catholic monk"; the diversity of their experiences testifies to the validity of their experiences. At the same time, she supports the validity of her own experience as a woman. Lutheran, Methodist, and Catholic doctrine and church polity would exclude her from participation in the most sacred religious exercises, but these exclusions do not matter when she reads hymns. Warner's assumption—that one should judge Christian experience by depth of feeling rather than by adherence to correct doctrine or church authority—challenges the right of anyone but God to determine another's spiritual condition.

The ideology of separate spheres allows Warner to mute the explosive nature of her challenge to ecclesiastical authority in the soft, nonthreatening language of the private sphere. But one remembers the fate of Anne Hutchinson, who asserted her right to hear the voice of God directly and trust her own feelings two centuries earlier. Hutchinson was banished from the Massachusetts Bay colony for breaking the fifth commandment ("Honor thy father and thy mother") or, in other words, for an intolerable challenge to male spiritual authority. By asserting the value of hymns as an aid to interpreting spiritual experience, Warner too risks a charge of antinomianism. If she listens to her own conscience and feelings, she could risk ignoring the guidance of established authority; indeed, she makes herself an authority. The issue, in the end, is not so much how to be saved as how to experience truth.

If the voice of truth comes from a God who is "outside or above this world," Carol Ochs says, then we must be saved "*from* this world" (24). If God is nonphysical, she argues, then the physical aspects of life are "suspect, if not absolutely evil" (21). In fact, in a traditional model for spirituality the primary experiences of a middle- or lower-class nineteenth-century woman's life (giving birth, nurturing the family, homemaking) are not the province of spiritual formation. However, Warner's suggestions for hymn use challenge the androcentric model by making concrete experience an avenue to the divine. On the page preceding the Scripture quoted above, she provides a dedication that quite specifically designates the home, not the church, as the place of spiritual renewal:

> These Hymns are here brought together for the Help of the Christian's life—the Joy and Comfort of the Sick Room—the Hope of the Doubting, and the Rest of the Weary in Heart. Under His Blessing

who has Promised to His People that "in the Days of Famine They shall be Satisfied."

Warner implies that hymns are the cultural property of women by suggesting their use in activities limited to the female sphere: nursing the sick, providing a quiet, harmonious place of rest, and feeding the hungry. The scriptural allusion in the last line is to Psalm 37, a psalm whose language in the King James Bible emphasizes the feminine qualities of God. For example, verse 1 speaks to the "righteous" in the language of a mother addressing a tired, emotionally distraught child: "Fret not thyself because of evildoers." Verse 3 promises that "trust in the Lord" and doing good will be rewarded because "verily thou shalt be fed."

In keeping with her emphasis on the private nature of faith, Warner suggests the personal journey of *The Pilgrim's Progress* in the title of *Wayfaring Hymns* and refers to Bunyan's work explicitly in her preface to *Hymns of the Church Militant*. Her references to Bunyan's allegory are neither surprising nor revolutionary; mid-nineteenth-century American writers allude to it so continually that such references are the mark of conventional, respectable evangelical Christianity. Its very respectability makes it safe. Yet Anna Warner's references change crucial aspects of the original allegory in ways that revise the original pilgrimage and recreate it for a new, nineteenth-century Christiana. Specifically, Warner manipulates the functions of allegory itself to challenge the Protestant social order that gave primary spiritual authority to men and relegated women to the role of second-class citizens in the kingdom of God.

The following lines from the preface to *Hymns of the Church Militant*, for example, use the language of *The Pilgrim's Progress* to show that singing hymns is an aid on the Christian pilgrimage and to suggest that those who use or promote the use of hymns would be following Christ in leading pilgrims toward the proper destination:

The Church are one here . . .—they suffer in mind, in body, in estate; with sometimes no sign of life but this—they would lie in the Slough of Despond for ever, rather than climb out on any side but that which is towards the Celestial City. . . . With one voice they sing,

"Heavenward the waves I'll breast
Till in heaven I am at rest."

Heavenward with Christ—after him. His headship over the Church is wonderfully set forth in their songs. (v)

In this passage, Christians travel toward the Celestial City, singing as they go as if singing allows them to maintain focus on the destination. But, in a hymnal that describes itself in terms of material for use in the female sphere, associating a private journey with hymns is also a way to associate the private journey with women. Nineteenth-century women were certainly expected to guide the spiritual journeys of their children, and hymns were a tool to use in this task.[5] In *The Mother's Book,* Lydia Maria Child advises mothers to assign hymns for their children to learn on Sunday:

> A little hymn every Sabbath is a pleasant and profitable lesson; and if it is simple enough to be understood, the child will amuse himself by repeating it through the week. Some of the very strongest impressions of childhood are made by the hymns learned at an early age. (70)

A few pages later, Child emphasizes the value of religious education (including hymn memorization) by saying it is "rearing beings for another world as well as for this" (74). However, she clearly describes the "other world" as an extension of this one when she suggests that death be beautified for children by sentimental funerary customs such as displaying the corpse attractively and making cemeteries landscaped "places of public promenade"; her aim is to help children regard death as "like going to a happy *home* [italics hers]" (81). The journey for Child is another cycle in a common repetitive activity of childhood: going home when the day is done.

The Pilgrim's Progress itself is full of hymns that aid Christian and Christiana; Secret, God's messenger, orders Christiana to use hymns on the journey when he tells her that the letter he bears from the King is "one of the Songs that thou must Sing while thou art in this House of thy Pilgrimage" (286). However, Bunyan assumes that Christiana is weaker spiritually than her husband. When she and her companion, Mercy, are nearly assaulted on the road, a character named Reliever comes to their aid and scolds these "*weak Women*" for not requesting a "*Conductor*" for their journey (299). Eventually, the women are assigned a guide, Mr. Great-Heart, who fights their battles for them and protects them from spiritual danger. In contrast, Warner's belief that hymns are both encouragement for the road and the cultural property of women reverses the roles of Christiana and Mr. Great-Heart: using hymns makes women spiritual guides because hymn use belongs to the sphere of genuine feeling, the province of women. As Angus Fletcher argues, because allegory creates a hierarchical model of reality, it does more than simply assign a person's "proper place"; it also describes his or her "legitimate powers" (22–23).

In general, however, traditional allegorical functions begin to disintegrate in Warner's rhetoric. Warner undermines the way allegory reduces complex human experience to an abstraction statable in a few words because she associates hymns with the concrete experiences of real life rather than with doctrine. She says, for example, that she wishes she knew the "history" of each hymn in *Hymns of the Church Militant* since she feels sure that "some special circumstances called it forth." She also names concrete details about the manuscripts she has studied as a way to evoke the personality of the hymnist or the owner of the text:

> The hymn on page 218, was found treasured up in a chest in some poor cottage in England—that on page 615 is a French hymn, written in Paris during the cholera summer of 1832. . . . The old leaf whereon I found "The Saviour's Merit," . . . was so worn through with use, though the rest of the book was perfect, that some few words had to be supplied. (iii–iv)

These words suggest spirituality that demonstrates itself in the everyday, the concrete, the world of feeling—in short, in the world of women. One hymn is found "treasured up in a chest," a suggestion of women's domestic focus on preservation rather than on "acquiring."[6] Another is a "French hymn" written during "the cholera summer of 1832," a time when unexpected tragedy would have forced many into a spiritual walk of "indeterminate" length. The third is the object of private devotional use; in other words, it belongs to the private sphere, where it is read, not sung. Warner's insistence on grounding her discussion of hymns in personal history also makes hymns into spiritual scripts; they provide models for other Christians in similar circumstances rather than state doctrine as a basis for faith. Many titles in *Wayfaring Hymns* suggest this practical function of hymns: "Walking with God," "Be of Good Cheer," "On Thee Do I Wait All the Day," "A Morning Song," "The Song of a Tired Servant."

This shift to a focus on the Christian walk requires a nonlinear view of time very different from Bunyan's concept. To explain to Christian the allegorical dichotomy represented by Passion and Patience, the Interpreter explains the necessity of focusing on the end of the journey:

> *Patience* will have to laugh at *Passion* because he had his best things *last;* for *first* must give place to *last,* because *last* must have his time to come, but *last* gives place to *nothing,* for there is not another to succeed. (164)

Having internalized the symbolic lesson, Christian concludes, "*I perceive, 'tis not best to covet things that are* now, *but to wait for things to* come" (164). Accordingly, in *The Pilgrim's Progress,* hymns are either encouragement to reach the goal or modes of instruction for those who follow the pilgrims. Warner, in contrast, views hymns in terms of the lives they represent and the way they create a community of spectators who cheer the Christian on during his or her "progress": "To me, the hymns have been like a vision of the 'great cloud of witnesses'" (*Hymns of the Church Militant* iv). Her quotation alludes to Hebrews 12:1, which describes the Christian life as a race witnessed by the faithful of all ages, those discussed earlier in my analysis of Hebrews 11. Saying that the hymns themselves "have been like a vision of the 'great cloud of witnesses'" associates hymns with lives rather than with ideas or goals. In this scheme, the hymns she has collected exist in a realm of cyclical and eternal time because the faithful appear in every age, yet all still remain by the path to witness her pilgrimage. Anna Warner implies that her goal is to join the group rather than just to finish the race honorably.

She also emphasizes the communal experience of Christianity. Warner's believer is like Christiana in the second book of Bunyan's allegory rather than like Christian because her believer travels always in the company of other pilgrims who are fighting interior spiritual battles. Warner claims in the preface to *Hymns of the Church Militant* that the repeated hymnic comparisons of Christianity to an internal battle with sin actually "[tells] us that the Church is one" (iv). In contrast, if the battle is on male property (sermons and theological treatises), the result is a pseudobattle that causes division among the ranks:

> In prose, one denomination will war with another,—war, and strive—as some of the disciples did—for a place above the rest. The Church Militant is to outward eyes, often a Church divided against itself—every banner attacking every other, forgetful that the great standard of the Prince of Peace floats over all.
> Yet this is but a difference of head—look here [i.e., in this hymnal] at their hearts. Read Luther and some old Catholic monk, side by side,—read Wesley, and all he ever opposed, or who ever opposed him. They fight still, but it is with themselves, with sin, with unbelief. (iv)

According to Warner, public Christianity is only "head" religion, a facade characterized by denominational battles in which the most celebrated warriors are those who gain "a place above the rest." But in a heart religion the battle rages in the interior world of private emotions and the struggle with sin and despair; this world is the domain of women, who are the ranking officers on their own turf. Used for "the Help of the Christian's life," then, hymns give women the spiritual authority of a commander directing the ordinary soldiers in the field while removing them as leaders from the spiritual corruption of active combat in the public sphere.

In short, the familiar martial imagery Anna Warner adopts is subversive: the spiritual authority women acquire by using hymns both challenges the hierarchy of command in Christendom and radically reorients the meaning of spirituality. If the battle is no longer among opponents trying to best each other (i.e., the various Christian denominations) but against a larger, more dangerous foe, then ecclesiastical authority is not as important as personal spiritual resources. If home is the place for spiritual renewal engineered by women, then battle imagery is no longer as important as domestic language for revealing spiritual truth. If God gives spiritual authority to women, then women must be made in the image of God. More to the point, if women act with spiritual authority, then God is female as well as male.

Hymns in Domestic Novels

Domestic or sentimental novels of the period help us contextualize the specific uses of hymns as cultural property within the culture of nineteenth-century Protestant women in America. Written by women and clergymen and targeted primarily for women, this popular literature frequently and characteristically refers to hymns and incorporates hymn texts into the narratives. These novels provide a fruitful way to explore the notions of nineteenth-century Americans because, as Jane Tompkins argues, they "[tap] into a storehouse of commonly held assumptions, reproducing what is already there in a typical and familiar form" (*Sensational Designs* xvi). Although, with some exceptions, the hymns reproduced or described in these novels were written by men, their use by women reveals nineteenth-century writers' and readers' assumptions about spiritual roles. In general, female characters in domestic novels use hymns in the private sphere in distinctive ways: to reinterpret God and spirituality in terms of a female epistemology that finds the divine in concrete experiences and envisions spiritual reality in domestic terms, to create community and promote the pleasure women find in each other's company, and to influence others' spiritual development. In contrast, both male and female novelists agree that men may use hymns to exert social control and to teach doctrine or codes of conduct in public.

In the social scheme above, women's roles are those that promote religious feelings, especially the perception of the immanence of divinity and the intense pleasure of religion. These are characteristics highly valued by nineteenth-century evangelicals. Edward Halsey Foster, biographer of Anna Warner and her sister, Susan Warner, defines *evangelicalism* by quoting the description of "Spiritual Religion" in a book by the women's pastor, Thomas Harvey Skinner. Skinner asserts that "Spiritual Religion" is that

> which can be satisfied with nothing merely external, however blameless and fair. The offering up of prayer and praise, meditation on the Scriptures, attendance upon ordinances, liberality toward the poor, the utmost exactness and irreproachableness of life—these do not meet its demands, unless there is correspondent sensibility and life in the

heart. There must be a feeling of the Divine presence; a relishing of the Divine excellence; a heart-assured persuasion of the Divine favour and complacency. God must be enjoyed. (qtd. in E. Foster 29)

As this passage suggests, the combination of hymns and novels about the home to be read in the home is particularly powerful because the home is associated with spiritual feelings, the hallmark of true religion for evangelical Christians. Thomas Harvey Skinner describes true religion in terms of "sensibility and life in the heart," "feeling of the Divine presence," "heart-assured persuasion." Therefore, the use of hymns in domestic novels endorses spiritual authority specifically associated with women, authority they were not granted in American Protestantism before the rise of nineteenth-century evangelicalism.

It is easy today to overlook the subversive nature of using hymns in novels rather than in private devotions or worship services. However, as Cathy N. Davidson argues, many nineteenth-century Protestants looked askance at novels because they challenged the male ministers' "role as the primary interpreters of American culture" (42). The reader of a novel, upon encountering a hymn, can interpret it within the created reality of the narrative. As Davidson and others have noted, the novel's effect is to "relocate authority in the individual response of the reading self" (14). In addition, the seductive, engrossing nature of fiction makes it a potentially devastating threat to the minister's authority (14, 43). Sermons and church administration rely more on rational analysis and didactic pronouncements by an indisputable authority than on the less controllable but, perhaps, more appealing motivation of religious emotion. But while domestic/sentimental novels with religious narratives certainly warranted the suspicion of those who controlled public religion, they also furthered the evangelical agenda of soul winning in ways that male religious authorities must have found hard to criticize.

Susan Warner's *The Wide, Wide World* (1850), for example, makes the discussion of hymns a vehicle for the young protagonist's conversion and a tool to aid her spiritual growth throughout the novel. In *The Wide, Wide World*, Ellen Montgomery leaves her saintly mother and uncaring father to live with her stern Aunt Fortune, who is literally a "Miss Fortune" (E. Foster 35), a woman who does her duty but has no love for the child. Hymns comfort, strengthen, and instruct the lonely girl; memorizing their words from a book given to her by a friendly stranger on the trip to Aunt Fortune's becomes her chief pleasure in life. Significantly, the volume is small enough to keep in her pocket (88).

In a pivotal scene, Ellen discusses one of these hymns, Charles Wesley's "A Charge to Keep I Have," with an older friend and spiritual guide, Alice Humphreys. The text describes a Christian's duty as that of a servant toward an exacting master:

> A charge to keep I have—
> A God to glorify;
> A never-dying soul to save,
> And fit it for the sky.
>
> To serve the present age,
> My calling to fulfill;
> Oh may it all my powers engage
> To do my father's will.
>
> Arm me with jealous care
> As in thy sight to live;
> And oh! thy servant, Lord, prepare
> A strict account to give.

Alice first recasts Wesley's eighteenth-century text for Ellen in terms of nineteenth-century domesticity. To define a "charge," she moves the usually public—thus, male—activity of accepting a charge on behalf of someone else to the private female sphere by relating an anecdote about being left at home in charge of her baby sister (238–39). More subversively, in explicating "A God to glorify," and doing her "father's will," she redefines God as female by saying that obedience to God is the equivalent of Ellen's obedience to her mother. Wesley's hymn is, in fact, one that Ellen's mother particularly loved (238). When Ellen asks how she can honor (glorify) God, Alice responds with, "Must not your behaviour speak either well or ill for the mother who has brought you up?" (239). Later, Alice compares the way Ellen's behavior reflects her mother's character to how a Christian's behavior testifies to the character of God: "I thought [your mother] must be a refined and cultivated person from the manner of your speech and behaviour; and I was sure she was a Christian, because she had taught you the truth, and evidently had tried to lead you in it" (240).

As Tompkins argues, this process of allying mothers with God in the novel creates "a feminist theology in which the godhead is refashioned into an image of maternal authority" (*Sensational Designs* 163). In keeping with this revised theology, Alice shrinks "the wide, wide world" to the home when she explains that Ellen's "calling to fulfill" is to serve others in her home "in the faithful, patient, self-denying performance of every duty as it comes to hand" (239). Alice also explicates in domestic terms the last stanza of the hymn, which begins with martial imagery ("Arm me with jealous care") and ends by describing a servant in a business who must give a strict accounting to the master. Once again, the field of activity is the home and the "master" is a mistress because Alice compares giving an account to handing her servant Thomas a dollar to buy something for use in the home and then expecting an "account" of how he spent it when he returns.

As part of her hymn explication, Alice relates salvation to action rather than to belief in correct doctrine. She views conversion as a process rather than as a single, decisive event occurring at a particular point in linear time. When she explains that Ellen will have to "give account" on the Day of Judgment, Ellen is worried that her name might not be in the "Lamb's book of life." Discerning if she is among the saved, Alice explains, comes from examining her actions rather than her beliefs. She adds that Ellen should act as if she loved God by being kind to her exasperating old grandmother and by showing perfect submission to Aunt Fortune and, thus, one infers, to her fate (241). Assurance of faith will come as the result of action. As Alice explains,

> "My dear child, . . . if you love Jesus Christ you may know you are his child, and none shall pluck you out of his hand."
> "But how can I tell whether I do love him really? sometimes I think I do, and then again sometimes I am afraid I don't at all."
> Alice answered in the words of Christ;—"He that hath my commandments and keepeth them, he it is that loveth me." (242)

This move from action to faith rather than from faith to action challenges the model for salvation proclaimed publicly in sermons of the period, which began with doctrine (reading of Scripture, then explication of the text) and ended with an application suggesting action in accordance with correct belief. In *The Model Preacher: Comprised in a Series of Letters Illustrating The Best Mode of Preaching the Gospel* (1860), one of the many homiletics manuals published during this period, Rev. William Taylor outlines the characteristic format. It is, he says, the model supplied by Jesus, the greatest preacher: "In presenting a point or proposition, or in defining and enforcing a duty, his plan was first to state the subject clearly, in the fewest and simplest words possible—then illustrate—then apply" (97). Alice Humphreys reverses this process with Ellen. The text for her private "sermon" is a hymn composed by Charles Wesley, an imposing authority but, nevertheless, a human being; she does not focus on Scripture, words from a sacred document delivered by God and, thus, beyond dispute. Alice suggests that Ellen apply the hymn's truths to test them; she leaves room for error or difference of opinion. In effect, when Alice counsels Ellen to act before she believes, she reverses a process that privileges abstract laws or norms, a part of public religion that women cannot control, over individual behavior, which they can. Alice also rejects the social or spatial position of a male minister. She does not stand above her student making pronouncements that can only be accepted, never openly questioned. She does not require a lonely individual response from Ellen; instead, she allows Ellen to acquire spiritual insight through interacting with her. Her teaching involves Ellen in the process of discerning truth through a discussion of concrete situations. For the young woman and the girl, salvation requires a personal relationship with another human being and a communal sense of shared experience.

During this episode, Ellen not only learns from her friend; she also establishes intimate physical contact with her. She begins the conversation in Alice's arms:

> "I am *so* glad you are come, dear Alice!" said Ellen. . . . "I wish I could have you always!" And the long, very close pressure of her two arms about her friend said as much. There was a long pause. The cheek of Alice rested on Ellen's head which nestled against her. (238)

Later, Ellen sobs with her head in Alice's lap, and the scene ends with her head on Alice's shoulder, which is now wet with her tears (240–43). Thus, the hymn not only provides a teaching tool for the two; reading and discussing it also provoke strong emotions that lead naturally to physical and emotional closeness. Ellen's spiritual awareness is intimately tied to her sense of community and connection with Alice.

In this scene between a young woman and a girl, a nineteenth-century reader would likely see a touching image of maternal affection: Alice's behavior expresses the love of God and emphasizes its feminine qualities while Ellen's response demonstrates a child's physical and emotional bonds with the mother. In an unpublished final chapter of *The Wide, Wide World*, in fact, Ellen and her new husband, John, contrast the effects of two pictures, one of a "recumbent Magdalen," the other of a Madonna and child that Warner describes in terms very similar to those she uses to describe Alice and Ellen:

> The mother's face in calm beauty bent over that of the infant as if about to give the kiss her lips were already pouting for; the expression of grave maternal dignity and love; but in the child's uplifted deep blue eye there was a perfect heaven of affection, while the little mouth was parted, it might be either for a kiss or a smile, ready for both. (578)

In the ensuing conversation, Ellen and John agree that the picture of maternal love represents "moral beauty" and "the immaterial soul" while the picture of the recumbent Magdalen, associated with sexual love, is beautiful but merely "physical" (578).[7]

Hymn sharing in *The Wide, Wide World* provides the context for what Lillian Faderman calls a "romantic friendship" between Alice and Ellen (74). When Alice and Ellen discuss a hymn, the conversation creates a bond of affection; learning is a matter of being drawn into communion with another person. Ellen associates reading hymns in her home with tenderness, physical intimacy, camaraderie, and the free expression of her feelings because these characteristics of love between women are also components of a spirituality that valorizes intense intimacy. As Faderman explains, nineteenth-century women saw such a relationship as "ennobling" because it was passionate but nonsexual (151, 159–61). Jane Tompkins argues that "the affection and closeness that women share in the sheltered spaces of domestic fiction . . . embody an intimacy that takes the place of heterosexual love" (Afterword 600). In contrast, when Ellen discusses or sings hymns with men, the experience emphasizes her lack of status and need to submit to the opinions of another. Discussing the hymn is, perhaps, a beneficial experience, but its benefit is the result of intensifying the distance between her and another person, not of creating a sense of communion.

In the scene where Alice and Ellen discuss "A Charge to Keep I Have," Ellen feels comforted and relaxed. She prays, and, afterward, "rose up comforted, her mind fixing on those most sweet words Alice had brought to her memory" (243). She and Alice are, in fact, physically demonstrative even at their first meeting, when Alice finds Ellen weeping convulsively on a hillside and gently counsels her. Ellen kisses Alice with no hesitation at the end of this meeting, and Alice, in fact, asks for another kiss before she leaves (155). In contrast, when Ellen receives a hymnal with several hymns marked for her to study from a man on the boat to Aunt Fortune's, she is overwhelmed with remorse because he helps her see that she loves her mother better than God. Her new friend does not explicate the hymns for her; he simply points out a hymn as illustration of the religious principles he has been expounding. She does not show physical affection for him although she leans against him and falls asleep at one point, implying her dependence on a stronger person (77). At the end of the scene, Ellen dries her tears "with a sort of despairing submission" (82). The phrase indicates that her friend's goal was to help her gain control of her emotions although his tender concern for her welfare is also obvious. He leaves her with kisses on her cheek "that sent a thrill of pleasure to Ellen's heart that she did not get over that evening, nor all the next day" (82). Here she is the recipient, not the giver of caresses, and her "thrill of pleasure" suggests awareness that these kisses bestow some honor on her.

The use of hymns as narrative elements in domestic novels suggests, then, that female spirituality operates on two levels and that women participate in two different cultures with two different sets of values. In female culture, they learn and develop by establishing community with others; in a sense, communion with others is in itself a spiritual process. Indeed, female characters often read or sing hymns at home in novels of the period specifically to establish or strengthen relationships and sometimes to invoke the presence of dead or absent family members. Such use of hymns lends an air of spiritual glory to women. In *Little Women* (1868), for example, Beth is both the musician who leads the others in singing hymns and the spiritual leader of the family, much more so than her father, who is absent for most of the story. The night before Marmee leaves to bring home the ailing Mr. March, "Beth went to the piano and played the father's favorite hymn; all began bravely, but broke down one by one till Beth was left alone, singing with all her heart, for to her music was always a sweet consoler" (152). The hymn invokes Mr. March's presence so strongly that the sisters leave the room "as silently as if the dear invalid lay in the next room" (152). Afterward, Meg and Jo go to their shared bed. In the night, Meg hears Jo crying over her hair, which she has sold for money to bring Mr. March home. Meg's response is to comfort her sister: she "kissed and caressed the afflicted heroine in the tenderest manner" (152). As the scene suggests, the hymn united the family in a tender web of concern that provoked physical expression. Beth, the promoter of hymn use, also acquires the status of a sacred object by the end of the story, where Alcott describes her as "a household saint in its shrine" (378). As "its" implies, she has transcended her sexual identity, yet her place is still in the home, where she influences others, but only when they come to her "shrine."

Despite their status within the domestic setting, however, nineteenth-century women were also part of a larger cultural community of Christians that included people of both sexes. Within this larger culture, women helped maintain an epistemology that valued hierarchy over communality. Even within the home, women did not use hymns to create community with those who were not part of the female world (which included servants and children of both sexes). However, they could use hymns indirectly to influence men. Spiritual guidance from women was acceptable only if it happened by accident or if a woman behaved so ingenuously that it could not be perceived as a challenge to male authority.[8] For example, when Alice dies, Ellen realizes that her father, Reverend Humphreys, is distraught with grief. Eventually, Alice's brother, John, suggests that she sing a hymn to comfort him. She sits on the sofa in a darkened room where Reverend Humphreys can hear but not see her and begins to sing, her spirit lightening as she sings hymns such as John Newton's "How Sweet the Name of Jesus Sounds" and Charles Wesley's "Jesus, Lover of My Soul." The narrator notes that Ellen's voice is not "powerful" but that the "feeling" with which she sings makes up for other deficiencies. With her physical presence concealed, Ellen's expression of the hymn itself, enhanced by the "feeling" she brings to it, becomes the medium of influence. At the end, Reverend Humphreys rises, embraces Ellen, and says she has been a comfort to him (451–54). Later, Ellen uses the same strategy to influence her uncle after her grandmother refuses to allow her the consolation of a daily devotional hour. Ellen's singing of "Rock of Ages" alone in her room is so moving that he intercedes to restore her quiet meditation time (545).

As these examples show, hymns are both real and powerful tools, especially for those denied a direct and public voice. Other domestic novels of the mid-nineteenth century show characters using hymns to empower those without formal spiritual authority, and, in some cases, that power transcends barriers of space, time, race, and class. In *Uncle Tom's Cabin* (1852), Harriet Beecher Stowe gives such authority to both women and slaves. Augustine St. Clare's mother, for example, is able to influence her son's conversion even from beyond the grave. St. Clare is converted on his deathbed through recalling his mother's transcription of the "Dies Irae" from Mozart's *Requiem*. Appropriately, when he dies, he cries not "Jesus," but "Mother!" (369–70). Uncle Tom, who has by far the greatest spiritual authority and power of any character in the novel, also sings and discusses hymns constantly. At one point, he infuriates his master, Simon Legree, by singing Isaac Watts's "When I Can Read My Title Clear" where Legree can overhear. The irony of the hymn choice is unmistakable: Tom cannot own himself, much less his own "cabin," yet he can sing with assurance of a title to "mansions in the sky." Enraged, Legree beats Tom, but he cannot "hide from himself that his power over his bond thrall was gone" (458–59). Throughout *Uncle Tom's Cabin*, Stowe often establishes an affinity between women and black slaves; she shows, for example, that both are "home-loving" and "naturally more impressible to religious sentiment than the white [man]" (118, 270). And both use hymns in the home to gain power over others.

In contrast, the public use of hymns is reserved for men in domestic novels. Bringing hymns into the public sphere does not remove them entirely from their association with women, however. By 1873, the publication date of the Rev. E. P. Roe's *Barriers Burned Away*, using hymns implies a refined sensibility that marks true religion, a religion of feeling. In the novel, the young protagonist, Dennis Fleet, is closely identified with his saintly mother. Roe says that "while he had the heart and courage of a man, he also had the quick supple hand and gentle bearing of a woman, when occasion required" (26). Dennis demonstrates a domesticated approach to religion when he is called upon to comfort his younger sisters upon the death of their father. His first response is to pull them into another room where they can "sing a pretty hymn about papa's sleep" (25).

Having established Dennis's spiritual authority through his use of hymns in the first chapter, Roe continues a tale that reveals the young man's social authority as well. Dennis is in love with Christine Ludolph, his employer's proud, haughty daughter, even though she is above him in social status; in fact, a major theme of the novel is that he has true nobility of character that can be revealed only in public situations that put him to the test. Christine's aristocratic lineage, in contrast, can only be proven by her submission to authority. When the great Chicago fire engulfs their city, Dennis rescues Christine from her burning house, demonstrating his role as the savior to whom she must submit if she is to be saved. Bursting into Christine's bedroom, he finds her in a drugged sleep. When she is unable to dress herself, Dennis decides that he must play the part of a "brother or husband" and cover "her wildly throbbing bosom" (415). Only by submitting her body and its sexual possibilities to him can Christine be saved either physically or spiritually.

In the next scene, in fact, Christine undergoes an emotional conversion experience, and Dennis proves his spiritual superiority by using hymns to control others. Standing in Lake Michigan with Christine and other hysterical people who have begun to fight to get farther into the water, Dennis sings Charles Wesley's "Jesus, Lover of My Soul." Dennis's singing calms and comforts the crowd, which then looks to him for direction (427). Later, in a church where Dennis and Christine take refuge along with many others, Christine asks him to sing something to help the refugees. He stands and sings a hymn in a "sweet, clear voice" that "penetrates every part of the large building." Afterward, Christine and the others are crying, and she says he has done them good, presumably by taking control as their spiritual leader (463–64).

In these scenes, Dennis is truly spiritual because he is like his mother, a trait confirmed by his love of hymns. But Roe shows him appropriating what has been associated with women and the home as a tool of social control. Roe claims that being a true man requires aggressive behavior if one is to be a spiritual leader. Speaking of men and women tried by difficult circumstances, he writes that True Women

> become unselfishly devoted to others, and by gentle, self-denying ways seek to impart to those about them the happiness denied to themselves. But with all manly young men, the instinct of Dennis is perhaps the most common. They will rise, shine, and dazzle the eyes that once looked scornfully or indifferently at them. (375)

In this passage, Roe could be contrasting Dennis with Ellen Montgomery. She uses hymns to establish community with others in a way that cancels her individuality through unselfish service; he uses hymns to individuate himself and establish control of others. She relates to a god who is like a good mother. He can "rise, shine, and dazzle the eyes," as if he were a god himself. Ellen behaves as if she loves God; then she has faith. In *Barriers Burned Away,* Christine, who despairs of having faith, follows the same pattern. As she and Dennis watch the fire on the shore of Lake Michigan, she has an epiphany that leads to faith when she helps an injured woman. Dennis, on the other hand, frequently recalls his religious instruction, then acts to express the principles he has been taught. Most important, while Ellen and Christine can only "influence" others, Dennis can use power directly in public. Susie Winthrop, one of Dennis and Christine's friends, also sings a hymn in the church building where Dennis sings, but Roe describes her as maddened with shock and grief so that she does not know where she is. His explanation is charitable in that it excuses Susie for usurping a man's prerogative.

Barriers Burned Away illustrates the way hymns used in the public sphere retain the spiritual authority associated with women and the feminine qualities of God but use that authority, ironically, to control the emotions and behavior of others. In *Stepping Heavenward* (1869), novelist and hymnist Elizabeth Prentiss hints that hymns lose their true spiritual significance once they become public. Her novel is a feminine revision of *The Pilgrim's Progress* in which the "steps" one takes toward heaven occur in a domestic context and represent a Christian walk that can be influenced by hymns. At one point, Katy Elliott, the protagonist, visits a dying friend and tries to direct her attention to the state of her soul by quoting lines from a hymn: "O Saviour, whose mercy severe in its kindness / Hath chastened my wanderings, and guided my way." Her friend Amelia, a vain, materialistic woman, is not interested:

> "I don't care much for hymns," she said. "When one is well, and everything goes quite to one's mind, it is nice to go to church and sing with the rest of them. But, sick as I am, it isn't so easy to be religious." (216)

The fact that Amelia associates hymns only with a pleasant experience of church music rather than with the serious business of her own salvation reveals her spiritual peril. As Prentiss implies, organized religion as expressed in church worship services can even hinder salvation if it diverts the sinner's attention to surface matters.

Hymns Move into the Public Sphere

A minister writing about this time shows, though, that in his mind hymns can be used in a worship service to evoke all the positive qualities of private religion as it is experienced in the home. The *Lectures on Preaching* given at Yale University by Henry Ward Beecher and published in 1873 include "Relations of Music to Worship." In this lecture, Beecher describes hymn singing and other music as the true "worshiping element" that inspires the imagination and "affect[s], not so much the understanding, as that part of man's nature which the sermon usually leaves comparatively barren" (115–16). At the end, he amplifies his remarks by classifying parts of the sermon according to their function in engaging elements of human nature:

> The sermon represents the intellectual nature. That is the foundation from which you start. Now, I do not think that the hymn does [represent the intellectual nature], nor the prayer. They commence at once with feeling as something already generated, and I have just said, represent and develop the emotional element of worship. (145)

These remarks by Beecher, probably the most popular preacher of his day, indicate his acceptance of, indeed, his reliance on hymns in public worship by the early 1870s. Early in the lecture, he describes music as a tool for encouraging worship and labels it "one of the most important auxiliaries of the preacher" and "the preacher's prime minister" (114, 116). But his separation of elements of worship maintains the dichotomy that associated hymns with the private sphere of emotion and sermons with the public sphere of intellectual activity. This polarization suggests that, as hymns became established parts of public worship, they brought with them strong associations with women and feminized religion. I have argued in this chapter that, as long as hymns were as important for private devotions as for public worship, they remained the cultural property of women. However, after about 1870,[9] hymns became more important in church worship services than they had been earlier in the century, and their power was appropriated in some ways by ministers, as I illustrate below. As if to demonstrate women's loss of control over hymns, late-nineteenth-century fiction portrays women using them in more rigidly prescribed roles than in the domestic novels.

This change implies that the evangelical community may have been questioning women's roles in relationship to church music. Since more women were writing published hymns by this time, perhaps women's connections to hymns threatened men in their churches in a way they had not before. Certainly, gospel hymns, first popularized through their distribution for Sunday schools, were making their way into hymnals published by Protestant denominations (Reynolds 19). These hymns were associated with women in two ways. First, Sunday schools were run primarily by women. According to William J. Reynolds, ministers and other church admin-istrators frequently thought of the Sunday school as a "'competitor' to the church" because its monetary collections were separate from church funds (20). Second, gospel hymns employed language that Sandra Sizer labels "evangelical domesticity" (87), the rhetoric of spiritual experience found in domestic novels and other popular lit-erature. In any case, the problems of making hymns public property and the consequent loss of control over them by women is graphi-cally illustrated in two novels published in 1896, Harold Frederic's *The Damnation of Theron Ware* and Charles Sheldon's *In His Steps*.

Harold Frederic satirizes women who would use hymns publicly to exert social control in his characterization of the "debt raiser," Sis-ter Soulsby, a woman brought in to raise funds needed to pay off the debt in Reverend Ware's Methodist Church. Frederic presents Sis-ter Soulsby as an almost uncontrollable force because she combines the power of the public and the private spheres. She uses the emo-tional appeal of hymns to control church members, but her motiva-tion and business acumen are those of a man for whom profit is the highest goal. Sister Soulsby's masculinity is, in fact, one of her most notable characteristics. During their first meeting, Ware notices that she is "like a busy man of affairs" and that she kisses his wife in a "masterful manner" (134). Another time, she offers to shake hands "in a frank, manly fashion" (143). Even though she depends on the emotions evoked by hymns for successful fund raising, she also dis-misses the value of emotions, telling Reverend Ware that she has been converted "dozens of times . . . but that's a matter of tempera-ment—of emotions" (178). In her eyes, good religion is a matter of "machinery, management, organization" (179).

Sister Soulsby's first tactic is to stand up during the quarterly "love feast" and sing "Rock of Ages" to an unfamiliar tune with her husband providing an unusual and beautiful "second" (149). Later, the reader discovers that she chooses tunes by Chopin as new set-tings for familiar words. Frederic describes how the audience, "lis-tening in rapt attention, felt the suggestion of reserved power in every sentence she uttered, and burst forth . . . in a loud chorus of ejaculations." Equating the event with the first battle of a war, the writer claims "the Soulsbys had captured Octavius with their first outer skirmish line" (150). The next day, when Sister Soulsby turns a revival meeting into a way to retire the church debt by locking the church doors until the congregation raises the necessary funds, individuals in the audience are willing to make pledges totaling the $1,500 required. Again, her "delightfully novel sacred duets" move the audience to do her bidding (160).

Sister Soulsby's use of the standard hymn texts made fresh by compelling music to excite the emotions of Theron Ware's congregation reminds a modern reader of nothing so much as the tactics of a televangelist. However, Sister Soulsby represents a sinister threat to the church because she is more than simply a clever con artist. Her strategy is a direct appropriation of power in a church that vests spiritual authority in the feelings of the individual believer. As she explains to Ware, she simply fills a vacuum:

> "Now a church is like everything else—it's got to have a boss, a head, an authority of some sort, that people will listen to and mind. The Catholics are different. . . . Their church is chuck-full of authority— all the way from the Pope down to the priest—and accordingly they do as they're told. But the Protestants—your Methodists most of all— they say 'No, we won't have any authority, we won't obey any boss.' Very well, what happens? We who are responsible for running the thing, and raising the money and so on—we have to put on a spurt every once in a while, and work up a general state of excitement, and while it's going, don't you see that *that* is the authority, the motive power, whatever you like to call it, by which things are done?" (178)

In this passage, Frederic illustrates the threat of women's authority that has always been feared in evangelical churches when he shows the power of a woman's hymns to move people to action. In the "opening skirmish," for example, Sister Soulsby chooses the powerful associations the congregation has with "Rock of Ages" to achieve her goal. Though most of Augustus M. Toplady's text was published in 1775 and 1776 (Reynolds 186), the theme of a pious woman clinging to the rock of ages is a frequent motif in sentimental art and literature and reappears in many gospel hymns.[10] As a familiar and well-loved cliche, it has the power to move people to act—both in the novel and in real life—without causing them to think. In fact, Frederick describes the members of this Methodist church as mesmerized by Sister Soulsby's "tranquillizing" overture to her fund raising. The next day, Sister Soulsby controls the congregation so completely that no one protests when she begins to preach to them. Sister Soulsby even mocks the biblical injunction against women preachers by saying that "she deferred to Paul's views about women preachers on Sundays . . . but on week-days she had just as much right to snatch brands from the burning as Paul, or Peter, or any other man" (159).

Sister Soulsby's comments about women preaching reveal the heart of evangelical fears about women's power in churches. The real issue was not whether women should participate in worship services but whether they should be allowed to speak before men, to have a public voice. Evangelical women who promoted women's missionary support groups encountered the same problem. Catherine B. Allen, historian of the Southern Baptist Woman's Missionary Union, explains that Baptist women in the South faced enormous opposition when they organized in 1888. The problem was not that anyone doubted their sincerity or value as supporters of missionary efforts. What men feared was that empowering women in any way would lead inevitably to women speaking in public. Allen gives numerous examples of pronouncements by men who feared the slippery slope of allowing women to organize.

A characteristic statement is this one from a committee of the Baptist General Association of Virginia:

> It is to be feared that a separate and distinct organization of the women of the churches for independent mission work might have a tendency, in its ultimate results at least, to compromise that womanly reserve and modesty, and as Paul styles it, that "shamefacedness," which is in our esteem . . . beyond all price. Not only so, but we further fear that such an independent organization of women naturally tends toward a violation of the divine interdict against women's becoming a public religious teacher and leader—a speaker before mixed assemblies, a platform declaimer, a pulpit proclaimer, street preacher, lyceum lecturer, stump orator. (Qtd. in Allen 30–31)

Although the committee frames its reservations in terms of biblical injunctions, Allen's interpretation is more pragmatic. As she says, "A primal fear was economic." Many men, concerned that women controlled the wealth of their families and impressed by church women's competence at money raising, feared that a public voice would change the way money was spent (30, 32, 42). Sister Soulsby's success as a fund raiser aptly illustrates the realization of these fears.

In the last analysis, Frederic satirizes a church that has lost its intellectual rigor, that depends on emotions to control people and "good frauds" like Sister Soulsby (179) to take care of business, that is vulnerable to what Scott Donaldson labels "the gospel of expediency" (xxvii). In this climate, women are dangerous without control because they have powerful cultural property that can aid them in seizing power. Although Frederic's portrayal of Methodists as simple-minded, materialistic dupes of a con artist is reductive, his picture of hymns as cultural property available by 1896 to anyone who wants to control the church is shrewd. What is at once the power and the danger of hymns is their powerful connection to the private domain of emotions, the world of women in which religious pleasure, even ecstasy is possible. Carol Ochs contends that recognition of such danger "results in society's trying to tame and control the experience by creating safe outlets for it and situations in which it can occur, such as institutionalized religious practices" (8).

The Appropriation of Women's Property

As Ochs argues further, though, controlling spiritual experience brings its own dangers, one of which is the possibility of "controlling something other than what was intended" (8). Charles Sheldon's social gospel novel *In His Steps,* published the same year as *The Damnation of Theron Ware,* illustrates the way a minister controls a woman by making her public use of hymns subordinate to his own agenda. As the novel shows, hymns as cultural property can be left ostensibly in the hands of women when they are encouraged to sing in worship services but denied a public voice other than the text of the hymn. In this way, men can appropriate the emotional power of hymns but control those in whose hands their power might be threatening.

At the beginning of the story, an existential crisis prompts the

Rev. Henry Maxwell to give his congregation an extraordinary challenge: he asks them to promise never to act without first asking "What would Jesus do?" His challenge eventually changes the character of the town of Raymond as the newspaper publisher refuses to print stories of prize fights and ends Sunday publications altogether, a rich socialite devotes her inheritance to the poor, a railroad man loses his job when he exposes corrupt dealings. Another parishioner who accepts Maxwell's challenge is Rachel Winslow, a soprano with a beautiful voice and the opportunity for a brilliant stage career. Instead of accepting offers to sing for pay, Rachel begins to spend her time singing in revival meetings held in Raymond's rough Rectangle district in addition to her position as soloist at First Church. Sheldon describes her singing both in terms of its power to sway the emotions of her audience and in its capacity for being used by men in the story. In the first worship service in the novel, for example, the pastor uses Rachel's singing to increase his own rhetorical power. As she begins to sing, Reverend Maxwell

> settled himself contentedly behind the pulpit. Rachel Winslow's singing always helped him. He generally arranged for a song before the sermon. It made possible a certain inspiration of feeling that made his delivery more impressive. (11)

However, once his attention turns from promoting himself to asking "What would Jesus do?," Maxwell loses his fluency in newfound humility. During this critical time, he relies more heavily on Rachel's hymn singing to calm the unruly crowd in the Rectangle so that it will listen to him. Her hymns have the same effect on the crowd that Sister Soulsby's had on Theron Ware's congregation in Octavius:

> Rachel had not sung the first line before the people in the tent were all turned toward her, hushed and reverent. Before she had finished the verse the Rectangle was subdued and tamed. It lay like some wild beast at her feet, and she sang it into harmlessness. (80)

After the song, Maxwell is calmer, able now to speak simply to the "transformed mob" (80–81). By the end of the novel, Maxwell has gained a new identity as an empowered preacher. He uses lines from hymns to amplify points in his sermon (281); Rachel is, in the end, only his auxiliary, still helpful, but no longer necessary to his success.

Meanwhile, Rachel's identity is gradually effaced. She equates spiritual submission with submission to men so strongly that she evaluates one suitor according to whether she can "give him [her] life" (103). These words echo the sentiments of many of the hymns she sings describing a relationship to Jesus: "I'll go with Him . . . all the way"; "Only to meet Thy will / My will shall be"; "All for Jesus / All for Jesus" (74, 80, 17). Meanwhile, her singing seems to increase her sexual attractiveness to two young men who want to marry her. After one revival service, Jasper Chase, a novelist, declares his love and asks Rachel to marry him because her attraction is irresistible:

> Never had her beauty and strength influenced him as tonight. While she was singing he saw and heard no one else. The tent swarmed with a confused crowd of faces and he knew he was sitting there hemmed in by a mob of people, but they had no meaning to him. He felt powerless to avoid speaking to her. (100)

As Chase painfully analyzes her refusal, he realizes that his timing was wrong because he had not understood "Rachel's tense, passionate absorption of all her feeling in the scenes at the tent" (101). In other words, her passionate hymn singing awakens religious feelings in her and sexual feelings in him. She has become an object of his desire, and she refuses him because the "spiritual factor" in the Rectangle moves her more strongly than her desire to belong even to a "strong man" whom she once loved (103). In the end, Rachel chooses to marry a man whose religious fervor matches her own. And she decides to give up her public role to became a wife and music teacher in a settlement house. She also begins to think of her voice as not belonging to her any more. By the end of the novel, Sheldon pictures her praying for her voice to be used as an instrument of God:

> When she began to sing to-night at this Settlement meeting, she had never prayed more deeply for results to come from her voice, the voice which she now regarded as the Master's, to be used for him. (271)

Predicting her future, Maxwell foresees her singing, not in church, but "in slums and dark places of despair and sin" (284). To follow "in his steps," she must take the role of the servant whose power is acceptable only when it is confined by being limited to specifically religious work.

In contrast to the men who vow never to act without asking what Jesus would do, her task is to give up her voice, both in the sense of yielding her singing to the cause and in the sense of silencing the individual expression of her personality. Sheldon notes, for example, that her singing is more spiritual and beautiful after she decides to follow Jesus and loses consciousness of her physical loveliness (47). And throughout the story, she sings hymns written by others.[11] However, assuming the role of, say, Alice Humphreys by explicating and individualizing the text, is not an option; she is confined to singing what is written. In contrast to Rachel, women in domestic novels are models of spiritual liberation.

Significantly, men in the story who take the same vow are required to make sacrifices, but their religious devotion is measured in their willingness to use their voices for public good. College president Donald Marsh, for example, is convicted of his selfishness in having "lived in a little world of literature and scholarly seclusion." Although it is what he most dreads, he plans to speak out against corrupt politicians and "the entire horrible whirlpool of deceit, bribery, political trickery, and saloonism as it exists in Raymond today" (109). Similarly, newspaperman Edward Norman envisions his risk in terms of speaking out against the saloon and endorsing ethical politics. By the final pages, Henry Maxwell himself is using his voice in a new way by speaking out against social ills.

The differences between Sheldon's *In His Steps* and a social gospel novel by a woman like Elizabeth Stuart Phelps [Mary Gray Phelps Ward] suggest that silencing women is an agenda of men within the social gospel movement rather than of the social gospel movement itself. Phelps's *A Singular Life* (1894) demonstrates that the re-formation of female character by social Christianity can be quite different from Sheldon's portrait of Rachel and that public hymn singing can demonstrate spiritual authority. In Phelps's novel, a prostitute named Lena (short for "Magdalena") comes to the attention of the protagonist, Emanuel Bayard, when he hears her sing "the chorus of a song which he had never heard before, and was not anxious to hear again." "You have a good voice," he tells her. "You can put it to a better use than that" (61). Bayard fulfills the promise of his first name and becomes known as "the Christman" because he labors to end the rum trade and restore the personal dignity of poor people in the fishing village of Windover.

When Lena agrees to become a woman Bayard can "respect," the young man realizes that she will have to find a new profession: "'Perhaps there may be some position—some form of household service,' he [ventures] with the groping masculine idea that a domestic career was the only one open to a girl like Lena." However, Lena laughs in his face as she asserts that she wants no part of domestic servitude. Instead, she takes a position in a gunpowder factory! She also redirects the explosive power of her voice in a new song: she employs hymns to "[make] people purer and better" instead of singing the songs that lead men "into damnation" (301–04). Phelps emphasizes the way this spiritually rejuvenated voice establishes Lena's value as an autonomous person. Just before Bayard is martyred during a dedication for his new chapel, Lena's voice is distinguished from the others as they sing Annie Hawks's "I Need Thee Every Hour" (1872): "her fine voice rose like a solo; it had a certain solitariness about it which was touching to hear" (407). After the son of a local liquor dealer fatally injures Bayard, it is this newly empowered Lena rather than one of the male followers who catches the perpetrator (410–11). And during the minister's funeral, Lena leads Bayard's followers in singing "the minister's hymn" again (426).

Sheldon also uses a public funeral to emphasize the deadly power of the rum trade, but in *In His Steps*, the martyr is a woman, the recovering alcoholic Loreen, who dies when she is hit in the head with a liquor bottle. At her public funeral, women bear the coffin, and "the Holy Spirit seemed to bless with special power the use of this senseless clay. For that night He swept more than a score of lost souls, mostly women, into the fold of the Good Shepherd" (150). Loreen's death strengthens the male-led movement to follow Jesus' steps and encourages Rachel Winslow and her friend, heiress Virginia Page, to give up powerful leadership positions for supporting roles as teacher and benefactor (151–56). In contrast, Phelps's *A Singular Life* casts a man as the suffering servant who must give up his life and lose his voice, leaving empowered women such as Lena and Bayard's new bride, Helen, to live out the demands of the social gospel. Phelps moves beyond the domestic ideal of influence to create Christian New Women who gain power through their public enactment of female spirituality.

Still, it was Sheldon's novel that became the best loved of the social gospel novels, perhaps in part because it idealized women that were more True than New. Ironically, the social gospel endorsed by Sheldon's book supports the very values associated with female spirituality in the domestic novels. It emphasizes social action over doctrine, moves from action to faith instead of from faith to action, and finds divinity immanent in the concrete details of daily life. And, as the title *In His Steps* suggests, it adopts the feminine version of *The Pilgrim's Progress,* in which the daily walk, not completing the journey, is the focus of Christianity. In short, the idealization of women with passive personalities and no personal ambition in the novel conflicts with its strong depiction of feminized spirituality. My conclusion is that once female spirituality became public property it was in danger of being co-opted by men who made its values their own but then silenced women. This effort was never entirely successful, as Phelps's novel shows, but a novel like *In His Steps* suggests that women could lose the flexible spiritual roles represented by their use of hymns in the world of domestic novels as they lost control over what had been their cultural property.

Evangelical women's voices were not completely silenced in popular culture because of resistance by writers like Phelps. More significantly, their voices were not silenced in their churches because, by 1870, women were writing hymns that have become the backbone of twentieth-century hymnody, particularly in typical evangelical churches of, say, fewer than three hundred regular members. Anna Warner's hymn collections are now of interest only to scholars and collectors of Victorian memorabilia, and few people read *The Wide, Wide World,* touted by Edward Foster as "with the sole exception of *Uncle Tom's Cabin,* the most famous and popular book of the day" (35). But the cultural property of women represented by hymns in nineteenth-century domestic/sentimental novels provided grounds on which to build a tradition of woman-centered hymns. Anna

Warner is still revered in Protestant circles, not as the collector of hymns or as a novelist, but as the author of "Jesus Loves Me," the most popular children's hymn of all time and the first religious song nearly every Protestant child in any denomination learns. Appropriately, "Jesus Loves Me" was first published in *Say and Seal* (1860), a domestic novel co-written by Susan and Anna Warner. In the story, the song is sung by a male schoolteacher and divinity student to comfort a dying child (2:115–16). The narrative context for this hymn emphasizes the maternal aspects of God and suggests that domesticated spirituality is a model applicable to all believers. In feminized hymnody, women drew upon the powerful associations hymns had as their cultural property to create scripts for all Christians in evangelical churches.

His Religion and Hers

If you are tired of the load of your sin,
Let Jesus come into your heart.
—MRS. C. H. MORRIS, 1898

Would you be free from the burden of sin?
There's pow'r in the blood . . .
—LEWIS E. JONES, 1899

Male and Female Spirituality

The flourishing market for sacred music after the Civil War created many opportunities for both men and women to publish hymns
(Rothenbusch 182).[1] In both content and rhetorical strategies, these
texts exemplify the enormous influence of women on American
hymnody. Most obviously, nondenominational "social" hymnals
published between 1870 and 1920 include many hymns that promote
the social concerns of women sacralized by association with the private sphere: the religious education of children, domestic and foreign missions, temperance, veneration of the Christian mother.
W. A. Ogden and A. J. Abbey's *Songs of the Bible for the Sunday
School* (1873), for example, offers a number of missionary hymns, one
of which supports home missions:

If you cannot cross the ocean,
And the heathen lands explore,
You can find the heathen nearer,
You can help them at your door. (81)

A characteristic example of temperance hymns in this volume, Abbey's "We Shall Never be Drunkards," is set to a lively tune that could easily be a drinking song (72–73). Ogden and Abbey also include a funeral hymn memorializing the Sunday school superintendent—"Death of Superintendent" by Fanny Crosby ("Mrs. Van Alstyne")[2]—and another urging the establishment of what were called "evergreen" Sunday schools:

> Are they talking of closing the Sunday school,
> Now that winter is coming on?
> Through storm and wind 'twil be hard to go,
> So "close the school," says one.
> No, keep the school open, don't close the school,
> Don't close the Sunday School. (86–87)

In addition to women's social concerns, the female spirituality already developed in domestic/sentimental novels characterizes gospel hymns of the period. Significantly, domestic novelists such as Harriet Beecher Stowe, Anna B. Warner, and Elizabeth Prentiss also wrote popular hymns. Stowe's "Still, Still with Thee," though not a gospel hymn, was published in 1855, before *Uncle Tom's Cabin*. Robert Guy McCutchan, author of a companion to the 1935 *Methodist Hymnal*, regarded it as more significant than the novel: "While Mrs. Stowe gained fame and fortune through *Uncle Tom's Cabin*, many thousands, doubtless, who never heard of that book nor ever will hear of it, have sung or will sing this hymn" (68). In addition to "Jesus Loves Me," Anna Warner is also known for "One More Day's Work for Jesus" (1874), a standard feature of evangelical hymnals at least through the 1940s. Elizabeth Prentiss's "More Love to Thee, O Christ" (1856) is in the 1991 edition of *The Baptist Hymnal*. The shift around 1870 from perceiving hymns as devotional aids to seeing them almost entirely as elements of communal worship allowed these women to use powerful language already associated with the domestic sphere in hymns that became community property. Female hymnists also authorized their hymns with composition narratives that emphasized divine inspiration and with rhetorical formulas that underscored orality in a community that placed high value on verbal expressions of faith.

Consider, for example, the way Mrs. C. H. Morris uses these for-

Temperance hymn from *Songs of the Bible for the Sunday School,* ed. W. A. Ogden and A. J. Abbey (Toledo: W. W. Whitney, 1873).

mulas of language and composition in "Let Jesus Come Into Your Heart," one of the hymns quoted in the epigraph at the beginning of the chapter. Morris's composition narrative emphasizes her role as a scribe who hears and records a message from God:

> At the Sunday morning service, Mountain Lake Park, Maryland, camp meeting, the minister preached with apostolic fervor. . . . His handling of his theme, "Repentance," brought many to the altar. One was a woman of culture and refinement. As she knelt and prayed, she gave evidence of the inner struggle taking place. She wanted to do something—to give, not receive. Mrs. C. H. Morris quietly joined her at the altar, put her arm around her, and prayed with her. Mrs. Morris said, "Just now your doubtings give o'er." Dr. H. L. Gilmour, song leader of the camp meeting, added another phrase, "Just now reject Him no more." L. H. Baker, the preacher of the sermon, earnestly importuned, "Just now throw open the door." Mrs. Morris made the last appeal, "Let Jesus Come Into Your Heart." (Sanville 28)

According to George W. Sanville, the four lines spoken by Morris, Gilmour, and Baker—rhymed, measured, and ordered just as they are in the narrative—became the refrain of Morris's hymn, for which she also wrote the music "before the close of the camp meeting" (28).

Sanville's narrative presents Morris's hymn as the product of spontaneous oral composition. Significantly, the verses are cast in the "call and response" style that Harry Eskew and Hugh T. McElrath describe as "a pattern developing out of the folk song tradition in non-literate societies" (23). In these verses, two of which I quote below, the performer describes a problem, then gives the solution in the tag line, "Let Jesus come into your heart":

> If you are tired of the load of your sin,
> Let Jesus come into your heart;
> If you desire a new life to begin,
> Let Jesus come into your heart.

> If 'tis for purity now that you sigh,
> Let Jesus come into your heart;
> Fountains for cleansing are flowing near by,
> Let Jesus come into your heart. (BH1956 230)

Although this hymn does not include all of the rhetorical features that Walter J. Ong describes as characteristic of oral composition

(37–49), it does illustrate most of them. It is "aggregative rather than analytic," combining a series of highly familiar formulas that appear over and over in gospel hymnody: sin as a burden, being born again or finding "new life," fountains of blood in which one can be ritually cleansed, letting Jesus into one's heart. It is "copious," repeating eight times in four stanzas the idea that letting "Jesus come into your heart" will solve spiritual problems. It does not build an argument from these ideas, moving ahead in a linear fashion; it merely repeats them. The hymn also serves a conservative purpose: it preserves the idea of a personal savior waiting on the sinner for admittance into the most intimate human space—the heart of the believer. At a time when theological modernism cast Jesus simply as a good man to imitate, the hymn creates what Ong calls "homeostasis," not just by "sloughing off memories [e.g., of Calvinistic election] which no longer have present relevance" (46), but also by supporting an invented tradition that counters the forces of modernity. Perhaps most important, the call and response form of the hymn assumes that performing the text is participatory; indeed, as Sanville records, the very composition of the refrain was a cooperative effort.

Male hymnists used all of these empowering formulas of evangelical hymnody too, but with variations that reveal conflicting models of spirituality. In 1899, a year after the publication of Morris's "Let Jesus Come Into Your Heart," Lewis E. Jones wrote his remarkably similar hymn "There Is Power in the Blood" at the same camp meeting in Mountain Lake Park, Maryland, where Morris composed her hymn. H. L. Gilmour, song leader of the camp meeting, purchased both Morris's and Lewis's hymns and, with his friend William J. Kirkpatrick, published the hymns a year apart in two different hymnals (Reynolds 110, 247). Jones recasts the ideas of Morris's hymn as a dialogue in which the problems Morris poses are solved, not by letting Jesus into one's heart, but by accepting the efficacy of blood sacrifice:

> Would you be free from the burden of sin?
> There's pow'r in the blood, pow'r in the blood;
> Would you o'er evil a victory win?
> There's wonderful pow'r in the blood.

Would you be free from your passion and pride?
There's pow'r in the blood, pow'r in the blood;
Come for a cleansing to Calvary's tide;
There's wonderful pow'r in the blood. (BH1956 193, GS 320)

Like "Let Jesus Come into Your Heart," "Power in the Blood" is composed of repeated cliches arranged in a predictable question-and-answer pattern; these rhetorical features serve as mnemonic devices for singers and encourage group participation. However, Morris and Jones use different figures of speech to describe the process of salvation—the business of getting rid of burdensome sin—and they present the relationship between the speaker of the hymn and the audience in different ways. Morris uses figures that could describe the behavior of a Christian woman who is a character in a domestic novel. "Let Jesus come into your heart" compares conversion to the reception of a guest in a private space and makes spiritual formation a matter of developing a relationship. Beginning each two-line segment with "if" implies that the speaker's suggestions may be taken or rejected; the deferential tone suggests that the speaker seeks to influence behavior rather than to control it. In this way, the speaker maintains affinity with the hearer. Morris also implies that action—throwing open the heart's door and admitting the Savior—will eventually lead to faith, symbolized by the believer's entering "the mansions of rest," presumably after death. In short, Morris endorses the values of the private sphere and the spiritual model developed by the characterization of women who use hymns in domestic novels.

Jones, on the other hand, alludes to the public virtues required in sacerdotal religious ceremony, commerce, and war. He envisions salvation as the result of a blood sacrifice, perhaps one performed in a public ritual by a priest: "There is pow'r, pow'r / Wonder working pow'r / In the precious blood of the Lamb." The power results from an economic exchange; blood money is required to buy forgiveness for transgression. This exchange also produces the power required for a military victory—winning the battle "o'er evil." Because Jones is a Protestant, his ideal of spiritual leadership comes not only from the authority to perform sacramental rituals but also from the authority to use words that give public instruction. The speaker in the hymn is like a Protestant preacher who asks rhetorical questions that have an obvious answer and elicit no true interaction with the audience. There is only one correct response to "Would you be free from the burden of sin?" An affirmative answer requires acceptance of the Christian doctrine of atonement, which must precede "service for Jesus."

What emerges from this comparison of the two hymns is a complicated picture of the evangelical textual community. Hymns represent a text around which the community organizes itself. The enactment of hymns—their composition and their performance—uses rhetorical techniques of oral texts, and this process both unites the community and authorizes its behavior in a culture that places high value on orality. Yet gospel hymns also draw upon and interpret written texts, including the King James Bible and the nineteenth-century sentimental/domestic novel. The female model of spirituality presented in Morris's "Let Jesus Come into Your Heart" relies heavily on the language and situations popularized by sentimental novelists, and these novels provide the fleshed-out narratives to clarify that model. As Jane Tompkins argues, the question to ask about one of these novels is not whether it is any good but "what kind of work" it is "trying to do." Her conclusion—and mine—is that domestic novels were written to establish a "tradition of evangelical piety" (*Sensational Designs* 38, 123).[3] But I would also add that the piety the novels represent is distinctly female in the sense that a nineteenth-century woman would have understood the word *female*. That is, the religiosity of the novels is filtered through the experience and language of the private female sphere to reveal an epistemology that differs from that associated with the evangelical male. I do not argue here or elsewhere that all women in the nineteenth century were fundamentally alike or that all men were alike, for that matter. My use of the term *female* refers to a culturally constructed notion of gender commonly articulated in popular literature and other texts of the period. Both men and women wrote sentimental novels, and both created remarkably similar views of what women and men were like.

Accounting for the differences in the way men and women make meaning while using the same language has engaged many literary critics and social historians. Brian Stock, for example, observes that "oral literature in formerly colonial lands has had to adopt the outsider's literary formats in order to be heard. So have women" (10). Similarly, Elaine Showalter, who uses a model originally developed by Edwin Ardener, argues that women are a "muted" group who must use the language of the dominant group to be taken seriously. She explains that "women's beliefs find expression through ritual and art, expressions which can be deciphered by the ethnographer, either female or male, who is willing to make the effort to perceive beyond the screens of the dominant structure" (200). Though neither of these writers was writing about American hymnists, of course, both explanations for differences in gendered language provide possible explanations for the phenomenon I describe. However, I find both explanations unsatisfying when applied to American gospel hymns in the years 1870–1920 if their application implies that female hymnists have no language of their own, that, at best, they can encode their meaning in rhetorical constructions available but only crudely appropriate for their use.

I argue instead that women had a well-articulated language of spirituality by this time. Nineteenth-century domestic novels had, by 1870, established the home as a center of spiritual development, created a model of the Christian life as a nonlinear walk rather than a journey, given spiritual authority to women—especially to mothers—in the private sphere, and developed a resonant language of the feelings to define spirituality. They had also established the idea that hymns themselves are the cultural property of women to be used in the home. That male hymnists used women's language in hymns is obvious; at times, they also overlaid the cultural tropes created by the domestic novels with patriarchal values or drew upon an earlier tradition of hymnody that emphasized an androcentric worldview. But female hymnists constantly reappropriated their own language. Historian Carlo Ginzburg, though writing of a premodern condition, proposes a useful model for this process. He suggests that socially subordinate groups read and express themselves through a filter that effectively blocks what lacks meaning for them or does not accord with their experience (33). Adapting this notion to the complex use of language in gospel hymns, then, I argue that women filter out patriarchal values that become attached to the cultural tropes made available to all hymn writers through domestic or sentimental novels.

To illustrate and support my thesis, I have chosen four sets of representative hymns written between approximately 1870 and 1920 that demonstrate how male and female hymnists use the same figures of speech and other rhetorical techniques in ways that demonstrate epistemological differences. I do not propose to prove that all female hymnists write hymns centered in female experience or that all men appropriate female language and use it to further an agenda of male domination. Rather, I argue that male and female uses of what Sandra Sizer calls the language of "evangelical domesticity" (87) represent a struggle between two kinds of authority within the evangelical community. Women in the evangelical textual community frequently employ the language of influential nineteenth-century literature produced for reading in the private sphere to shape behavior and beliefs while men often use the rhetorical techniques of sermons and the values of the public sphere to challenge female values.[4] From this gendered contest emerge distinctly male and female models of spirituality.[5]

Coming Home to Jesus

As Mary G. De Jong observes, the favorite parable of Victorian hymnists was the Prodigal Son (467). Gospel hymnists compress this narrative into the figure of coming home to Jesus and use it to describe both conversion and going to heaven. Male and female approaches to this metaphor differ primarily in the position of the narrator or speaker in the hymn. Men tend to identify with the prodigal and to speak as one who is out on the road and being called home. Women, understandably, are more likely to situate themselves within the home and to speak on God's behalf, thus identifying themselves with the forgiving father.

Examples of a male approach to coming home to Jesus are William J. Kirkpatrick's "Lord, I'm Coming Home" (1892) and Will L. Thompson's "Softly and Tenderly Jesus Is Calling" (1880).[6] Kirkpatrick takes the perspective of a man returning home, tired and battered after battles in a sinful world. He says that he's "wandered far away from God" and that, like an adulterous husband, he's "tired of sin and straying." Home is to him an oasis of comfort, and he prays, "My strength renew, my hope restore." This imagery culminates in the chorus, which creates a scene that sounds like an errant husband's plea to his long-suffering wife:

> Coming home, coming home,
> Nevermore to roam,
> Open wide Thine arms of love,
> Lord, I'm coming home. (BH1956 237, GS 104)

Similarly, Thompson's narrator associates himself with the sinner who is away from home and must heed God's call, which comes "softly and tenderly" like the voice of a beloved woman. Throughout the hymn, he often speaks in first-person plural, emphasizing his identification with other sinners. In the first verse, he encourages the fellow sinner to whom he speaks to visualize Jesus waiting at home:

> Softly and tenderly Jesus is calling,
> Calling for you and for me;
> See, on the portals He's waiting and watching,
> Watching for you and for me.

Thompson clearly associates going home with conversion when he urges the sinner to go home quickly because "shadows are gathering, deathbeds are coming." And he envisions God in terms of unconditional welcome, love, and pardon:

> Oh! for the wonderful love He has promised,
> Promised for you and for me;
> Tho' we have sinn'd, He has mercy and pardon,
> Pardon for you and for me. (BR 100, CWH 137, GS 213)

This hymn characterizes God as a good nineteenth-century woman.[7] She is stationary in the home; the sinner must come to her. Her identity is created by family relationships—in Kirkpatrick's hymn, that of husband to wife; in Thompson's, that of child to mother.[8] She shows no anger in the face of transgression, yet her suffering is apparent because she is "pleading" for the sinner to allow her restorative work.[9]

Twentieth-century critic Barbara Welter describes this same woman as a "hostage in the home" who redeems men's contamination in "a materialistic society" (151). In other words, women's sphere is for the nineteenth-century male a retreat wherein to restore emotional, moral, and spiritual wholeness. As Harvey Green argues, the "division between commerce and morality" in nineteenth-century America created a separation between secular and sacred because "by the mid-nineteenth century the economy operated as a theoretical antagonist to the principles of Christian behavior" (181). Green concludes that restoring order in society depended on centering morality and goodness in the home, away from the economic demands of capitalism.[10] In terms of a popular biblical metaphor used to describe the American mission, the idea that American communities would provide a moral "beacon on a hill" was reduced to the notion of the "light in the home" provided by women, who created a retreat from the corrupting world of commerce (181).[11]

The spiritual values that emerge most clearly from Kirkpatrick's and Thompson's hymns are those created by the division Green suggests between "morality and feeling," which belong to the private sphere, and "material well-being," which requires going out into the sinful world where one is necessarily contaminated. It is not surprising, then, that for these hymnists spiritual reality exists in dichotomies: sin and pardon, traveling and arriving at home, dissipation and restoration of feelings, sinful man and all-accepting God.[12] Conversion is a matter of submission to a female standard that requires privileging one's feelings, the compulsion to give in to that soft and tender voice. However, assigning gender-specific traits to God means that God, like women, can be confined, and thus controlled, in the home. One can apparently go on with one's necessary economic activities in the public space so long as one goes home from time to time to set things right.

Female hymnists do not see it that way. In "Jesus Is Tenderly Calling Thee Home" (1883), Fanny J. Crosby positions herself in the home calling on behalf of the Savior. The first two stanzas describe the sinner's position as "away" and entreat the sinner to "bring" the burden of sin home, not "take" it to another place:

Jesus is tenderly calling thee home,
Calling today, calling today;
Why from the sunshine of love wilt thou roam
Farther and farther away?

Jesus is calling the weary to rest,
Calling today, calling today;
Bring Him thy burden and thou shalt be blest;
He will not turn thee away. (BR 57, CWH 128, GS 125)

Kirkpatrick speaks of the past when he regrets the fact that he "wandered far away from God" and "wasted many precious years," and Thompson speaks of future "death beds . . . coming." But Crosby's speaker ignores linear time; she exists, like God, in a timeless present. She emphasizes the importance of the present in the phrase "quickly arise and away," and the repeated verbals in the phrase "calling today, calling today" describe action without restricting it to a particular time. The words keep the future from intruding.[13]

Even more important than a different sense of place and time in the hymn is the implication that a woman's position in the home identifies her with God. Thus, she transcends her confinement by becoming like God, who can move at will through influence. In *The Wide, Wide World*, Ellen Montgomery uses the influence of hymns both to cure Reverend Humphreys of despair and to preserve the devotional hour that provides her transcendence. In Crosby's hymn, the speaker, like God, can move the hearer/performer to return home, an action that empowers her. She even envisions the sinner bowing at the feet of the one who calls. Many hymns of the period also make women ubiquitous in spirit though their bodies stay in the home. In Lizzie DeArmond's "Mother's Prayers Have Followed Me," for example, the speaker says he's "coming home / To live my wasted life anew / For mother's pray'rs have followed me . . . the whole world thro'" (Sanville 65).[14]

These elements of female spirituality—emphasis on eternal or cyclical time, operating out of the home, and power in the form of influence—were standard features of domestic novels in the nineteenth century. The most resonant scene of Harriet Beecher Stowe's *Uncle Tom's Cabin* (1852) brings together all three. Eliza and Harry, slaves who have escaped and been aided by the underground railroad, are reunited in the Quaker Hallidays' kitchen, where women reign supreme:

> Everything went on so sociably, so quietly, so harmoniously, in the great kitchen,—it seemed so pleasant to every one to do just what they were doing, there was such an atmosphere of mutual confidence and good fellowship everywhere,—even the knives and forks had a social clatter as they went on to the table; and the chicken and ham had a cheerful and joyous fizzle in the pan, as if they rather enjoyed being cooked than otherwise. . . .
>
> It was the first time that ever George had sat down on equal terms at any white man's table; and he sat down, at first, with some constraint and awkwardness; but they all exhaled and went off like fog, in the genial morning rays of the simple, overflowing kindness.
>
> This indeed, was a home,—*home*,—a word that George had never yet known a meaning for, and a belief in God and trust in his providence, began to encircle his heart. (169–70)

The name Halliday suggests the "holy day of the Lord," or the marriage feast of the Lamb predicted in Revelation 19: 7–9. In Stowe's novel, the expected hierarchies that place men over women and free people over slaves dissolve in this scene just as they will at the end of time when all Christians sit down together at the same table. Yet the scene can be enacted over and over because the activities of the kitchen are cyclical. What happens in a kitchen has deep spiritual significance that can literally change the world because it challenges the social order.[15]

Thus, for Stowe and Crosby heaven does not have to wait for the end of time. It can be a feature of present life within the home. This conflation of home and heaven occurs in other hymns as well. For example, Mariana B. Slade describes going to heaven as going home in "Gathering Home" (BR 128, CWH 208). Reynolds points out that Crosby intended "Jesus Is Tenderly Calling Thee Home" to be an invitation hymn (122), one urging the sinner to conversion during an altar call; and Slade's hymn is clearly a hymn about heaven.[16] Yet both use nearly identical metaphors. Crosby's voice lures the sinner by asking, "Why from the sunshine of love wilt thou roam?" Slade describes a place "where falleth no night" and where one is "never to roam." Both speak of rest, a tender welcome, and great joy.

Elizabeth Stuart Phelps [Ward]'s *Beyond the Gates* (1883), published the same year as "Jesus Is Tenderly Calling Thee Home," describes heaven in amazingly concrete terms that include details of dress, eating, recreation, and courtship after death.[17] In the novel, Mary, a forty-year-old woman, dies and goes to heaven, where she is taken to "a small and quiet house built of curiously inlaid woods"; surrounded by trees, it has all the accouterments of a pleasant home, including "a fine dog sunning himself upon the steps" (124–25). She discovers that this home has been prepared for her and asks,

> Was Heaven an aggregate of homes like this? Did everlasting life move on in the same dear ordered channel—the dearest that human experiment had ever found—the channel of family love? Had one, after death, the old blessedness without the old burden? . . . Was there always in the eternal world "somebody to come home to"? And was there always the knowledge that it could not be the wrong person? (126–27).

Mary quickly learns that the answer to all her questions is "yes." Her father, the first family member to arrive in heaven and himself glad to have "somebody to come home to," explains that Mary's "new life had but now, in the practical sense of the word, begun; since a human home was the centre of all growth and blessedness" (128).

The influence of Phelps's novels on evangelical society in general and evangelical hymnody in particular was enormous. One telling piece of evidence is the frequent allusions in gospel hymns to *The Gates Ajar* (1868), the title of the first book in her "Gates" trilogy; Lydia Baxter's hymn "The Gate Ajar for Me," (CWH 126) is a good example.[18] The characterization of the human home as "the centre of all growth and blessedness" implies that relationships provide the context for spiritual growth. This growth within a relationship is another central feature of female spirituality. Mary finds that heaven simply refines what has been a feature of the earthly home. After death, she discovers a "social economy of the new life" in which relationships themselves exist in a state of "eternal permanency" because old mistakes are rectified. For example, Mary rediscovers a man she loved and lost twenty years earlier. The woman he committed himself to is fortunately absent, and Jesus himself blesses the resumption of their love (Phelps, *Beyond* 129, 190–94). As Slade's hymn describes, heaven is the place where the "dear ones" gather. It is this gathering, the creation of what Carol Gilligan calls a "web of relationships" (59), that distinguishes female spirituality.

In a heavenly social economy women acquire the authority denied to them in a capitalistic society and in the churches that support its values. At the end of Harriet Beecher Stowe's *The Minister's Wooing* (1859), the novelist describes a newly married woman as a priestess guarding a holy fire:

> The fair poetic maiden, the seeress, the saint, has passed into that appointed shrine for woman, more holy than cloister, more saintly and pure than church or altar,—*a Christian home*. Priestess, wife, and mother, there she ministers daily in holy works of household peace, and by faith and prayer and love redeems from grossness and earthliness the common toils and wants of life. (870)

In contrast to its probable reception in 1859, this vision of the saintly woman revered but cloistered in her home grates at a modern sensibility. Mary Kelley argues in *Private Woman, Public Stage* (1984) that domestic novelists did not think it possible to enter "the wide world," and so they "thought to make woman's private domestic world wider" by "influencing and controlling men" (308). Kelley claims that these women worked at cross purposes because their goal to influence men and, thus, gain identity in society relied on their dependent status and on the creation of subjectivity through relationship, which denied them autonomous identity (286, 296–97, 304–09, 333). Kelley labels their sense of power and identity a "fantasy" (286, 309).

However, Kelley's reading of the literary domestics—and certainly their number could include female hymnists—judges nineteenth-century women by androcentric twentieth-century standards that define maturity as differentiation from others. In contrast, Nancy Chodorow argues that

> in any given society, feminine personality comes to define itself in relation and connection to other people more than masculine personality does. (In psychoanalytic terms, women are less individuated than men; they have more flexible ego boundaries.) (44)

Chodorow acknowledges that "the language that describes personality structure is itself embedded with value judgment," especially the notion that weak ego boundaries indicate pathology (44 n. 3). Ochs extends Chodorow's argument in her discussion of spirituality by explaining that "traditional spirituality has been male-centered" because it is based on a "male maturational process" that values "individuation—coming into selfhood." The female maturational process, according to Ochs, emphasizes "coming into relationship" (2).[19] In other words, Kelley's argument affirms male values.[20]

But, more than that, Kelley's analysis is anachronistic because it fails to take into account the religious standards of nineteenth-century evangelical culture and because it ignores the nineteenth-century evangelical woman's sense of developing a new identity in her society. In the first place, the most important role model for all nineteenth-century evangelicals was the biblical description of Christ as the Suffering Servant, or what Tompkins calls the "pervasive cultural myth which invests the suffering and death of an innocent victim with . . . the power to work in, and change, the world" (*Sensational Designs* 130). This myth inverted the social order, challenged the nineteenth-century notion of progress, and assigned worth on the basis of service to others. In addition, as I explain in chapter 1, part of a new sense of identity for middle-class nineteenth-century women was their sense of connection to other women; in other words, these women created identity and power by creating relationships.

Submission to Sexual Authority

Despite her empowerment by feminized religion, a woman's spiritual influence within the evangelical community came at the price of total submission to divine authority. In fact, the figure of conversion as surrender is common to both male and female hymnists; it implies a common standard for all believers. J. W. Van Deventer's "I Surrender All" (1896) exemplifies the use of this theme in a hymn that mixes images of military and sexual surrender.[21] For example, the second verse envisions the speaker bowing at Jesus' feet and renouncing "worldly pleasure" to join his side, yet the verse ends with the words "Take me, Jesus, take me now"; this last phrase could be a plea to be admitted into the ranks of believers, or it could be an expression of sexual surrender.

Domestic novels also equate conversion with emotional and physical surrender. *The Wide, Wide World* makes the connection explicit. John Humphreys, Ellen Montgomery's adopted older brother and eventual husband, requires total submission, both to God and to him. At one point, he advises Ellen to "be humbled in the dust" before God after she confesses to choosing a treat from a grab bag because she had accidentally seen and desired it even though the other children participating in the game would have considered it the best prize (297). As John teaches her, the only Christian pleasure is in submission to the will of others. A scene near the end of the novel describes a sobbing, passionate teenaged Ellen greeting John in exile at her grandmother's home in Scotland. John will not permit her spontaneous emotion or caresses and firmly imprisons her hand until she "checks herself." Ellen sits passively at last, "quieting down into fulness of happiness" (560–61). The submission required of Ellen suggests a connection "between punishment and sexual pleasure, humiliation, and bliss" so great that Jane Tompkins equates it with the sexual submission in a contemporary sadomasochistic novel, *The Story of O* (*Sensational Designs* 180–81).

In gospel hymns, male and female versions of the metaphor describing conversion as submission to sexual authority differ in meaningful ways. In the male figure, the speaker in the hymn gives advice to the believer and thus implies that the speaker is teaching correct doctrine. In the female version, the speaker addresses God, and the focus is on their relationship. Further, the androcentric view of submission to sexual authority makes it part of an economic exchange, but a women's view is that it leads to transcendence and a mystical union. Hymns by Cyrus S. Nusbaum and Adelaide A. Pollard illustrate these differences.

Nusbaum's hymn, "His Way with Thee" (1899), is an address to the sinner by an authority figure giving advice. Each stanza begins with three rhetorical questions that promise a worthy outcome if the hearer takes the speaker's counsel to "let Him have His way with thee." The first stanza, for example, says,

Would you live for Jesus, and be always pure and good?
Would you walk with Him within the narrow road?
Would you have Him bear your burden, carry all your load?
Let Him have His way with thee.

(BR 122, CWH 99, GS 321)

Other rewards for submission to Jesus include freedom, peace, and rest. Nusbaum also suggests that the convert will work better and be saved from failure, asking, "Would you in His service labor always at your best?" and "Would you have Him save you so that you can never fall?" The chorus reiterates the benefits of Jesus' "power," which can, among other things, "make you what you ought to be." It ends with the claim that "you will see / 'Twas best for Him to have His way with thee."

Although the phrase "let Him have His way with thee" is a euphemistic description of a woman's submission to intercourse, Nusbaum's hymn ignores physical union, focusing instead on conversion as an economic exchange. Those who spend enough—"[give] all"—in the enterprise will gain an enormous profit. Hearing this hymn, one can imagine a loving father admonishing his daughter to submit to the man chosen to be her husband in order to reap the rewards of the relationship. The authoritative male speaker employs rhetorical questions, endorses values of the public sphere, and envisions sex as something to be enacted upon a passive partner. Thus, even though the believer in the hymn is clearly female, the male hymnist can retain social authority by separating his social functions from his spiritual role. And, as De Jong observes, such hymns can resolve the conflict created for men by a religion that requires female-style submission for all believers in an era that "insisted on female inferiority in all realms but domesticity and piety" (468). Hymns that cast Christ as the powerful bridegroom in a marriage contract allowed "male singers" to "perceive their own social dominance as Christlike" (469).

In contrast, Adelaide A. Pollard's "Have Thine Own Way, Lord"[22] emphasizes the transcendent nature of sexual union. This hymn also concerns itself with power, but Pollard envisions her female believer empowered in a consummation that makes her one with God. "Have Thine Own Way, Lord," still sung every Sunday in

No. 63.

Oh, to be Nothing.

"Neither is he that planteth, anything, neither he that watereth."—1 Cor. 3: 7.

Georgiana M. Taylor, 1869.   R. Geo. Halls.   Arr. by P. P. Bliss.

Very slow.

1. Oh, to be nothing, noth-ing,   On-ly to lie at His feet,

Cho. Oh, to be nothing, noth-ing,   On-ly to lie at His feet,

FINE.

A broken and emptied ves-sel. For the Mas-ter's use made meet.

A broken and emptied ves-sel, For the Mas-ter's use made meet.

Emptied that He might fill me As forth to His service I go;

D. C. CHORUS.

Broken, that so un-hin-dered, His life through me might flow

2 Oh, to be nothing, nothing,
     Only as led by His hand;
A messenger at His gateway,
     Only waiting for His command,
Only an instrument ready
     His praises to sound at His will,
Willing, should He not require me,
     In silence to wait on Him still. *Cho.*

3 Oh, to be nothing, nothing,
     Painful the humbling may be,
Yet low in the dust I'd lay me
     That the world might my Saviour see.
Rather be nothing, nothing,
     To Him let their voices be raised,
He is the Fountain of blessing,
     He only is meet to be praised. *Cho.*

65

Georgiana M. Taylor's "Oh, to be Nothing" (1869), from *Gospel Hymns No. 2,* ed.
P. P. Bliss and Ira D. Sankey (New York: Biglow & Main and John Church,
1876). The hymn elaborates on advice given to Ellen Montgomery in Susan
Warner's *The Wide, Wide World:* "Be humbled in the dust" before God.

evangelical churches as an invitation hymn, is a very intimate prayer in which the speaker asks God to use her to his purpose. In the first verse, Pollard writes:

> Have Thine own way, Lord!
> Have Thine own way!
> Thou art the Potter;
> I am the clay.
> Mould me and make me
> After Thy will,
> While I am waiting,
> Yielded and still. (BR 254, CWH 72, GS 55)

The god of Pollard's hymn is not a businessman but an artist. Pollard's god could even be a woman in parts of the hymn. At any rate, the hymnist uses artistic and domestic figures to describe what "have Thine own way" means. She asks God, for example, to "mould" her like a potter, to "wash" her like a housewife, to "touch and heal" her like a mother caring for a sick child. While the language of submission to sexual authority emphasizes the masculinity of Christ and the separation of bride and bridegroom in "His Way with Thee," here it feminizes the deity and endorses a female spirituality in which conversion requires "coming into relationship." As if to underscore the priority of relationship, "Have Thine Own Way, Lord" is usually sung to a hymn tune with a waltz rhythm, suggesting fusion in a sort of dance between God and the believer.[23]

Pollard's focus on domestic tasks also provides an important contrast to Nusbaum's mercantile metaphor by making home, not church, a public place where men exercise authority, the locus of spiritual activity. In so doing, Pollard gives sacramental value to the ordinary activities of caring for others. As Josephine Donovan argues,

> The housewife is immersed in the daily world of concrete realities in a way that most men are not, and the qualitative nature of her products—that they have been personalized by her touch—gives women an avenue to the sacred that most men, immersed as they are in the profane, alienated world of exchange or commodity production, do not have. (103)

Thus Pollard, like Stowe in her description of the Halliday home, endorses the values of the kitchen, where the cyclical process of preparing raw materials, using what is prepared, and beginning the process again is the norm. In addition, Pollard's model for conversion stresses the importance of "usefulness" or benevolent activity, religious behavior designated to women in the nineteenth century and denigrated as a function of feelings and behavior rather than of reason and the intellect.[24] The metaphor describing God as a potter and the believer as clay alludes to Jeremiah 18:6, Isaiah 64:8, and Romans 9:21, passages in which the relationship between God and the chosen vessel depends entirely on the adaptability of the clay. In other words, the spiritual relationship requires that the believer, like a piece of pottery, be useful to God, not that the believer be a valuable commodity. The form of the vessel—by implication the physical body—is recast by God's spirit and put to use. Thus, sexual differences do not hinder or restrict full spirituality.[25]

In the terms of the sexual metaphor, conversion is a penetration of the believer's very essence by the spirit of God. Total submission means God can enter the believer and live through her, an idea articulated in the last line of Pollard's hymn:

Fill with Thy Spirit
Till all shall see
Christ only, always
Living in me.

Fanny Crosby's "More Like Jesus Would I Be" (1868), offers another version of salvation as consummation. In the last verse, she wishes to "rest me by [Jesus'] side," to find "by His love my will subdued," and to "let my Saviour dwell in me." However, this submission is not simple, mindless passivity and acceptance of humiliation. It is a conscious choice on the part of the believer to open herself to God, a matter of throwing off restrictions and inhibitions on perception and behavior.

Similarly, Clara H. Scott's[26] "Open My Eyes That I May See" (1895) describes a progressive opening of the eyes, ears, mouth, and heart to God. The first verse speaks of receiving God as liberating and compares this reception to being infused with light:

Open my eyes, that I may see
Glimpses of truth Thou hast for me;
Place in my hands the wonderful key

That shall unclasp, and set me free.
Silently now I wait for Thee,
Ready, my God, Thy will to see;
Open my eyes, illumine me, Spirit divine!
(BR 351, CWH 89)

Best of all, in the last verse the Spirit of God gives a voice to one restricted from public speaking: "Open my mouth, and let me bear / Gladly the warm truth ev'rywhere." These lines suggest an interesting parallel between physical intercourse, which can lead to childbearing, and spiritual intercourse, which reaches fulfillment when the believer "bear[s] . . . the truth." No longer restricted to the functions of her body, Scott's believer can express her creativity with language.

In the Garden

Despite frequent references to sexuality in gospel hymns, evangelical hymnody of the nineteenth and early twentieth centuries lacks the sensuality of earlier Protestant hymns. De Jong cites these lines from early American hymnist Lucy Allen to illustrate the concrete nature of sexuality in eighteenth-century hymns:

> Then I should fly away,
> Into my Saviour's arms,
> Where he would ever let me stay,
> And drown me with his charms. (465)

Madeleine Forell Marshall and Janet Todd trace the emphasis on graphic physical details in such hymns to the Pietist Moravians who influenced John and Charles Wesley (21–22). Marshall and Todd quote the following translation of a Moravian hymn to illustrate the "bizarre extremes" to which portraying intimacy between Christ and the believer could lead:

> God's Side-hole, hear my Prayer,
> Accept my Meditation:
> On thee I cast my Care
> With Child-like Adoration.
> While Days and Ages pass, and endless periods roll,
> An everlasting Blaze shall sparkle from that Hole.

Lovely Side-hole, dearest Side-hole,
Sweetest Side-hole made for me,
O my most beloved Side-hole,
I wish to be lost in thee.
O my dearest Side-hole,
Thou art to my Bride soul,
The most dear and loveliest Place: Pleura's Space!
Soul and Body in thee pass. (22–23)

These lyrics portray all believers as female brides of Christ, physically ravished by their lover. In Allen's hymn, Christ is male, but the Moravian hymn transcends sexual designations. Christ is both the bridegroom and a womblike retreat for his beloved.[27] In both hymns, the hymnist celebrates the sensuous aspects of a physical embrace to describe the intimacy between God and the believer. A century later, though, while gospel hymns retain the erotic theme of conversion as sexual union, they usually reduce the physical aspects of consummation to descriptions of entering closed spaces. In addition, a male version of the relationship between sensuality and spirituality devalues spirituality by associating it with nature rather than culture. The female version, however, separates physical intimacy from sexual expression and makes a romantic friendship between two women the model for idealized spirituality. Both versions describe a relationship with Christ in terms of entering a garden.

C. Austin Miles's version of this metaphor in his hymn "In the Garden" (1912) eroticizes this relationship. Miles describes a meeting with Christ in a garden the believer enters alone "while the dew is still on the roses." Paula Bennett explains the importance of such a setting in her discussion of the erotic suggestiveness of flower imagery for a Victorian audience:

the Language of Flowers has been Western culture's language of women. Most specifically, it has been the language through which woman's body and . . . women's genitals have been represented and inscribed. (242)[28]

In addition, Bennett describes "flower language" as

so widely deployed for sexual purposes that Freud, writing in the first decades of the twentieth century, could casually refer to its erotics as "'popular' symbolism" and assume his audience would not demur. (241)[29]

In this cultural context, the speaker's withdrawal into an enclosed place filled with flowers suggests sexual intercourse. The intimacy of the relationship and the speaker's sense of privacy and exclusivity reinforce this idea. In the chorus, for example, Miles narrates a scenario of romantic love:

> And He walks with me, and He talks with me,
> And He tells me I am His own;
> And the joy we share as we tarry there,
> None other has ever known. (BR 356, CWH 62, GS 177)

The idea of God walking and talking in a garden with a human being recalls the innocence of the Garden of Eden (Gen. 3:8).[30] But attention to sensory details in the hymn suggests both spirituality and sexuality. The voice of Christ, for example, "is so sweet the birds hush their singing."

The third verse of "In the Garden" portrays the believer sorrowfully leaving to return to the real world:

> I'd stay in the garden with Him
> Though the night around me be falling,
> But He bids me go;
> Thro' the voice of woe
> His voice to me is calling.

The pastoral aspects of the garden—its remove from real time and public space and its function as a retreat—make it much like the heavenly home described in *Beyond the Gates*. Leaving the "Son of God" behind in the garden, where He calls the believer to return in a "voice of woe," assigns to Christ the role of a woman and underscores the general irrelevancy of spirituality to real life. Presumably, the believer is sent out into the world because "the night . . . be falling" and the world must be brought to redemption. Time in the garden renews the believer and gives him pleasure so compelling he can scarcely bear to leave, but the real test comes in his separation from the female world.[31]

The hymn allies women with nature and men with culture, which Sherry B. Ortner says "generate[s] and sustain[s] systems of meaningful forms (symbols, artifacts, etc.) by means of which humanity transcends the givens of natural existence, bends them to its purposes, controls them in its interest" (72). Ortner argues that women become mediators between culture and nature (80)—represented in the hymn by references to birds and flowers, the suggestion of sexual intimacy, and the desire to renew the nurturing, exclusive bond between mother and child. Miles's hymn implies that the female world is necessary to salvation, a process described in Puritan sermons as changing a natural man into a regenerated one. As Ortner explains, women engage in "*mediation* (i.e., performing conversion functions)." Though Ortner describes "conversion" in terms of socializing infants and turning raw food into cooked (84–85), the word is also used to describe spiritual salvation.[32] As mediators, however, women can be safely confined to "the garden," and their activities can be controlled by making "gardening" their prime activity.[33] Thus, their spiritual authority is unquestioned, but their real power is limited.

In contrast to the sensual implications of "In the Garden," Eleanor Allen Schroll's "The Beautiful Garden of Prayer" (1920) seems curiously abstract and flat. Schroll describes the waiting Savior without the intimate, specific characteristics of Miles's hymn. The garden itself has no concrete details; it is simply "wondrously fair" and "it glows with the light of His presence." Jesus is not a lover, but a friend who "waits," "opens the gates," and speaks "words of comfort" rather than expressions of romantic love to the believer who meets him. Like Clara H. Scott in "Open My Eyes That I May See," Schroll is concerned with light—a symbol for spiritual and intellectual insight—and with opening what has been closed. But the garden is spiritualized, shorn of its physical characteristics. As in hymns describing conversion as submission to sexual authority, female hymnists split sexual response into intimate but pure expressions of love and the sexuality that characterizes Miles's garden. Omitting the latter to focus on the former is perhaps a way of asserting spiritual autonomy and of gaining power. Michelle Zimbalist Rosaldo argues, "If assertions of sexuality can give power to women, so too can its denial. Victorian women won status by denying their own sexuality and treating male sex drives as a sin" (38).

Louisa May Alcott aptly illustrates the concept of sexuality spiritualized by references to gardening in *Work* (published serially 1872–73). Near the end of this story set in the early 1860s, Christie

Devon marries a gardener named David Sterling shortly before he is to report for duty in the Union army. After the ceremony, the minister tells the young couple, "One hour more is all you have, so make the most of it, dearly beloved. You young folks take a wedding-trip to the green-house, while we see how well we can get on without you" (379). Sarah Elbert explains that the novel draws heavily on transcendentalism, including the idea that "the spirit could transcend the prison of the flesh through an original relationship with Nature" (xxxiv–xxxv). Thus, the consummation of Christie and David's marriage takes place in the context of flowers, symbols of female sexuality that for Alcott replace physical relations with spiritual intercourse. Entering the closed world of the greenhouse is immersion in nature to achieve transcendence rather than a retreat from culture to the periphery where nature and culture meet, and it does not require subordination of either Christie or David.[34] Afterward both of them go off to war because Christie has decided to "enlist" as a nurse (362).

When David conveniently dies of wounds received in battle, Christie is left to the satisfying communion of other women, relationships unvexed by sexuality or, more accurately, by the associations of heterosexual relations with corruption and subordination. Her household consists of her daughter, David's mother, and David's sister. The final scene in the novel describes Christie sitting around a table holding hands with her women friends as they discuss her part in a reform movement to improve the lot of working women. Her name is, of course, no accident, for she becomes a Christlike friend to other women.

Symbolic of her connections with female friends are tender physical gestures that occur frequently in the novel. Christie's most eloquent caresses are given to her romantic friend, Rachel, whom she later learns is David's sister. Christie "wooed this shy, cold girl as patiently and as gently as a lover might" when they were seamstresses together. When Rachel finally consents to be her friend, "Christie kissed her warmly, whisked away the tear, and began to paint the delights in store for them" (131–32). Later, Christie learns that Rachel is a reformed "fallen woman," corrupted by a former sexual liaison with a man that, when discovered by their employer, causes her to lose her position as a seamstress (134–38). In contrast, the relationship between the two women does both of them good because it is pure love in which physical caresses do not carry the weight of sexual sin or the obligation of subordination.

Despite gaining through their relationship, Christie loses her job when she stands by Rachel. Eventually, reduced to poverty and illness, she decides to drown herself. But Christie is saved at the last moment when Rachel finds her and pulls her back from danger. The scene that follows is a scenario of romantic friendship often associated with Christ in gospel hymns: Rachel "tenderly laid the poor, white face upon her breast, and wrapped her shawl about the trembling figure clinging to her with such passionate delight" (160). Symbolically, Christie has lost her life (as a seamstress) to save it in relationship with her friend.[35] She trades physical security for spiritual security and manages to retain sensory comfort as well.

An example of this version of evangelical spirituality in gospel hymnody is Fanny Crosby's "Safe in the Arms of Jesus" (1869), probably her best-loved hymn until well into the twentieth century:[36]

> Safe in the arms of Jesus,
> Safe on His gentle breast,
> There by His love o'er-shaded,
> Sweetly my soul shall rest. (BR 353, GS 194)

These words describe the believer and Jesus in an embrace appropriate for a woman and her "bosom companion."[37] The second verse of the hymn stresses the purity of the relationship with Christ and contrasts it with figures of decay and corruption: "in the arms of Jesus," the believer is "safe from corroding care" and "free from the blight of sorrow." Like Christie clinging to Rachel, Crosby's speaker is "firm on the Rock of Ages," where "sin cannot harm" her.

Physical expression of love for Christ is thus passionate but pure, representing for the original audience love between women rather than love between a man and a woman. As Crosby reiterates in the first two verses and the chorus, it is "safe." In addition, De Jong argues that both Christ's willingness to suffer and his nurturance are feminine characteristics for the original audience of these hymns and that this nurturant Christ served a function for Protestants similar to that filled for Catholics by the Holy Mother: in their compassion, supportiveness, and self-effacement, both are "feminine"; both afford emotional, even sensual, gratification yet are sexless by virtue of their purity. (471)

In a sense, then, the Christ of "Safe in the Arms of Jesus" is not a male Jesus but his sister.[38]

The Evangelical Imperative

The modern missionary movement, which began around 1800 in the United States, characterizes evangelicals as people devoted not only to hearing but to telling the "good news." Many hymns interpreted and promoted the Scripture known as the Great Commission: "Go ye therefore, and teach all nations, baptizing them in the name of the Father, and of the Son, and of the Holy Ghost: Teaching them to observe all things whatsoever I have commanded you (Matt. 28:19–20, KJV). Male versions of the notion that those who have been saved must make disciples cast missions in imperialistic terms of conquest and surrender; female versions of going on mission stress establishing community with others.

A good example of the androcentric version of missions is William P. Merrill's "Rise Up, O Men of God" (1911). That this is a hymn about male experience is obvious from the title, which is echoed in the first line, and from Merrill's account of how the hymn came to be written:

> Nolan R. Best, then editor of *The Continent*, happened to say to me that there was urgent need of a brotherhood hymn. . . . The suggestion lingered in my mind, and just about that time (1911) I came upon an article by Gerald Stanley Lee, entitled "The Church of the Strong Men." I was on one of the Lake Michigan steamers going back to Chicago for a Sunday at my own church when suddenly this hymn came up, almost without conscious thought or effort. (qtd. in Reynolds 186)

In "Rise Up, O Men of God," Merrill creates a picture of strong men going to do battle in service of "the King of kings." He instructs the warriors to "lift high the cross of Christ!" like the banner carried before an army, to gather the resources—"heart and mind and soul and strength"—and to "end the night of wrong" (BR 186, CWH 147). Sandra Sizer claims that the central metaphor in such a hymn is "the spread of empire" (43) because "mission is equated with ideological conquest" (44). In Will Thompson's "The Whole, Wide World for Jesus" (1908), evangelical goals of the period sound a great deal like the motivation for the Crusades:

> The whole wide world for Jesus!
> Be this our battle-cry
> The Crucified shall conquer
> And victory is nigh. (BH 1926 270)

As these examples show, mission hymns of conquest focus on the male activity of going to war. In addition, "Rise Up, O Men of God" draws some of its figurative language from a sexuality intent upon domination and display of power. The hymn presents "men of God" as having a machismo that glories in an erection of strength and the impregnation (making great with child) of a feeble woman, which is the way Merrill describes the church in stanza three:

> Rise up, O men of God!
> The church for you doth wait,
> Her strength unequal to her task;
> Rise up and make her great!

A mission is then both a war to be fought and a way to prove one's manhood since "the day of brotherhood" is what can bring about "His kingdom." De Jong argues that military hymns focus more on the characteristics of the soldier in battle than on those of Jesus, the captain, as a way of promoting an "energetic, 'martial,' bodily ideal of manhood" (476). Her conclusion is that hymns stressing "manly Christianity" indicate a reaction to the feminization of American Protestantism:

> The late-Victorian obsession with "muscular Christianity" coincided with the emergence of the New Woman and the disintegration of the notion of the "manly" man as a courageous, self-reliant achiever, a dominant but benevolent provider of the material needs of women and children. (475)

But muscular Christianity makes missions a restorative activity, not a lifestyle. Like coming-home-to-Jesus and garden hymns, male mission hymns are scenarios of activity that take a man away temporarily from the "real" world of business: Merrill exhorts the "men of God" to "have done with lesser things" in going to battle, but the soldier does return, eventually, to ordinary life. And, like hymns that equate conversion with submission to sexual authority, they stress a solid return for one's investment: a renewed and vigorous masculinity.

A perfect counter to "Rise Up, O Men of God" is Fanny Crosby's "Rescue the Perishing" (1869), which describes what Sizer calls a "rescue mission" (43). While Merrill's account of writing "Rise Up, O Men of God" emphasizes its call to brotherhood, Crosby's composition narrative shows that it comes from her conscious use of a woman's experience:

> As I was addressing a large company of working men one hot summer evening, the thought kept forcing itself on my mind that some mother's boy must be rescued that night or perhaps not at all. So I requested that, if there was any boy present, who had wandered away from mother's teaching, he would come to the platform at the conclusion of the service. A young man of eighteen came forward and said,
> "Did you mean me? I have promised my mother to meet her in heaven; but as I am now living that would be impossible." We prayed for him; he finally arose with a new light in his eyes; and exclaimed triumphantly,
> "Now I can meet mother in heaven; for I have found her God." (Crosby, *Memories* 144–45)

In keeping with the story, "Rescue the Perishing" begs the audience to deal with sinners as a loving mother would deal with a wayward child, to "plead with them earnestly" and "gently," to "wake[n]" them "with kindness," to "patiently win them." Crosby's rescue deals with individual human beings, very possibly the sort of "lesser things" that Merrill admonishes men of God to "have done with" in order to fight an abstract battle against "wrong." The concrete reality of sitting down to attend to another's needs is, in Donovan's words, "an avenue to the sacred" (102). And Crosby seems to agree with Alcott's Christie Devon that domestic missions are an important focus for female Christianity. When asked her "opinion of missionaries," Christie replies, "If I had any money to leave them, I should bequeath it to those who help the heathen here at home, and should let the innocent Feejee Islanders worship their idols a little longer in benighted peace" (421).

After she was sixty years old, Crosby devoted her life to home missions, and "Rescue the Perishing" became the theme song of the home missions movement (Ruffin 104–36). Thus, she fits Carroll Smith-Rosenberg's definition of the "public mother" who moved the functions of the home into the public sphere ("The New Woman" 263). Appropriately, then, "Rescue the Perishing" focuses on life instead of death. Her object is not to "end the night of wrong" and establish the kingdom of God by annihilating the enemy but to save sinners from death:

> Rescue the perishing
> Care for the dying
> Snatch them in pity
> From sin and the grave.
> (BR 80, CWH 143, GS 193)

In a deeper sense, her goal is to give new life to the sinner by what Sizer terms the "inward restoration of the emotions" (34). Verse three, for example, reads:

> Down in the human heart,
> Crushed by the tempter,
> Feelings lie buried that grace can restore;
> Touched by a loving heart,
> Wakened by kindness,
> Chords that are broken will vibrate once more.

Thus, for Crosby religious experience is an individual rather than a collective experience although individual experience leads to connection with others. Harriet Beecher Stowe also emphasizes the restorative value of harmonious feelings for both the individual and the community in the conclusion to *Uncle Tom's Cabin*. The solution to slavery, as she sees it, is proper feelings:

There is one thing that every individual can do—they can see to it that *they feel right.* . . . See, then, to your sympathies in this matter! Are they in harmony with the sympathies of Christ? or are they swayed and perverted by the sophistries of worldly policy? (515)

Excluded from the public world of politics, Stowe endorses a solution to slavery that would not have required the bloodiest war in American history. Her reference to a "day of vengeance" in her "Concluding Remarks" is not a call to arms but a prediction of eschatalogical punishment for those who fail to attend to feeings that affirm life (*Uncle Tom's Cabin* 519).

His Religion and Hers

Harriet Beecher Stowe's grandniece, Charlotte Perkins Gilman, argues in *His Religion and Hers: A Study of the Faith of Our Fathers and the Work of Our Mothers* (1923) that Christianity is a death-based religion because death "was the principal crisis in the life of primitive men" (37). Since hunting and fighting were the main events for a primitive man, death became

> the event, the purpose of his efforts, the success, the glory. If he was the dead one, we cannot follow further; but if he triumphed and saw his "kill" before him, here was cause for thought. The death-crisis, coming as the crashing climax to the most intense activity, naturally focused his attention on the strange result. Here was something which had been alive and was dead; what had happened to it? (37–38)[39]

To this intense interest in death, Gilman attributes Christianity's focus on eternal life after death and the reward for individual merit. However, she claims that this development was actually imposed upon the "teaching of Jesus, heart-warming, truth-filled doctrine of 'God in man,' of 'Thy kingdom come on earth,' of worship in love and service" (41–47). Hymns by male hymnists illustrate this male version of Christianity. Their coming-home hymns could well be scenes of men returning home after battle to a reward or escape. These texts require a linear concept of time and place their primary emphasis on the future. In addition, male hymnists who envision conversion as submission to sexual authority cast Christ as the lord of the manor who rewards sexual surrender. Further, garden hymns eroticize the relationship with Christ but make pleasure—a vital part of life—something to be left behind upon returning to the real world of military or mercantile battles. Finally, hymns such as "Rise

Up, O Men of God" describe going on a mission as riding into battle, ready to die a glorious death for the cause.

In contrast, Gilman argues that if Christianity had developed "through the minds of women," it would have been a "birth-based religion," concerned with the beginning of life rather than its end. Accordingly, "with birth as the major crisis of life, awakening thought leads inevitably to that love and service, to defense and care and teaching, to all the labors that maintain and improve life" (46–47). Although Gilman proposes woman-based Christianity as a goal, hymns by female hymnists suggest that it was, in a sense, already a fact. Hymns that connect women at home to conversion sacralize a place where service, rather than exchange, is the order of the day. Coming home hymns by women portray home as heaven on earth; they emphasize the present over the future, cyclical or eternal time over linearity. In addition, female hymns that use submission to sexual authority as a metaphor to describe union with God echo Gilman's vision of a birth-based religion: "Seeing God as within us, to be expressed, instead of above us, to be worshipped, is enough to change heaven and earth in our minds, and gradually to bring heaven on earth by our actions" (292). Female hymnists even retain the concrete pleasure of physical contact with others by making Christ a romantic friend instead of the lord of the manor. Finally, Gilman says, "her" religion can change society by giving it new life through "charity, that social osmosis by which withheld nutrition has forced its way through diseased tissues of the body politic" (281). In a sense, Crosby really can "rescue the perishing" because birth-based religion sees "human life as one unbroken line, visibly immortal, readily improvable" (Gilman 292). In other words, in "her" religion, eternal life is ours as long as the race of humanity can be nurtured and kept alive.

These male and female versions of the same cultural tropes and themes in evangelical hymns written between 1870 and 1920 suggest a struggle for authority between male and female versions of Christianity. As Rosemary Radford Ruether and Rosemary Skinner Keller argue, the nineteenth century represents a unique period for American women, a time in which "progressive feminism" and "progressive Christianity" were closely linked. During this period, the language and epistemology of the private sphere, which were well developed in domestic novels by 1870, gave women a powerful public voice that spoke through evangelical hymnody. Meanwhile, evangelical men faced a choice either of identifying with a feminized Christianity that perhaps failed to accord with their sense of masculinity or of appropriating women's language and repositioning it to restore their lost power. Ruether and Keller observe that by 1920, when American women won the right to vote and began to enter the public sphere on men's terms, Christianity was no longer a power base for women; by the 1960s, "the assumption that the Christian churches are inherently antiwoman" was widespread (xiii). But for half a century female hymnists created texts that undermined patriarchal religion by centering power in the home rather than in the church, by locating God within themselves, by separating physical intimacy from sexual submission, and by emphasizing service rather than conquest.

Women's Hymns as Narrative Models

What matters is that lives do not serve as models; only stories do that. And it is a hard thing to make up stories to live by. We can only retell and live by the stories we have read and heard. We live our lives through texts. . . . Whatever their form or medium, these stories have formed us all; they are what we must use to make new fictions, new narratives.
—CAROLYN G. HEILBRUN, *Writing a Woman's Life* (1988)

> This is my story, this is my song
> Praising my Saviour all the day long.
> —FANNY J. CROSBY, "Blessed Assurance" (1873)

Scripts for Living: The Walk of Faith and the Voyage of Life

In 1874 blind gospel hymnist Fanny Crosby prayed in utter simplicity one day for money to pay her rent (Ruffin 141).[1] Her autobiography records:

> Not long after I had prayed for the money, a gentleman came into the house, "passed the time of day", shook hands with me, and went out immediately. When I closed my hand, after the friendly salutation, I found in it a five-dollar bill, which he had left there.
>
> I have no way to account for this, except to believe that God, in answer to my prayer, put it into the heart of this good man, to bring me the money.

Crosby's response to this sign of God's providence was to write the hymn "All the Way My Saviour Leads Me." The testimony that she adds at the end of the anecdote moves inductively from her concrete experience to a general principle: "I have never had the least reason to doubt the practical usefulness of that promise that if we ask we shall receive" (*Fanny Crosby's Life-Story* 128–29).

The hymn itself transforms a particular experience into a guide for living that pictures Jesus as a companion on the path of life:

> All the way my Saviour leads me;
> What have I to ask beside?
> Can I doubt His tender mercy,
> Who through life has been my Guide?
> Heavenly peace, divinest comfort,
> Here by faith in Him to dwell!
> For I know whate'er befall me,
> Jesus doeth all things well. (BR 369, GS 334)

Within the evangelical community, this hymn is a testimony to "blind" faith written by a blind woman. Cecilia Margaret Rudin, for example, assumes that Crosby's hymn is autobiographical when she says in *Stories of Hymns We Love* (1934) that "'All the Way My Saviour Leads Me' suggests how much a strong guiding hand means to the blind" (n.p.). As Rudin's comment implies, the hymn's authority comes from the fact that it is a narrative of personal experience; it is valuable in the same way that eyewitness testimony is valuable in a court of law.[2] The editors of Duncan Campbell's *Hymns and Hymn Makers* (1912), in fact, emphasize in a "prefatory note" the chronological and perceptual details that would carry weight in a court of law:

> Those who use a hymn want to know not only the date of the composition and its author's name, but something also about the author himself, and the times and circumstance in which his work found voice in sacred song. For those who have read this book the hymn will always be associated with the lights and shadows of the singer's experience. (n.p.)

Many such testimonies are preserved in the numerous hymnal companions or collections of hymn stories published during the last century. These collections suggest that the story of a hymn is almost as important as the hymn itself and that hymns are perceived as autobiographical statements. Rudin interprets "All the Way My Saviour Leads Me" in light of common knowledge about Crosby's life even though she does not connect the hymn to a specific composition narrative.

Crosby also obviously intends for the "All the Way" to be viewed as a personal testimony. It is in first person, and the last line uses the evangelical formula that equates having faith with having a song: "This my song thro' endless ages: Jesus led me all the way." But more than that, the hymn is a script for living a "walk" of faith; in Crosby's words, it articulates "the practical usefulness" of accepting literally a biblical commandment: "Ask and it shall be given you" (Matt. 7:7). The singer who verbalizes and internalizes the hymn can use the narrative in "practical" ways such as praying for help with the rent. However, envisioning life as a walk with a divine guide allows the singer to adapt the model to particular circumstances. Jesus provides "living bread," "a spring of joy" when the traveler is thirsty, and "grace for every trial," but the specific details of the walk will vary from person to person.

While a hymn like Crosby's can empower women by authorizing their experiences, however, it also allows their stories to be marginalized as idiosyncratic. For example, Nicholas Smith, editor of a 1903 collection of hymn stories called *Songs from the Hearts of Women*, emphasizes a gendered association of women's hymns with sentiment and personal experience. He implies that women write within the small, individual scope of personal feelings, unaware of a larger audience and disconnected from the large scale of public discourse. He indicates, for instance, that Phoebe Cary's "Nearer Home" (1852) is an example of writing produced as a private act of devotion when he observes that "its author never designed that it should be sung" (161); as far as Smith is concerned, it is accidental that Cary's hymn was, in the words of her biographer, "printed on Sabbath-school cards, embodied in books of sacred song, pasted into scrap-books, read with tearful eyes by patient invalids in twilight sick chambers" (Ames 175). Or perhaps Smith is protecting Cary from a charge of unseemly female behavior by asserting that she did not seek fame. Cary's biographer, Mary Clemmer Ames, tells a rather different story. Though Ames emphasizes Cary's modesty, she describes the hymnist's delight on hearing the story of two gamblers who were set on the road to Christian virtue when one began to sing her hymn during a card game. Cary clipped the story from the *Boston Daily News* and sent it to a friend with a letter that stated, "It makes me very happy to think that any word I could say has done a little good in the world" (176–77). Cary might have agreed with Nicholas Smith's preface, which claims that "the language of woman's soul in the hours of sorrow [has] given the Church many of the tenderest and sweetest of the world's best hymns" (ix). But she might not have agreed with Smith's implication that women's hymns are like the women themselves—soft, emotional, and nonthreatening.[3] Perhaps unconsciously, Smith trivializes hymns by female hymnists in the guise of praise. As Sidonie Smith argues, interpreting women's writings as autobiographical is a way to devalue them because it denies their universal significance (*A Poetics* 16).[4]

Women's hymns can also be marginalized because they do not conform to master narratives of spiritual formation valued during a particular period in history. Crosby's hymn, for example, is very different from the less flexible script offered by Edward Hopper's "Jesus, Saviour, Pilot Me" (1871):

> Jesus, Saviour, pilot me
> Over life's tempestuous sea:
> Unknown waves before me roll,
> Hiding rocks and treacherous shoal;
> Chart and compass come from Thee,
> Jesus, Saviour, pilot me.
> (CWH 71–72, BR 158, GS 424)

Robert Guy McCutchan says that this hymn was written "especially for sailors, who, in large numbers, attended Doctor Hopper's Church of the Sea and Land, in New York City" (307). It is a description of a human experience that many men share, but it does not describe the author's personal experience. Instead, the authority of "Jesus, Saviour, Pilot Me" comes from the fact that the allegory of life as a sea voyage was already a master script for a nineteenth-century audience. The text creates a one-on-one correspondence between concrete entities and abstract truths: a frightened passenger in a boat is the believer, a pilot with "chart and compass" represents Jesus, and "life's tempestuous sea" pictures the treacherous route a

Christian must travel to reach safe harbor at last. It is absolute truth applied deductively to human lives.

Like *The Pilgrim's Progress* and other allegories, the sea voyage relies upon fixed conventions that interpret the life narrative of believers.[5] First, the Christian's voyage in this hymn is on a route marked by familiar milestones; the "fearful breakers" just before the shore (v. 3), for example, are to be expected. The "chart and compass" imply that the territory has been explored before and that travel requires directions as unvarying as the points of a compass. The most important part of the journey is reaching what Hopper calls "the shore," the place of "peaceful rest." Jesus is a pilot rather than a companion, as Crosby portrays him, because the path is so treacherous that relaxing with the pilot must wait until the end. The second convention is the use of scriptural allusions. Ultimately, the idea that life is a voyage on a fixed path comes from the descriptions in Psalms, Revelation, and elsewhere of the river of life flowing in heaven from the throne of God.[6] It is also biblical because it articulates a typological pattern: the voyage "over life's tempestuous sea" recreates Elijah's flight from Jezebel (1 Kings 19), the children of Israel's wandering in the wilderness, and Christ's journey to face temptation in the desert (Mark 1, Matt. 4, Luke 4). Travel into a wild, untamed part of nature pictures the separation from civilization that is crucial to replacing self-reliance with reliance on God. This convention has special resonance for Americans, for whom conquering the wilderness was also a way to fulfill their manifest destiny.[7] Third, the journey progresses from imperfection to perfection: at the end, the traveler quits the dangerous journey to enter "peaceful rest." Finally, the soul is alone in the boat on the sea; spiritual formation pictured as a sea voyage is a lonely, isolated experience that creates an integrated self.[8]

According to Ellwood C. Parry, the allegory of life as a voyage is the subject of numerous nineteenth-century sermons, poems, and essays (228). A visual representation of Hopper's hymn is Thomas Cole's series of four paintings titled *The Voyage of Life* (1842). The first picture, *Childhood,* is of an ornamental boat departing from a cave at dawn. In the boat is a chubby infant, surrounded by flowers and accompanied by an angel whose hand is on the rudder. In *Youth,* the second picture, the baby is now a young man gliding down a quiet stream. The "Guardian Spirit," as Cole designated the angel, waves good-bye from the shore, and the traveler steers the boat himself toward an ethereal palace in the air although the stream turns abruptly toward a "rocky ravine" without reaching the cloud castle (Powell 89). *Manhood* shows the traveler on the turbulent stream that pours into the "rocky ravine," the "tempestuous sea" of Hopper's hymn. The boat lacks a pilot since the pilgrim's hands are clasped together in prayer. Above him, the angel smiles calmly from a break in the clouds beyond the traveler's field of vision. Finally, *Old Age* envisions spiritual maturity as a battered boat gliding into quiet waters. The angelic figurehead at the prow of the boat is broken off, the hourglass that has been in its hands is missing, and the rudder is gone. The Guardian Spirit points the now gray and bearded traveler toward a light-filled opening in the clouds filled with angels.

The narrative conventions that inform Cole's painting and Hopper's hymn create what Patricia Meyer Spacks and others describe as a predictable script that is valued because it declares "the permanence of God's patterns" (55).[9] However, the script is also one that would deny or limit the spiritual identity of a nineteenth-century evangelical woman. Most basically, the voyage of life did not describe an experience the nineteenth-century woman would know firsthand. The ideology of separate spheres meant that a woman did not normally work as a sailor. At the same time, the religious and secular establishment limited public speech so that she could not develop an alternative script in sermons, public prayers, or even public testimony. Denied the opportunity to preach, she found that her use of typology—the biblical narratives used as prototypes for spiritual formation—was also suspect even in public testimony because it suggested she was interpreting Scripture as well as herself.[10] Another limitation was that the master script required every Christian to engage the wilderness, yet the cult of domesticity confined a woman to the home and encouraged conformity, not separation from civilization.[11] In the home, her daily activities were repetitive and cyclical; they did not move toward the perfection represented by an ultimate goal such as financial independence or public recognition. Nor could she progress from imperfection to the perfection suggested by leaving connections with others and with her own body behind; her imposed identity came from relationships to others.[12] Indeed, the nineteenth-century evangelical woman supported the master script by her absence, for she represented the antithesis of the self-sufficient isolate.[13]

A few women openly engaged the limitations of the master script. One might argue, for example, that domestic novels and short stories created fictional pulpits for some evangelical women—Harriet Beecher Stowe is an obvious example.[14] However, these forums were written rather than spoken texts and thus suspect to evangelicals, who associated orality with divine inspiration and textual authenticity. In any case, women willing to engage in both written and oratorical challenges of such deeply embedded cultural ideals were rare. The ultimate status and authority of these public women may have come in part from their willingness to use oral public discourse. In her last public speech, "The Solitude of Self" (1892), for example, Elizabeth Cady Stanton addressed the plight of nineteenth-century women who cannot act out the normative script because they lack the tools of a formal education, legal and social equality, and a public voice. Stanton emphasizes the loneliness of trying to live a man's script without a man's identity:

> No matter how much women prefer to lean, to be protected and supported, nor how much men desire to have them do so, they must make the voyage of life alone, and for safety in an emergency they must know something of the laws of navigation. To guide our own craft, we must be captain, pilot, engineer; with chart and compass to stand at the wheel; to watch the wind and waves and know when to take in the sail, and to read the signs in the firmament over all. . . . We come into the world alone, unlike all who have gone before us; we leave it alone under circumstances peculiar to ourselves. No mortal ever has been, no mortal ever will be like the soul just launched on the sea of life. (160)

In this passage, Stanton envisions herself as a male encumbered by nineteenth-century standards. A woman who regularly spoke in public and rewrote Scripture in *The Woman's Bible,* Stanton represents the iconoclastic reformer demanding her right to an identity that allowed autonomy, agency, and power.[15]

Evangelical women hymnists were reformers too, but they ignored the icon of master narratives to focus instead on creating alternative scripts based on their experiences as women. They consciously incorporate life experiences into their hymns in ways that, ironically, reverse the effect of the very characteristics Nicholas Smith employs to trivialize their efforts: the inductive nature of their writing, their location in a private world rather than in public discourse, and the characteristic use of sentimental appeals. Composition narratives of personal experience authorize hymns by relating autobiographical information that would otherwise be seen as idiosyncratic and trivial. The hymns themselves provide a form that allows women to have a voice in a community that proscribes their public speech: congregational singing gives oral presence to printed words. Through hymn writing, women can also subvert the conventions of scripts that deny the value of their lives. For example, because hymns are personal testimony rather than preaching, they give women a way to use Scripture in nonthreatening ways, to describe themselves as actors in biblical narratives rather than as biblical "types" playing out a fixed script. Hymns also allow women to create alternative epistemologies of space and time that endorse domestic space and cyclical time schemes. Ultimately, hymns based on personal experiences allow women to validate the formation of spiritual identity through relationship and affinity rather than through separation and individuation. Through hymn writing, evangelical women refuse to be the victims of scripts that exclude them; instead, they are empowered through exclusion.

The Convention of Silence

The most stubborn exclusionary practice was the limitation on public speech, which created a dilemma of identity for a nineteenth-century evangelical woman. As an evangelical, she must by definition be a "bearer of good news"; as a woman, she was denied a voice within her church by the literal interpretation of such Scriptures as I Corinthians 14:34: "Let your women keep silence in the churches: for it is not permitted unto them to speak."[16] She must choose between being a good Christian or a good woman, but to lose either was to lose both. Similarly, in writing or rewriting her life, any nineteenth-century woman faced the loss of her gender identity but no real access to any other self. Margo Culley puts it like this: "In defying the traditional injunction to silence for women, the autobiographical act contests WOMAN" ("What a Piece of Work" 11). That female hymnists managed to create an identity for themselves without choosing the silence of absence or the absence of silence is remarkable.

The evangelical woman's dilemma is well represented in the two published memoirs and many hymns of Fanny Crosby. A particularly illuminating pairing of a life event and its hymnic representation is her conversion narrative in *Memories of Eighty Years* and her retelling of the experience in the hymn "Redeemed, How I Love to Proclaim It" (1882). Paradox riddles both narratives as she confronts both her need to speak and the perception of her place within religious practice that would deny her a voice. The conversion narrative begins with the description of a dream in which she promised to meet a dying friend in heaven. Then, some weeks later, Crosby attended a series of revival services in a Methodist church. After responding to two altar calls, she still "did not find the joy I craved." However, on November 20, 1850, she was moved by a line from Isaac Watts's hymn "Alas! And Did My Savior Bleed" (1707). Upon hearing the words "Here Lord, I give myself away," Crosby records that her "very soul was flooded with a celestial light." Her first reaction was verbal: "I sprang to my feet, shouting 'hallelujah.'" A few days later, she "gave a public testimony at our class meeting." This was not an entirely felicitous experience, however, because Crosby immediately felt anxious and guilty about speaking well: "when I finished the tempter [Satan] said to me, 'Well, Fanny, you made a good speech, didn't you?' and I realized at once that this was the old pride returning again to reign in my heart" (*Memories* 95–97).

Crosby is able to solve her dilemma by denying herself autonomy and agency in public. At a friend's suggestion, she makes a more "complete surrender of [her] will" to God. The result is that she can violate the restriction on public speaking without feeling guilty since she now acts in obedience to the will of God rather than on her own behalf. A later incident shows that speaking has become acceptable because she no longer wants to do it:

Not many weeks later Mr. Stephen Merritt asked me to close one of our class meetings with a brief prayer. My first thought was "I can't"; then the voice of conscience said, "but your promise"; and from that hour, I believe I have never refused to pray or speak in a public service, with the result that I have been richly blessed. (*Memories* 97)

The paradox in Crosby's experience creates two rhetorical problems. Her spiritual experience seems beyond the bounds of language and everyday reality; it is the stuff of dreams and glimpses of what she calls a "Better Land." Yet she cannot realize spiritual growth without casting the experience in language.[17] More important, she believes that salvation compels a public testimony even though her identity as a woman speaking in public creates, in her mind, unjustifiable pride, then guilt and disorder.[18] Crosby reconciles these conflicting demands by applying Isaac Watts's words quite literally: "Here Lord, I give myself away." Watts's scriptural allusion is to Jesus' admonition in the synoptic gospels: "Whoever finds his life will lose it, and whoever loses his life for my sake will find it" (Matt. 10:39).[19] Crosby's narrative emphasizes giving up her desires, but not giving up desire in general. Instead, she learns to desire for God's sake, to substitute the divine identity for her restricted subjectivity as a woman. Thus, she chooses the course of Adelaide Pollard, whose hymn "Have Thine Own Way, Lord" ends with a prayer that others may see "Christ only, always / Living in me" (BH1926 384).

Some thirty years after her conversion but twenty-four years before her memoir was published, Crosby generalized the evangelical woman's dilemma in her hymn "Redeemed, How I Love to Proclaim It" (1882). The second verse describes her position outside the bounds of language:

> Redeemed and so happy in Jesus,
> No language my rapture can tell;
> I know that the light of His presence
> With me doth continually dwell. (BR 92)

In words that recall her conversion experience of receiving "celestial light," Crosby defines the paradoxical nature of her identity. She is beyond language perhaps because, as a woman, she cannot fit her experience into a logical system. Her "rapture" is ineffable. She "knows" her experience, but she cannot "tell" it. Sidonie Smith argues that this claim to rapture beyond language is a traditional method of empowerment for "those who were denied access to the realm of formalized theological discourse" because mysticism represents an "exaggeration of the quintessential model of the feminine" (*A Poetics* 10). That is, mystic experience is beyond the realm of language and reason just as women were thought to be. But, as the next verse of "Redeemed" articulates, Crosby is an evangelical, and, thus, she must speak:

> I think of my blessed Redeemer,
> I think of Him all the day long;
> I sing, for I cannot be silent;
> His love is the theme of my song.

Thought leads inevitably to speech. If the choice is to "sing" or to "be silent," Crosby must sing. The hymn testifies on her behalf and preserves her story while it erases her identity as an autonomous person. Casting her experience in the art form of a hymn has exactly the same effect as speaking while denying her desire to do so. The autobiographical statements in both her memoir and her hymn create the subjectivity of Puritan spiritual autobiographies in which, Ann Taves explains, "the self that was empowered was a self-in-relation-with God, not a modern 'autonomous' self" (59).

To a modern reader who regards psychological suppression as a factor in mental illness, Crosby's strategy makes her an object of pity even though it is also an agent of empowerment. However, our pity would likely shock Crosby, Pollard, and other evangelical women of their era who regarded the loss of personal identity as a necessary prerequisite to literal spiritual fulfillment rather than as a psychological tragedy. The erotic overtones of many hymns by female hymnists suggest that the loss of personal identity they seek is that experienced in lovemaking, not that evidenced in mental illness. Quaker Hannah Whitall Smith articulates in *The Christian's Secret of a Happy Life* (1870) an attitude toward desire and the will in relationship to God that seems much closer to that of Crosby and Pollard:

> God's promise is that He will work in us to *will* as well as to do of His good pleasure.[20] This means, of course, that He will take possession of our will, and work it for us; and that His suggestions will come to us, not so much commands from the outside as desires springing up with-

in. They will originate in our will; we shall feel as though we *desired* to do so and so, not as though we *must*. And this makes it a service of perfect liberty; for it is always easy to do what we desire to do. (71–72)

These lines recall, then, the model of conversion as submission to sexual authority in which total submission brings union with the divine and pleasure so great that, in Crosby's words, "no language my rapture can tell." Hymns like Adelaide Pollard's "Have Thine Own Way Lord" describe the paradox of John Donne's "Batter My Heart, Three Personed God": total submission to God is the only avenue to perfect freedom. Donne equates bondage with freedom and sexual submission with spiritual fidelity:

> Take me to you, imprison me, for I
> Except you enthral me, never shall be free,
> Nor ever chaste, except you ravish me. (314–15)

However, in contrast to Donne's suggestion of the necessary pain of imprisonment and rape, evangelical women characteristically associate voluntary submission to God with sexual pleasure that transcends the limitations of reason and rhetoric. They empower themselves by using a female model of sexuality in which a woman's desires are the same as her master's. He can neither confine nor rape her if she chooses to live in his space and be his lover.

The Use of Typology

The underlying issue in denying public speech to evangelical women was, of course, the fear that they would preach. For evangelicals, reverence for the Bible as the Word of God complicated the issue since women's use of language has been associated historically with contamination. For example, among American Puritans, who required public testimony by women seeking church membership, women singing psalms with men was controversial (Ninde 19–20, 73–74); the practice was referred to as "promiscuous singing" (Hammons), a designation that implies women were alien elements in the worship service.[21] Later, when missionary support societies began to expand church roles for evangelical women and required that some speak at least to groups of other women, Southern Baptist Theological Seminary professor John A. Broadus warned the Southern Baptist convention against "the idea of women speaking before promiscuous assemblies" (qtd. in Allen 327). Broadus may simply have been referring here to the biblical injunction against women speaking to groups composed of both men and women; however, by 1881 when Broadus made this statement, the word *promiscuous* had begun to acquire its current connotations of sexual misconduct.[22] Certainly, nineteenth-century women who spoke in public endangered their reputations as chaste, respectable ladies. Sidonie Smith argues that the contamination suggested by the word *promiscuous* comes from an association of women with their bodies and a corresponding dissociation of women and reason. Within Christian churches, the anxiety seems to originate in the idea that language, with its connections in Christian theology to divine creation, judgment, and salvation, might lose its purity and power if employed by women, whose bodies signify the mutability of individual human lives. In Smith's words:

> The surrender of "woman's" reason before embodiment also contaminates her relationship to the word. Allying her still with the seductive Eve and the serpent, words return her via yet another route to her biological essence. Cultural practices of the early nineteenth century reaffirmed this association of the hole in her face and the hole between her legs. Women could not preach publicly; nor could they recite poetry before mixed groups of people and maintain their reputation; nor could they participate in formal education. ("Resisting" 82)

Hymns allowed evangelical women to use exclusion from public discourse to their advantage. Because hymns were seen as personal testimony and as ideas received by divine inspiration rather than as the result of human craft, women could use biblical allusions while bypassing the vexing issue of interpreting Scripture. If anything, using the language of the King James Bible in hymns strengthened their authority by associating hymn language with a text already perceived as transcribed rather than composed. Although both male and female gospel hymnists alluded to biblical stories in hymns, the use of these narratives by women is particularly significant because it signals the appropriation of scriptural narratives for all Christians.[23] Three specific uses of typology allow women to identify with male heroes in the Bible, to become actors in the biographical narrative of Jesus' life, and to create a spiritual pilgrimage in which the journey follows a path broken by Christ.

Mary Artemisia Lathbury's "Day Is Dying in the West" (1877) illustrates the way a female hymnist can appropriate the role of a biblical hero. In her own time, Lathbury was known as "The Laureate of Chautauqua" because she wrote hymns to be used at Methodist camp meetings on Lake Chautauqua.[24] "Day Is Dying in the West" was written on request for use at vespers (Ninde 308–13; McCutchan 72). One can imagine singing this hymn at a late afternoon or early evening service at the lake because the first verse is a call to worship at sunset:

> Day is dying in the west;
> Heaven is touching earth with rest;
> Wait and worship while the night
> Sets her evening lamps alight
> Thro' all the sky. (BR 87, GS 30, CWH 116)

Throughout the hymn, Lathbury pictures natural images of "deep'ning shadows," stars, and the return of morning. The refrain, however, alludes to the commissioning of the prophet Isaiah in Isaiah 6. The last verse of the hymn addresses God as "Lord of angels," and the refrain recalls the words of the angels praising God on the throne in Isaiah's vision: "Holy, holy, holy is the Lord of Hosts; the whole earth is full of his glory" (Isaiah 6:3, KJV). Echoing this passage, Lathbury's refrain casts the singers in the roles of angels adoring God and allows her to assume the role of Isaiah, watching the scene unfold in her mind:

> Holy, Holy, Holy
> Lord God of Hosts!
> Heaven and earth are full of Thee!
> Heaven and earth are praising Thee,
> O Lord Most High!

Isaiah's vision is set in the temple (Isaiah 6:1), but Lathbury moves the scene to the outdoors, "beneath the dome of the universe, Thy home." Setting the worship service out of doors instead of in a space reserved for the rituals of organized religion frees the narrator from the restrictions on speech in a sacramental place. If one presumes that the hymn derives its authority from personal experience—and a contemporary evangelical would have made this assumption—changing the setting of Isaiah's vision suggests that Lathbury is thinking of her own geographical location in relationship to her authority. Her leadership position as assistant to John H. Vincent, leader of the Chautauqua movement (Ninde 309), might be suspect if it were played out in a church. But at a camp meeting on the lake, the rules are less rigid.

More important, Lathbury's change of setting allows her to appropriate the narrative details of the commissioning of a prophet. For example, Isaiah's immediate reaction to his vision is fear that he will contaminate the word of God: "Woe is me! for I am undone; because I am a man of unclean lips, and I dwell in the midst of a people of unclean lips: for mine eyes have seen the King, the Lord of Hosts" (v. 5). But one of the angels touches his lips with a "live coal" from the altar, thus purging his sin and purifying his ability to speak; then God orders Isaiah to address the chosen people (vv. 6–13). The scenario of vision, purification, and heavenly authorization can also apply to Lathbury, who sees God in nature, perceives that she is purified by her contact with the divine, and then feels authorized to write a hymn. The ritual of purification—a burning coal applied to the lips—has double meaning for a female Isaiah: the lips of the "hole between her legs" must be purified to allow the lips of "the hole in her face" to speak sacred words. Lathbury's use of alternative space creates a script that allows her to cast herself in the role of a prophet. In identifying herself with Isaiah, Lathbury ignores the problem with authorship of the book raised by proponents of higher criticism of the Bible: the fact that there may, in fact, have been three Isaiahs.[25] Instead, she adopts the antimodern stance that the textual authority of Isaiah's narrative comes from the unquestionable truth of personal testimony. Evidence of Isaiah's embodiment in history is not as important as the words with which he articulates an encounter with God: "In the year that king Uzziah died I saw also the Lord sitting upon a throne, high and lifted up" (Isaiah 6:1). Separating Isaiah, prophetic author of the holy text, from Isaiah, prophet to his people some seven or eight centuries before the birth of Christ, permits Lathbury to separate her textual identity from her vexing embodiment as a woman. The fact that evangelicals are "Word centered" both excludes Lathbury from interpretation of Scripture and creates the ideology that permits an alternative typology.

Another Lathbury hymn written for use at the Methodist camp meeting allows the hymnist to escape the restrictions of time and space and insert herself into a scene in the life of Jesus. In "Break Thou the Bread of Life" (1877), Lake Chautauqua becomes the Sea of Galilee, and Lathbury participates in the feeding of the five thousand, when Jesus miraculously fed a great multitude with five loaves of bread and two fish (Matt. 14:13–21).[26] Rich with biblical allusions, the first verse also alludes to Psalm 42:1, John 1:1, and the narratives of the Last Supper:

> Break Thou the bread of life,
> Dear Lord, to me,
> As Thou didst break the loaves
> Beside the sea;
> Beyond the sacred page
> I seek thee, Lord;
> My spirit pants for Thee,
> O living Word! (BR 192, GS 354, CWH 88)

The second verse strengthens the reference to the feeding of the five thousand because Lathbury prays that God will bless "the truth" she receives just as Jesus blessed the loaves broken to share by the Sea of Galilee.

The parallels between the biblical story and Lathbury's location at a camp meeting are striking. In the scriptural narrative, Jesus has retreated to "a solitary place" (Matt. 14:13) to escape the religious and secular authorities. His followers leave civilization behind to follow him. Lathbury also must have known this familiar story from the sixth chapter of the gospel of John, in which Jesus identifies himself to his disciples as "the bread of life" (v. 35). With this other record of the story in mind, it is possible to interpret the actions of Jesus' followers as indications of spiritual hunger: they are so desperate for the "bread of life" that they are willing to seek it in a remote place where literal food is not available. Similarly, those at the camp meeting leave behind the formalities of organized churches to seek unmediated—thus, more genuine—spiritual truth. As Lathbury puts it, they seek God "beyond the sacred page," that is, in the realm of their own experience rather than in words. Like Fanny Crosby, who writes "no language my rapture can tell," they assume that spiritual reality exists unbounded by printed texts.

Spiritual identity for the five thousand fed through Jesus' miracle is a direct result of experience with the divine Word incarnate, the personality of Jesus, rather than a cognitive experience of Scripture. Here, then, Lathbury invokes the platonic elements of the New Testament to validate her notion of spiritual reality: an encounter with "the Word" is the ideal; knowledge of Scripture is but a shadow of truth. In the same way, a Protestant communion service symbolizes the idea that the bread of life is available in communion with Christ; one does not literally receive the bread of life in the process. In short, Lathbury, as a good Protestant, subordinates doctrine and religious practice to personal experience.

At the same time, she suggests a more flexible typology than that portrayed in the voyage of life and other master scripts. Envisioning herself within the general parameters of a historical event instead of as someone assigned a specific role in a narrative model allows her to credit her own experience. The five thousand fed by the Sea of Galilee may have had five thousand variations of the experience to relate when they returned home, and each one of them would be valid. In truth, the phrase *feeding of the five thousand* underestimates the number of personal experiences possible because, as Matt. 14:21 comments, the head count was "about five thousand men, beside women and children." As a person identified with those too insignificant to be counted in the scriptural narrative, Lathbury demands spiritual recognition. Perhaps she also takes advantage of her marginalization in the gospel account to authorize a different interpretation of the event. In any case, her hymn asserts that subjective spiritual identity comes from a relationship with the divine, which cannot be denied by social status or precisely prescribed by organized religion.

This spiritual identity also transcends the limitations of historical time and space because it does not depend upon making the concrete details of human experience fit a pattern established in another time and place. By becoming an actor improvising her role in a sacred drama, Lathbury creates a typology different from the Puritan model, which, as Sacvan Bercovitch puts it, works "to impose a sacred *telos* upon secular events" (52). Instead, her relationship to sacred history remains fluid because she makes truth relative to her experience of her own body. Desiring communion with Jesus takes on the immediate physical reality of sexual desire: her "spirit pants" for the Lord; she longs to fill herself with the bread of life. Instead of contaminating the Word with her body, she longs to sanctify her body with the Word. Her strategy has a historical dimension in that she projects herself back into an earlier time when Jesus was mortal. But it lacks the connection between two events on a time line, the move from "promise" to "fulfillment" that Thomas M. Davis says characterizes traditional Christian typology (15). If anything, the exquisite pain and pleasure of unsatisfied desire make time stand still in the hymn because it has no absolute beginning and no absolute end. Through flexible typology Lathbury creates what Julia Kristeva identifies as a particularly "female subjectivity" based on time: Lathbury's hymns emphasize the temporal modality of "repetition" that replicates the cycles of the female body and the modality of "eternity" or "monumental temporality, without cleavage or escape, which has so little to do with linear time (which passes) that the very word 'temporality' hardly fits" (191). More simply, she inscribes her female body when she creates a typology that emphasizes repetition without the ultimate fulfillment that would signal an end to historical time.

A third—and most characteristic—way that women use typology is to imagine themselves following the peripatetic ministry of Jesus, another way of inhabiting holy space and time. Gospel hymns are full of "pilgrim pathways" and of metaphors comparing Jesus to a pilot, a shepherd, a guide, a captain leading the believer into battle. But following Jesus takes on new significance when a woman uses this figure in her hymn because Jesus, both as a Jewish male and as the Christian high priest and Savior, went places no nineteenth-century woman could follow. A hymn like Mary B. C. Slade's "Footsteps of Jesus" (1871) stuns the reader with its boldness. Consider the first three verses:

Sweetly, Lord, have we heard Thee calling,
"Come, follow Me!"
And we see where Thy footprints falling,
Lead us to Thee.

Though they lead o'er the cold, dark mountain,
Seeking His sheep,
Or along by Siloam's fountains,
Helping the weak.

If they lead thro' the temple holy,
Preaching the Word;
Or in homes of the poor and lowly,
Serving the Lord.

Chorus:
Footprints of Jesus, that make the pathway glow;
We will follow the steps of Jesus where'er they go.
(BR 228, GS 223)

Because she can "follow the steps of Jesus where'er they go," Slade can take on men's roles: she can be a physician, as Jesus was by the Pool of Siloam, where he cured a man's blindness (John 9:1–11); she can preach in the temple if her path leads that way. And all this from a woman identified first in McCutchan's Methodist hymnal companion as "the wife of a clergyman" (467). At the same time Slade suggests that men must assume the lowly tasks of Jesus, those shunned because "serving" in the "homes of the poor and lowly" was women's work.

Perhaps the most obvious and compelling difference between Slade's life journey and Hopper's voyage is its transference to dry land. The advantage in this change is that it lets Slade capitalize on the model of Jesus' ministry, with its rambling, digressive movement in response to the dangers of encountering established religious authorities, the needs of the followers, the impulse of divine direction. At first glance, the land journey imitates the pilgrimage of Christian in *The Pilgrim's Progress*. However, Slade's hymn owes less to the allegory than to gospel narratives that emphasize the teaching and ministry of the historical Jesus. There are patterns, but the historical record cannot be comfortably reduced to a simple plot with a generalized hero. The personalities of believers intrude and affect the stories of Jesus. What Slade does is to create correspondence between the words of the Bible—the literal "prints" of Jesus—and the "foot-prints" he left as a record of his mortal life. Then she goes further to create correspondence between her own words or "prints" in the hymn and the narrative of Jesus' life "printed" in the Bible. The key to her authorization as a woman ministering as Jesus ministered is connecting the printed narratives through the oral medium of a hymn.

The idea that footprints on a page tell a story of spiritual forma-tion has so influenced the imagination of evangelicals in the Bible Belt that gift and card shops have been inundated in the past ten years or so with a sort of narrative poem usually titled something like "Footprints." This story describes a man surveying his life—perhaps from the vantage of heaven—and envisioning it as two sets of footprints, one for him and one for Jesus. The man complains to God that the hardest struggles in his life are marked by only one set of prints and asks why he was abandoned at these critical moments. The story ends with God telling him that at his weakest moments he couldn't walk on his own and Jesus had to carry him. I have sel-dom seen this narrative accompanied by any attribution; I first en-countered it, in fact, as an anonymous photocopied typescript being passed around in a Baptist church. Like gospel hymns, it seemed to be transcribed words transmitted by divine inspiration.

The most astonishing thing about this narrative—aside from its ubiquitous presence on plates, plaques, greeting cards, key chains, even packets of vacuum cleaner freshener—is what it owes to Slade's hymn. "Footsteps of Jesus" is one of the most popular gospel hymns of all time, and it is almost surely the source of the notion that Jesus' footprints have narrative significance that influences the way believ-ers construct their life stories. Although the twentieth-century ver-sion of the footprints loses the biblical allusions that allow Slade to increase her opportunities for ministry, it retains the flexible typolo-gy that allows Jesus and a believer to inhabit the same space at the same time. Reconceptualized more than a century later, the central figure of "Footsteps of Jesus" allows innumerable versions of a narra-tive wherein Jesus travels the path of the believer, instead of the oth-er way around.

The Devaluation of Domestic Space

While denying women the use of typology for self-interpretation restricted their identity in significant ways, the literal and spiritual confinement of women to domestic space that had obtained by 1870 was an even more effective way to deny their spiritual identity. In a community that valued wilderness experience as a crucial element in the voyage of life, the protective segregation and ostensibly beneficent enclosure of women in the home takes on sinister overtones, especially when it is explained in terms of a woman's highest duty, to care for other family members. George Sanville, compiler of *Forty Gospel Hymn Stories* (1940), illustrates these attitudes in a collection of biographical sketches of the authors of some well-known gospel hymns. Sanville claims in the preface to his book to have known personally the hymnists whose stories he tells. He regards the details of spiritual autobiography he has collected as the "personal testimony" of these hymnists, and he clearly sees the hymns he pairs with the stories as synecdochic expressions of those testimonies. He claims that the stories "[confirm] the transformation wrought in the lives by the Gospel" and that, thus, the gospel hymns "make a unique and invaluable contribution to the preaching of the Word" (n.p.).

Several of Sanville's stories demonstrate the extent to which he values female hymnists and women in general in direct proportion to their self-restriction and sacrifice of "masculine" ambition. For example, he glowingly describes what he terms the "defeat" of Ina Duley Ogdon's career plans:

> Mrs. Ina Duley Ogdon, who would have been satisfied to have had an audience of thousands on the Chautauqua circuits, actually reached many millions because the denial of her great ambition opened the door into a far wider field. Her well-planned and well-prepared-for career was abandoned through necessity. Her cherished ambition was defeated by the invalidism of her father. Mrs. Ogdon, who had hoped to reach the multitudes of Chautauqua circuits, had to compromise with an audience of one in the seclusion of a home. . . . The difficulty of reconciling herself to the loss of a great ambition, added to the duties which accompany the care of an invalid father, seemed almost unbearable. The transition from resentment to quiet acceptance was rapid. (20)

Sanville cites the success of Ogdon's hymn "Brighten the Corner Where You Are" (c. 1912) as proof of providential intervention to confine her to her home and as divine authorization of household chores: "'To the many duties ever near you now be true'—she was thinking of dish-washing, sweeping, and the commonplace household duties—'Brighten the corner where you are'" (20).

At first glance, it is hard to take Ogdon's hymn seriously because a more overused set of cliches than those she employs can scarcely be imagined. The chorus of "Brighten the Corner," for example, is insufferably cheerful in its attitude toward restricted spaces and in its references to a woman as the light of the home:

> Brighten the corner where you are!
> Brighten the corner where you are!
> Some one far from harbor you may guide across the bar,
> Brighten the corner where you are! (Sanville 21)

A troubling component of these saccharine lines is their reference to the voyage of life and the homebound woman's exclusion from it. Her identity comes not from making the voyage, but from acting as the light in a lighthouse for those in peril of shipwreck. Unless she brightens her corner (and stays in it), the whole enterprise is endangered. Taken in connection with Sanville's telling of Ogdon's story, the hymn suggests that the speaker's affliction is a necessary corrective to one who has forgotten "her place."

However, the last verse of "Brighten the Corner" presents a conflict between Sanville's version of Ogdon's sacrifice and her own interpretation of her confinement and restricted agency. In these lines, the hymnist compares her opportunity for service to that of Christ, the Suffering Servant:

> Here for all your talent you may surely find a need,
> Here reflect the Bright and Morning Star,
> Even from your humble hand the bread of life may feed,
> Brighten the corner where you are.

In confinement, Ogdon's light in the corner takes on apocalyptic significance: it reflects the "bright and morning star," the metaphor by which Christ identifies himself in Rev. 22:16. The hymnist's loss is, thus, analogous to Christ's. She may lose her self, represented by her talent, but the loss is redemptive for others. The last two lines of the verse assign to the speaker the role of Christ in the narrative of the feeding of the five thousand. In her corner, the believer distributes "bread" to others, but that bread becomes the "bread of life," the physical symbol of Christ himself.[27] While Lathbury imagines herself "panting" to receive the divine bread of life, Ogdon pictures fulfillment of that desire. Her union with Christ has been fruitful. She is the lady—literally the "breadgiver"—of her master's house.[28] In terms of Christian ritual, Ogdon replaces the priest who distributes communion bread with the priestess at the hearth.

Like Lathbury, Ogdon inserts herself into sacred history, but she makes Christ's narrative her own instead of imagining herself in a peripheral role. Challenging the convention that credits only wilderness experience, she changes the setting of the story to domestic space, which, like the lake shore, is beyond the bounds of organized religion. More important, the change subtly emphasizes Ogdon's identification with the hero of the story and, indirectly, criticizes an interpretation of self that finds normative scripts only in narratives such as Jesus' temptation or the withdrawal of John the Baptist. In the gospel accounts of the feeding of the five thousand, Jesus goes off by boat "privately" to a "solitary place" (Matt. 14:13). But the crowds follow, and Jesus compassionately heals the sick and feeds the hungry. The test of true spirituality in this story is not separation from others; the Christian most like her master withdraws to a place where others intrude and sacrifices privacy and autonomy to care for human needs.

Another way in which the script can be enacted is that domestic space can become a site for reliving the historical events of the crucifixion. Jennie Evelyn Hussey's "Lead Me to Calvary" (1921) illustrates this revaluation of confinement to the home. However, the autobiographical interpretation suggested by the hymn is available only if the reader knows the story behind it. Sanville's account adds his interpretation of her life:

Sacrificial service plants a garden in the heart. This labor of love flowers forth in endless beauty. "Lead Me to Calvary" is such a bloom.

The care of an invalid sister nearly all her adult life was the uncomplaining task of Jennie Hussey. During this time-devouring and strength-testing task, she wrote her many poems. They show keen understanding of the meaning of the Cross. She, too, carried a cross, so knew its joy and source of strength.

In "Lead Me to Calvary" she bares her love and loyalty to Christ. Through Gethsemane she has come to the rich possession of obedience and surrender. This made her service a joy, and not a burden. (Sanville 44)

Sanville's reference to "a garden in the heart" is a rather self-conscious allusion to the gardens of the hymn, in which Hussey begs Jesus, "the King of [her] life," to "Lead [her] to Calvary." The second and third verses of the hymn "lead" her to the garden that is the site of Jesus' tomb. The chorus mentions the garden of Gethsemane, where Jesus agonized over the coming crucifixion. In the hymn's subjective chronology, both places are on the path to Calvary. In the hymn's subjective geography, both are places within the unrestricted space of the speaker's own heart.

On the way to Calvary, Hussey comes first to the garden of the tomb because that is where she acknowledges the primacy of relationship in her salvation. She compares herself to Mary Magdalene, who witnessed the first appearance of Jesus after the resurrection: "Let me like Mary, thru the gloom / Come with a gift to Thee" (CWH 242, Sanville 45). She asks to be shown the "empty tomb" on her way to Calvary even though the resurrection follows the crucifixion in the gospel account. Hussey's chronology suggests that Calvary in the hymn is the site, not of Jesus' death, but of her own and that she is appropriating narrative details from the gospel of John (see 20:10–18) to show how interaction with Christ prepares her for her own sacrifice. In the biblical story, Mary has come to the tomb early on the morning of the resurrection. Distraught, she confuses Jesus with the gardener. The climax of the story comes when Jesus names her. As he says her name, she recognizes and names him as well: "Jesus said to her, 'Mary.' She turned toward him and cried out in Aramaic, 'Rabboni'" (v. 16). Thus, Mary's identity is conferred by the master himself on a person too insignificant even to be counted in the story of the feeding of the five thousand. Mary's naming brings her into being as an individual as it brings her into relationship with the divine.

As this drama unfolds within for the hymnist and the singer of her hymn, the setting becomes the human heart. For Jennie Evelyn Hussey, as Sanville indicates, the human heart internalizes the domestic space that figures so often in gospel hymns as the locus of spiritual development. If this hymn is read as an autobiographical statement, home becomes a Gethsemane in which the speaker must face her own death and a Calvary where that death becomes redemptive. Named and brought into spiritual selfhood by Jesus, her identity remains intimately connected to his: she asks, "May I be willing, Lord, to bear / Daily my cross for Thee" and she imagines sharing Christ's "cup of grief." Like Jesus, the believer must die daily in the unending tasks of the home. Her cross is the agent of her own death, which must occur to allow identification with one whose death makes him an element in a divine plan rather than a victim of circumstance.

While "Lead Me to Calvary" suggests a trip, it is not into the wilderness of the soul where the task is to distinguish what is "natural" from what is spiritual. The trip is not one of self-discovery, nor does it inspire self-protection. Rather, the suffering self of Hussey's hymn extinguishes itself by imitating Christ's journey. In *Manhood*, one of Thomas Cole's paintings from *The Voyage of Life*, the dangers of adulthood are pictured as three demonic forms scowling grimly from a dark cloud over a man in a boat headed for some dangerous rapids. Cole says that these figures represent "Suicide, Intemperance and Murder" (qtd. in Powell 92). In this visual representation of a master script, anything that threatens individual identity is demonic. Suicide is killing the self, Intemperance means slaying the soul through indulgence of the body, and Murder suggests failing to separate positively from some other self that is allowed too much influence over one's identity. In contrast, the suffering self in domestic space imitates Christ by annihilating the self, attending to the physical needs of others' bodies, and dying daily on behalf of someone else. The emphasis is not on suffering for its own sake; evangelical women like Ogdon and Hussey would find very foreign the notion of mortifying the flesh to save the spirit.[29] The point is that domestic space is where suffering is both redeemed and redemptive because it is borne in service to others. Suffering grants identity only when it is purposeful and when it models Christ's passion.

The American Myth of Progress

The notion of the suffering self also challenges the American myth of progress, itself a product of Protestant theology. William C. Spengemann and L. R. Lundquist observe, for example, that the myth is "an adaptation of Christian mythology to the particular problems of American life" (503). This cultural convention, exemplified by the progress of Bunyan's Christian from the City of Destruction to the Celestial City, excludes most late-nineteenth- and early-twentieth-century women by making movement from one place to another its central feature. The journey or voyage of faith is a crucial shaping element, and those who cannot move are denied adult selfhood and mature spirituality.

Also significant to the myth is a pattern of loss and gain based on a theological economy in which spiritual progress requires loss of the world to gain a heavenly reward. In both sacred and secular terms, the pattern takes several forms, all of which suggest a commercial "deal": the loss of immediate, sensory gratification in favor of a huge spiritual reward somewhere down the road; the repression of human nature to achieve a new, improved, regenerate nature; the sacrifice of relationships and endurance of affliction to reach a goal. The suffering that evangelicals expected of nineteenth-century foreign missionaries exemplifies the idea of sacrificing to advance the kingdom of God and, not infrequently, to promote the culture of the United States. Missionaries were expected to give up family ties, personal comfort, and safety when they went to the mission field to convert the heathen. Even furloughs to attend to health problems were frowned upon. The Southern Baptist Lottie Moon was and is highly revered in Baptist circles because she was, as Catherine Allen notes, "the first fully appointed woman missionary of the [Southern Baptist] Foreign Mission Board" (147). In other words, she was the first woman missionary authorized to travel and suffer in a way usually reserved for men. Moon, who literally starved herself to death after forty years in China, gained the status of a Catholic virgin martyr after her tragic death in 1912. Her epitaph on the gravestone erected by the Virginia Woman's Missionary Union in Crewe, Virginia, reads "faithful unto death." And Crewe Baptist Church boasts a stained glass window with a picture of Moon, an unusual feature for a Baptist church. Ultimately, the pattern of loss and gain results in an unencumbered traveler, a spiritually "self-made" man or woman.[30]

In life narratives, incidents of affliction or suffering can support the myth of progress. Sacvan Bercovitch argues, for example, that "the notion of gracious affliction" works on two levels for the Puritan biographer: affliction "prepared the saint for heaven by making visible the prospect of hell"; it also "prodded the colony forward by stressing God's untoward providences" (53–54). Both meanings affirm the idea that, individually and collectively, Americans move by God's gracious design from imperfection to perfection. However, accounts of suffering can also challenge the myth by proposing an alternative story. In "Brighten the Corner Where You Are" and "Lead Me to Calvary," for example, Ogdon and Hussey focus less on the typological journey than on a christology that emphasizes sacrifice as a way to redeem both the individual and the community. Jane Tompkins argues that sentimental novelists challenge the American myth in this same way, and her observations clarify my point that the challenge is crucial to some evangelical women's self-definition:

> They used the central myth of their culture—the story of Christ's death for the sins of mankind—as the basis for a new myth which reflected their own interests. They regarded their vision of the Christian home as the fulfillment of the Gospel, "the end . . . which Jesus Christ came into this world to secure," in exactly the same way that the Puritans believed that their mission was to found the "American city of God," and that Christians believe the New Testament to be a fulfillment of the Old. (*Sensational Designs* 220, n. 31)

In other words, the point of affliction—which may include the restriction and consequent suffering of the self—is not concerned with some future arrival. Its real concern is an apocalyptic reordering of a value system based on secular economics and an ideology of delayed gratification. Domestic space is very valuable indeed if it is the place in which the self can be formed now in the image of Christ, the place in which the normative Christian narrative is what Tompkins calls the "pervasive cultural myth" of the "innocent victim" who gains power through dying on behalf of others (*Sensational Designs* 130). This subversion of the economic model also requires the believer to look at things from the perspective of "woman's time." If the Christian home is "God's kingdom on earth," then linear time is an impractical concept; the fulfillment of God's purpose can be a daily reality in the cyclical activities of the kitchen.

One example of this revision of the American myth is Mary Ann Thomson's hymn "O Zion, Haste, Thy Mission High Fulfilling" (1868).[31] Thomson casts the American mission in terms of proclaiming the sacrifice of Christ and of taking responsibility for the welfare of the world, not of recreating the Exodus to reach the promised land and there becoming the exemplary "City on the Hill." She emphasizes liberating rather than conquering others for the kingdom of God; thus, she denies the creation of an identity articulated through the figures of winning a battle or achieving a goal. At the same time, the hymn describes the necessary sacrifices of the domestic sufferer for the good of humanity.

The autobiographical significance of this final aspect of the hymn becomes apparent if one considers Thomson's story of how she came to write it:

> I wrote the greater part of the hymn, "O Sion, Haste," in the year 1868. I had written many hymns before, and one night, while I was sitting up with one of my children who was ill with typhoid fever, I thought I should like to write a missionary hymn to the tune of the hymn, "Hark, Hark my Soul! Angelic Songs are Swelling." (Reynolds 172)

Here we have a Christian who defines herself through suffering. She is tired, worried, and confined by the needs of another. Yet even in these circumstances, she creates herself in contrast to the male hero of the myth of progress. Her rhetorical power allows her to change the world even if she cannot leave her child. If anything, suffering intensifies her power to focus on the goal of spreading the gospel because she can identify with those in need of "redemption and release," as she describes the unsaved world in the chorus. Some hymnals include a verse to this hymn in which Thomson describes the unsaved as "bound in the darksome prison house of sin" until someone "tell[s] them of the Savior's dying."[32] It is not hard to see that Thomson can identify with both the imprisoned and their lib-

erators; by speaking to others, she releases herself. As spiritual autobiography, her hymn represents what Mary G. Mason terms "the
autobiography of imprisonment." However, in contrast to the auto-
biographers such as Charlotte Perkins Gilman and Sylvia Plath that
Mason analyzes, Thomson is not permanently imprisoned, "kept
from coming into her own self" because of another person (Mason
234). Instead, she uses identification with others to liberate herself
rhetorically. References to speaking occur frequently: Thomson admonishes her audience to "tell to all the world that God is Light," to
"publish glad tidings," to "make known to ev'ry heart His saving
grace"; she accuses those who fail to do these things of "neglect."
These admonitions mandate speech. They also suggest that the true
Christian can be the one who sends the messenger as well as the one
who makes the trip to "ev'ry people, tongue, and nation." One verse
speaks directly to women confined to their home:

> Give of thy sons to bear the message glorious;
> Give of thy wealth to speed them on their way;
> Pour out thy soul for them in prayer victorious;
> And all thou spendest Jesus will repay.
> (BR 151, GS 474, CWH 16)

The activities Thomson endorses in this verse—encouraging
children to become missionaries, raising money for the cause, and
praying for specific missions endeavors—were characteristic objec-
tives of nineteenth-century women's missionary societies in evangelical churches.[33] Such support roles were acceptable outlets for evangelical women; they could be played out without leaving home and
church settings, and they directed women's time and energy away
from preaching.

However safe these religious roles were for women by the late
nineteenth century, though, the last line of this verse challenges the
economic aspects of the American myth of progress. The line "all
thou spendest Jesus will repay" paraphrases the words of the Good
Samaritan, who instructs an innkeeper to care for the wounded man
he has rescued: "Take care of him: and whatsoever thou spendest
more, when I come again, I will repay thee" (Luke 10:35b, KJV).
What the believer spends, then, is not on his or her own behalf. In
addition, the parable is told to answer a question: "Who is my

neighbor?" (Luke 10:29). The parable itself is a subversive examination of social status and ethnic identity that emphasizes self-sacrificing benevolence over competition and individual achievement. Thomson identifies the self-sacrificing believer with the Samaritan, the outcast from Jewish society, rather than with the priest or the Levite, religious leaders in the community who ignore the demands of being a real neighbor by "pass[ing] by on the other side" when they see a wounded man in the road (vv. 31–32). The representatives of organized religion focus on completing their journey rather than on the requirement that a real neighbor will have a more flexible script that allows halting forward movement to help a person in need. In this parable—and in Thomson's hymn—truly spiritual identity comes from identification with the marginalized hero as well as with the marginalized victim.

To appreciate how far Thomson moves from the myth of progress in late-nineteenth-century America, consider its economic articulation in the words of industrialist Andrew Carnegie, who urges a wholehearted adoption of social Darwinism in "The Gospel of Wealth." Carnegie's premise is that "upon the sacredness of property civilization itself depends" (18). He urges benevolence as a sacred duty, but only after one has proven one's social superiority by amassing as much property as possible. He refutes, with horror, the notion that individualism is not the highest good:

> We might as well urge the destruction of the highest existing type of man because he failed to reach our ideal as to favor the destruction of Individualism, Private Property, the Law of Accumulation of Wealth, and the Law of Competition; for these are the highest result of human experience, the soil in which society, so far, has produced the best fruit. (19)

Urging progress toward a utopia in which wealthy philanthropists provide "ladders" on which their less gifted fellow humans can "rise" to "improve the general condition of the people," Carnegie describes the ultimate secularization of the myth of progress in an essay that still couches itself in religious terms as a new "gospel." He ends the piece by announcing the advent of a new age that can achieve its own redemption through material means: "Such, in my opinion is the true gospel concerning wealth, obedience to which is destined some day to solve the problem of the rich and the poor, and to bring 'Peace on earth, among men good will'" (28–29). Carnegie's article perhaps takes the myth of progress to an economic extreme, but it still provides a usefully stark contrast to "O Zion, Haste," in which the suffering self acquires spiritual subjectivity by identification with others, rejection of competition, and receiving payment in spiritual coin.

The Spiritual Isolate

A final exclusionary convention challenged by female hymnists is the notion of the spiritual isolate, the idea that mature spirituality is characterized by independence from others within the community of faith and even from God. Intimately connected to the conventional metaphor of the spiritual journey into the wilderness, "isolate individualism," as Susan Stanford Friedman calls it (39), also requires denial of the encumbering body as the soul achieves total freedom and autonomy. In describing moments from their own spiritual progress through the medium of hymns, women challenge this definition of spiritual maturity in two ways. First, many female hymnists identify themselves so closely with Christ that the passionate longing for his presence becomes an identity; ultimately, Christ's story becomes the hymnist's story. Mary G. Mason finds versions of this paradigm to be characteristic of women's autobiography:

> The self discovery of female identity seems to acknowledge the real presence and recognition of another consciousness, and the disclosure of female self is linked to the identification of some "other." This recognition of another consciousness . . . this grounding of identity through relation to the chosen other, seems . . . to enable women to write openly about themselves. (210)

Describing this "relation to the chosen other" in erotic terms allows evangelical women to view their physical bodies as a medium for spiritual experience rather than as an encumbrance. Moreover, a female hymnist can present herself as representative of Christian women, thus indicating in another way that her spiritual identity is intimately related to her sense of her physical body and to identification with a group. Friedman describes the subjectivity produced by strong identification with other women as a "collective identity" characterized by a "collective consciousness of self" (39, 56).

Autobiographical fragments indicate that Elizabeth Payson Prentiss, hymnist and author of the novel *Stepping Heavenward* (1869), was a woman who told her own story only by making Christ her subject. Her contemporary, Scottish minister Duncan Campbell, quotes Prentiss as saying, "I write in verse whenever I am deeply stirred, because, though as full of tears as other people, I cannot shed them" (172). Her hymn "More Love to Thee, O Christ" (1869)[34] channels her feelings toward their desired object so that what she loves becomes what she is.[35] This conscious effort to describe herself in terms of losing everything but emotion is especially apparent in the first two verses:

> More love to Thee, O Christ,
> More love to Thee!
> Hear Thou the prayer I make
> On bended knee;
> This is my earnest plea:
> More love, O Christ, to Thee,
> More love to Thee, More love to Thee!

> Once earthly joy I craved,
> Sought peace and rest;
> Now Thee alone I seek,
> Give what is best;
> This all my prayer shall be;
> More love, O Christ, to Thee,
> More love to Thee, More love to Thee!
> (BR 218, GS 148, CWH 17)

Most biographical accounts of Prentiss emphasize her precarious physical and emotional health, probably caused by the bearing and care of six children, two of whom died early (see Campbell 172; Douglas 216; Reynolds 142). These life events may explain the sense of resignation in Prentiss's hymn and the transcendence she achieves by separating "earthly joy" from the pleasure of loving Christ. Clearly, however, her identity in the hymn comes from a passionate desire for communion. Her reference to seeking her love in the second verse recalls the words of the most sensual of biblical texts, the Song of Solomon: "By night on my bed I sought him whom my soul loveth: I sought him, but I found him not. I will rise now, and go about the city in the streets, and in the broad ways I will seek him whom my soul loveth" (3:1–2). Prentiss's threefold repetition of the phrase "more love to Thee" in the last two lines of each stanza suggests the increasing strength of her focus on the object of her love and her desire to receive him into herself when she implores, "Give what is best."

Annie S. Hawks also articulates her desire for heavenly communion in "I Need Thee Every Hour" (1872). In this hymn, she speaks to Christ in the words of a woman to her lover:

> I need Thee every hour,
> Most Holy One;
> O make me Thine indeed,
> Thou blessed Son.
> I need Thee, O, I need Thee;
> Every hour I need Thee!
> O bless me now, my Saviour,
> I come to Thee. (BR 193, GS 91, CWH 54)

Hawks describes the composition of this hymn in terms of divine possession, in which her intense need for God brings him into her: "I was so filled with the sense of nearness to the Master that, wondering how one could live without Him, either in joy or pain, these words, 'I Need Thee Every Hour,' were ushered into my mind, the thought at once taking full possession of me" (qtd. in Reynolds 104). In this revealing statement, Hawks emphasizes that her knowledge of the divine presence is parallel to her divine inspiration as a hymnist. The hymn enacts her spiritual development as a matter of coming into relationship: it articulates her sense that her identity somehow cannot sustain itself alone; its composition narrative makes divine inspiration of a passive recipient a rhetorical metaphor for establishing a relationship with God; its performance recreates the prayer by which the performer/audience join her in invoking God's presence.

Ultimately, identity defined as fusion with a divine consciousness means that two identities become one. A hymn by Anna B. Warner, for example, expresses the idea that daily existence means a continual substitution of painful service on Jesus' behalf for her own life: "One more day's work for Jesus / One less of life for me!" (BR 55). More directly, many hymnists frame their sense of being as a believer in terms of having a song to sing or a story to tell; the song interprets the believer's life in terms of a relationship to Jesus and his life narrative. Fanny Crosby's "Blessed Assurance" (1873) proclaims "This is my story, this is my song / Praising my Saviour all the day long" (BR 120, GS 21, GS 64). Annie B. Russell's "Wonderful, Wonderful Jesus" (1921)[36] stresses the divine origin of her "song" and suggests that she is impregnated by her heavenly relationship: "Wonderful, wonderful Jesus / In the heart He implanteth a song" (BR 69). In addition, many hymns stress the value of retelling the historical facts of Jesus' life. Crosby's "Tell Me the Story of Jesus" (1880) and Mary B. C. Slade's "Tell It Again"[37] are good examples. All of these hymns suggest that Christian identity can originate in a new narrative or hymn received as a gift of grace from a divine source.

Another way in which a nineteenth-century female hymnist can challenge the convention of the spiritual isolate is by defining herself as part of the community of women. As Susan Friedman argues, "Isolate individualism is an illusion. It is also the privilege of power. A white man has the luxury of forgetting his skin color and sex. . . . Women and minorities . . . have no such luxury" (39). Defined in contrast to men, women cannot escape their embodiment; however, a woman can exploit this identification with other women as a way to gain power in numbers. An excellent example of this utilization of collective identity is Fannie Exile Scudder Heck's "The Woman's Hymn."

The details of Heck's life indicate her strong identification with a community of other women. Heck was at the organizational meeting of the Southern Baptist Woman's Missionary Union (WMU) in 1888, and she served as its president for fifteen years in three terms between 1892 and 1915 ("Hall of Fame" 20). She devoted her life to an organization that both sustained women through missionary support "circles" in local churches and united them in a powerful national endeavor.[38] Under Heck's leadership, WMU raised millions of dollars to support foreign and domestic missionary causes, established a graduate school for women training to be missionaries, started a number of popular periodicals, and generally gave Baptist women the first real voice they had ever had in the running of their churches.[39] It is no wonder that Heck's most powerful autobiographical statement is *In Royal Service* (1913), a history of WMU written to celebrate its twenty-fifth anniversary as an organization. Her book celebrates the resiliency of Southern women after the Civil War and views that crisis as a precipitating factor in formulating a new collective identity for women:

> Amid these unwanted cares and deprivations [i.e., the hardships of the Reconstruction period] the new calls of woman to women is [sic] growing louder.
>
> Mother and daughter and the young granddaughter, now beside them, often talk of the Woman's Mission work, which is coming to be a distinct feature in the lives of Christian women everywhere. Here is work fitted to all the impulses of womanhood—love, pity and tenderness for woman; obedience to and confidence in God. These are the motives which shall spur her to action; these are the forces which shall develop in her that which is highest and best, which shall lead her to wider visions of life and higher reaches of faith; these shall be God's pillar of fire to guide her to her appointed place in the army which wages the long but always triumphant war for world-wide righteousness. (126)

Near the end of this passage, Heck envisions a new Exodus of women led through the desert like the children of Israel by a "pillar of fire." The "forces" that "spur" them on to fight the battles needed to win the Promised Land are those of relationship—"love, pity and tenderness for woman" and "obedience to and confidence in God." These same sentiments are the message of the first two verses of "The Woman's Hymn":

> Come, women, wide proclaim
> Life through your Saviour slain;
> Sing evermore.
> Christ, God's effulgence bright,
> Christ, who arose in might,
> Christ, who crowns you with light,
> Praise and adore.
>
> Come, clasping children's hands,
> Sisters from many lands,

Teach to adore,
For the sinsick and worn,
The weak and overborne,
All who in darkness mourn,
Pray, work, yet more. (BR 214)

In these verses, Heck calls upon the bonds of shared womanhood. Other Christian women are her "sisters" even if they live in
other countries; she celebrates their motherhood by inviting them to
"come, clasping children's hands."

Like other female hymnists of her time, Heck presents an apocalyptic vision in which women lead a new order of Christians into a
triumphant era. The phrase "Christ, who crowns you with light" and
Heck's promise in the third verse that "stars shall your brow adorn"
invoke the battle of Revelation 12, in which "a woman clothed with
the sun, and the moon under her feet, and upon her head a crown of
twelve stars" gives birth to a male child "who was to rule all nations
with a rod of iron." Representative perhaps of the twelve tribes of
Israel, the woman first produces a Messiah and then finds herself
and "the remnant of her seed" to be the deadly enemy of a dragon
representing the forces of evil. Thus, Heck refashions Christian history in allegorical terms to give women top billing and place the fate
of the religion in their hands. In the last pages of *In Royal Service*,
she calls for a Christian army to do the work of God: "The salvation
of the world waits the unreserved enlistment for life of the great
mass of Christians" (358). But as she makes clear, women are the
officers in this "royal service," and their identity comes from membership in their select group.

The title *In Royal Service* also suggests that Heck regards women
as a Christian aristocracy. This aspect of female identity formation
within Baptist circles was fully realized in Girl's Auxiliary (G.A.s), a
missions organization for preteen and young teenaged girls that began in 1914 during Heck's presidency (Allen 109). Eventually, G.A.s
developed a study program in which girls were rewarded for learning Scripture, performing service projects, and studying denominational work by designations describing their increasing status in the
missions aristocracy. Thousands of girls have become a "maiden,"
"lady-in-waiting," "princess," "queen," "queen with scepter," or

"queen regent" in elaborate coronation ceremonies as they advanced through the "Forward Steps" program sponsored by Woman's Missionary Union. The G.A. hymn, chosen in 1924, is H. Ernest Nichol's "We've a Story to Tell to the Nations" (Allen 109).[40] Though written by a man, the hymn appropriates the female hymnist's challenge to the convention of spiritual isolation: it creates subjectivity through telling someone else's story, singing someone else's song.

New Scripts

Carolyn G. Heilbrun writes that women have not been allowed to "assume power over—take control of—their own lives" because they have been denied the narratives available to men (17). She speaks specifically of narratives that express anger and those that allow the male autobiographer to describe his accomplishments in terms of overcoming difficulties and obstacles to transcend the limitations of human life (15–20). As I see it, the female hymnists about whom I write are actively engaged, not in writing spiritual autobiography that claims men's scripts, but in challenging what Natalie Zemon Davis calls the "fictional" aspects, that is, the "forming, shaping, and molding elements" of the conventional spiritual narratives (3). By writing new narratives of spiritual formation, these women proposed alternative scripts that allowed them to experience Christianity on their own terms.

Remembering her experience of writing "I Need Thee Every Hour," for example, Annie S. Hawks describes both the sense of longing for divine companionship one morning that led her to compose the hymn and the sense that the narrative it provided would eventually help her cope with her own life:

> For myself the hymn was prophetic rather than expressive of my own experience at the time it was written, and I do not understand why it so touched the great throbbing heart of humanity. It was not until long years after, when the shadow fell over my way—the shadow of a great loss—that I understood something of the comforting in the words I had been permitted to write and give out to others in my hours of sweet security and peace. (Qtd. in McCutchan 275)

On a larger scale, the gospel hymns created alternative identities and narratives of life experience for generations of believers. Another set of familiar and often repeated stories about hymns tells how they gave someone a script to follow during a crisis. A tale well-known in the secular community, for example, narrates how English hymnist Sarah Flower Adams's "Nearer, My God, to Thee" was sung as the *Titanic* sank on April 14, 1912 (Reynolds 151).[41]

Fanny Crosby's *Memories of Eighty Years* is full of tales in which a conversion or deathbed experience framed itself in the language of one of her hymns. She tells, for example, of a sailor who experienced his conversion in terms of being "safe in the arms of Jesus":

> Another incident of the singing of "Safe in the Arms of Jesus" was related by a sea captain, who was in the habit of holding services on board his vessel. From Sabbath to Sabbath he noticed that there was a certain man who did not unite with the others when they sang that hymn. At last he approached the sailor and inquired if he did not enjoy the meetings.
>
> "Oh, yes," the latter replied, "but I am not 'Safe in the arms of Jesus'; and I cannot sing that hymn." The captain prayed with him, and as a direct result of the interview, ere the next Sabbath, the sailor was singing the piece with the rest. (176)

Crosby also tells several touching stories about her hymn "Saved by Grace." In one, a woman faced with a "great temptation" happened into a chapel where the hymn was being sung and felt "that God had spoken to me through the voice of that song; and I at once decided to take the right path" (185). In another story, an actress is convicted of her sinful condition because hearing "Saved by Grace" sung in a public park brings back childhood memories (186). It is not uncommon even today for evangelicals to choose hymns for their own funerals based on the fact that a particular text provided a needed script at some pivotal moment in their lives.

As these stories show, then, hymns provide procedural knowledge of how a believer can behave and experience life. In addition, narratives about hymns working "miracles" serve a hagiographical function. Like stories of miracles told in the Roman Catholic tradition to argue for the canonization of a worthy Christian, stories of miracles wrought by hymns establish the "sainthood" of their composers, for whom the hymns are autobiographical statements. McCutchan's companion to *The Methodist Hymnal* of 1935 even includes a "hymn calendar"—in effect, a calendar of saints—that lists hymnists who were born, died, or were baptized on each day of the year. In the evangelical tradition, of course, a "saint" is simply any true Christian, not an example of extraordinary piety or a believer blessed with supernatural powers. But narratives that confer on Fanny Crosby the same sainthood as Isaac Watts or Charles Wesley were perceived to have given evangelical women a powerful identity that makes their voices ones to be reckoned with. Though these women remained in their churches, they used their power to push on the walls and widen their sphere of activity, to dismantle or refurbish some of the furniture, and to create a new pulpit through their hymns. More important, they authorized new narratives of spiritual formation based on their experiences of a woman's life.

[5]

The Patriarchal Backlash

Jesus "was no dough-faced, lick-spittle proposition. Jesus was the greatest scrapper that ever lived."
—BILLY SUNDAY

Backlash in the Evangelical Community

A religion that equates salvation with submission to a divine lover and makes the home more important than the church can make men profoundly uncomfortable. Shirley Abbott got it right when she described the Baptist experience on the American frontier in terms of an effort to "redefine masculinity":

> Something in the fundamentalist experience worked to redefine what a man had the right to do. . . . The metaphor of salvation—giving in to Christ, submitting to his will, accepting Him as Master—came naturally to women. Salvation was and is a poetic transformation of a relationship that women learn from early childhood. They trust and obey their fathers, look to their brothers for protection, and then become wives. Becoming the bride of Christ is not part of a man's training. Washed in that fount of blood, he will never be purely masculine afterward. Out in the wilderness in the nineteenth century, women surely realized that to get a man to kneel down before Christ was the first step in domesticating him and taming him. (146)

Perhaps unconsciously, Abbott weaves into her description the words of a well-known gospel hymn, John H. Sammis's "Trust and Obey" (1887). As this hymn implies, the evangelical model for salvation does seem to describe the social and sexual roles expected of a nineteenth-century woman: "Trust and obey, for there's no other way / To be happy in Jesus / But to trust and obey" (BR 390). The intellectual submission required "to be happy in Jesus" is obvious in the words of a young man who testified at a Dwight L. Moody revival that "I am not quite sure—but I am going to trust, and I am going to obey." Jotted down by Daniel B. Towner, who composed the hymn tune, these words were Sammis's inspiration for the hymn (Reynolds 243). However, such experiences seemed to have caused as much distress as inspiration. The stories of male reactions to feminized religion suggest that the evangelical domination of Protestant Christianity at the turn of the century may have owed much to the gender battles that enlivened the evangelical community.

Dwight Moody's successor, evangelist Billy Sunday, was one religious leader who apparently found the feminized Christianity of gospel hymns disturbing. Preaching in large cities across the country during the peak of his career from 1896–1912, Sunday carefully distanced himself from evangelicalism that would domesticate and feminize Christian men. Where Moody favored hymns such as "Oh, to Be Nothing," Sunday encouraged his "singer," Homer Rodeheaver, to lead revival congregations in "Onward Christian Soldiers," "The Battle Hymn of the Republic," and "The Fight Is On" (McLoughlin 84).[1] Sunday also made much of his background as a professional baseball player and described Christ as a man's man:

> [Sunday] declared that Jesus "was no dough-faced, lick-spittle proposition. Jesus was the greatest scrapper that ever lived." . . . Sunday repudiated the view that a Christian must be a "sort of dishrag proposition, a wishy-washy sissified sort of galoot that lets everybody make a doormat out of him. Let me tell you, the manliest man is the man who will acknowledge Jesus Christ." (McLoughlin 179)

Sunday's biographer records that the evangelist did use "old favorites"—that is, the gospel hymns already accepted as an invented tradition—in his revivals. However, he tended to secularize their lyrics or to choose hymns with little religious content to begin with. Rodeheaver also enjoyed suiting the hymns to the audience, and he encouraged humorous requests. Insurance salesmen might ask for "Blessed Assurance" while laundry workers favored "Wash Me and I

Shall Be Whiter than Snow." All of these strategies diminished the power of gospel hymns to teach doctrine or prescribe social roles while they enhanced their ability to create a feeling of community. Sunday and Rodeheaver were particularly careful to choose familiar invitation hymns that would play upon the emotions of potential "trail hitters," as the people who "walked the sawdust trail" to shake the preacher's hand and record their professions of faith were called (McLoughlin 84–85, 94, 97). Sunday's reaction to gospel hymns and the feminizing power they represented, then, was not to repudiate them but to manipulate them for his own purposes. And he was firmly evangelical in his assumptions that oral expressions of faith are flexible and sensitive to divine direction and that they translate spiritual pleasure into physical experience. The tension between feminine and masculine versions of evangelical Christianity probably accounted in part for Sunday's theatrics such as jumping on the pulpit and "wav[ing] two American flags" at the end of a sermon (McLoughlin 101). The desire to prove he was a red-blooded American man even as he promoted a feminized religion filled Sunday's especially constructed tabernacles and resulted in thousands of "trail hitters" per campaign.

An even more obvious exploitation of feminized Christianity was the shabby treatment of evangelical women hymnists within the sacred music business. The problem was that women usually wrote hymns but seldom composed hymn tunes, and copyrights were the exclusive property of the composers. Even a cursory examination of the paperback revival hymnals produced in the early decades of the twentieth century is telling: on page after page are hymn texts attributed to women and copyright notices informing the public that the rights to the hymns are the exclusive property of male composers. For example, in Homer Rodeheaver and B. D. Ackley's *Great Revival Hymns* (1911), the hymnal my grandmother personalized by altering the hymn titles, Nellie Talbot's "I'll Be a Sunbeam" (1900) carries a copyright notice that the words and music belong to E. O. Excell, and Excell has written a dedication beneath the title: "To my grandson, Edwin O. Excell, Jr" (144). To make matters worse, Rodeheaver and Ackley sold their hymnals for a tidy profit during Billy Sunday revivals. Rodeheaver was apparently an excellent salesman who created a demand for the songs his company published by teaching them to the congregation before the services (McLoughlin 78, 84–85).

Part of the problem was what Esther Rothenbusch calls "the low regard for lyricists, male or female, in the popular song industry." Fanny Crosby, who wrote popular secular lyrics before she began to write hymns, for example, collaborated with George Root in writing several popular songs. Rothenbusch reports that Crosby was not acknowledged as the lyricist on the sheet music of one of these, "Rosalie the Prairie Flower," and that she probably shared none of the "nearly three thousand dollars in royalties" (184). But at least "Rosalie" was a secular song. The hypocrisy of sacred music publishers— who worked ostensibly for the purest of motives and who knew they were producing what their audiences viewed as sacred texts—is harder to explain. A preface written by Billy Sunday for *Great Revival Hymns* claims that Rodeheaver and Ackley have "spared no expense" to advance "the work of bringing the unsaved to Christ." One wonders exactly what expenses were not spared. The female hymnists—including Fanny Crosby—who provided many of the texts for their book probably received nothing at all.

Crosby's career as a hymnist is a sad and probably representative tale of the exploitation of female hymn writers. From the late 1860s on, according to Bernard Ruffin, she wrote most of the hymn texts for publishers Biglow and Main of New York City and the John Church Company of Cincinnati. These companies became so dependent on her, in fact, that they persuaded her to use at least 204 pseudonyms to conceal the fact that she was producing one-third to one-half of the hymns in their popular hymnals. Yet Ruffin reports that she never received more than "a dollar or two" per hymn and that, once her hymns were sold, she lost all control over her work (105, 145–46). By the time Crosby published *Fanny Crosby's Life-Story* in 1903 when she was eighty-three, the publishers included this poignant notice in an advertisement at the front of the book:

> It is sincerely hoped by the publishers that this book may have as large a sale as possible, in order that the story of its loved author may be an inspiration to many people, and that she may be enabled to have a home of her own, in which to pass the remainder of her days.

Crosby's exploitation represents a literal appropriation of her work by male evangelicals, most of whom she regarded as close personal friends (Ruffin 146). It was a way to control her talent and limit her possibilities by creating dependence upon those who made a commodity of sacred texts. It also suggests that the real issue for some evangelical men was not evangelizing the world, as they piously claimed, but a need to control and profit from what powered the ordinary believer in the pew. As with Sunday's revivals, however, both economic and religious motivation fired the thriving sacred music business.

The Rhetoric of the Social Gospel

A more interesting rhetorical challenge to feminized evangelical hymnody—and one much less successful in promoting a particular brand of Christianity than Sunday's manipulation or the exploitation of music publishers—was social gospel hymns. With a few exceptions, these hymns are no longer included in denominational hymnals. However, at the turn of the century, social gospel spokesman Walter Rauschenbusch declared that they were essential to support his side of a conflict between what he termed male and female versions of Christianity. In 1909, Rauschenbusch complained in his *Prayers of the Social Awakening* that "the ordinary church hymnal rarely contains more than two or three hymns in which the triumphant chords of the social hope are struck" (10). Jon Michael Spencer identifies Rauschenbusch as "the first national figure to seriously espouse the promulgation of a social gospel hymnody." Although he did not write hymns himself, Rauschenbusch's call seems to have been the catalyst for at least three collections of hymns that supported the movement (19).[2] The ultimate failure of these hymnals testifies to the power of feminized religion to keep Protestantism alive.

The texts designated as social gospel hymns promote the masculine religion that Rauschenbusch called for in 1907 to address the American social crisis brought on by urbanization and industrialization. His book, *Christianity and the Social Crisis,* argues that Christian socialism can save America by relieving working men and women of the "economic fear" that lowers the marriage and birth rates and endangers the welfare of women (271–79). In other words, he promotes a religion that attends to the physical welfare of human beings at the expense of attention to doctrine and ritual. He supports reform measures to create safe working conditions for laborers, guard the food supply, and make taxation more equitable. All of these changes are necessary to promote the stability of families because "to create a maximum number of happy families might well be considered the end of all statesmanship" (272). The health of the nation clearly depends, says Rauschenbusch, "on the welfare of the home." However, the rhetoric that supports his social agenda sounds suspiciously like the nineteenth-century cult of domesticity with its interest in keeping healthy, pure women within their proper sphere of influence. He asks anxiously, "What . . . will be the outcome if the unmarried multiply; if homes remain childless; if families are homeless; if girls do not know housework; and if men come to distrust the purity of women?" (279).

To avoid these calamities, Rauschenbusch suggests that Christian men once again take up the duties of their appointed sphere and put women back in their proper place:

> There are two great entities in human life,—the human soul and the human race,—and religion is to save both. The soul is to seek righteousness and eternal life; the race is to seek righteousness and the kingdom of God. The social preacher is apt to overlook the one. But the evangelical preacher has long overlooked the other. It is due to that protracted neglect that we are now deluged by the social problem in its present acute form. It is partly due to the same neglect that our churches are overwhelmingly feminine. Woman nurtures the individual in the home, and God has equipped her with an intuitive insight into the problems of the individual life. Man's life faces the outward world, and his instincts and interests lie that way. . . . Our individualistic religion has helped to feminize our churches. A very protracted one-sidedness in preaching has to be balanced up, and if some now go to the other extreme, those who have created the situation hardly have the right to cast the first stone. (367)

A Baptist who learned firsthand the suffering of the urban poor in a pastorate near Hell's Kitchen in New York City, Rauschenbusch perceives a conflict between evangelicalism—which he associates with women—and Christian socialism—which he associates with men. He blames the church's neglect of the physical and social needs of humanity on the "feminization" of Christianity and Christian churches. Rhetorically, perhaps, the term *feminization* refers to the language of evangelical domesticity that dominated the fiction, sermons, and hymns of evangelicals and created the stereotype that evangelicalism was interested only in saving souls for eternity through sentimental appeals to home and mother. Socially, *feminization* may refer to a turf battle. As the women's missionary movement encouraged more women to view social service as a form of domestic missions, women—even among conservative Southern Baptists, who especially feared the social gospel—had taken the lead in benevolence work enacted in the public sphere.[3] Faced with the enormous social problems of his day, Rauschenbusch calls for action to remasculinize public Christianity.

Ironically, Rauschenbusch reverses the gender associations Charlotte Perkins Gilman makes with these aspects of Christianity in *His Religion and Hers: A Study of the Faith of Our Fathers and the Work of Our Mothers* (1923). Gilman argues that individualized religion focused primarily on death and eternal reward has been the province of men but that concern with relationships and "all the labors that maintain and improve life" has traditionally been the female version of Christianity (46). In other words, she associates faith in abstract doctrine with men and a commitment to practical Christianity with women. As gospel hymns themselves demonstrate, "her religion" stresses identity through community, views spirituality as coming into relationship rather than as an economic exchange, and resists the conventions that make the spiritual isolate the only model for spiritual maturity. More practically, Protestant Christianity in the Woman's Century was feminized partly because women led crusades for moral reform to improve the lives of impoverished or otherwise underprivileged people. Women also volunteered their time to work in settlement houses, teach English to immigrants, and run mother's clubs for women working in factories who needed encouragement and training in practical homemaking. The eventual professionalization of Christian social work was almost entirely the work of women. All of these things had been going on for years when the governor of Tennessee called the first Southern Sociological Congress in 1912 to consider the relationship between the church and social service. Walter Rauschenbusch spoke to the congress, but in the audience were laywomen who had created the prototypes for social gospel ministries (Allen 211–33).[4] Rauschenbusch's association of community and material concerns with public, masculine religion, then, ignores what women had actually been doing and, worse, appropriates the model of spirituality that fueled what Baptist women then called "personal service" and today speak of as "mission action."

   Christianity and the Social Crisis contains few practical suggestions for social service. Instead, it seems more concerned with an ideological basis for social roles that will keep women in their place while allowing men to appropriate their power. For example, Rauschenbusch suggests that masculine Christianity assume a social role frequently associated with mid-nineteenth-century women, one that emphasizes influencing others at the expense of more direct action. Vague about specific tactics, he argues that the church should solve the problems of a modern age through its ability to inspire and regenerate individuals rather than through using the financial and human resources of a social organization to affect public policy (348).[5] This strategy casts the man who supports Social Christianity in the popular role of the nineteenth-century woman who influences by example. "Such a man," says Rauschenbusch, "will in some measure incarnate the principles of a higher social order in his attitude to all questions and in all his relations to men, and will be a well-spring of regenerating influences" (351–52). By changing "such a man" to "such a woman," he could be describing Mrs. Shelby or Mrs. Bird in *Uncle Tom's Cabin*. These female characters exemplify the True Womanhood that supposedly enhances the social order through a superior spirituality and morality. The point is that True Women do not have to act; they just have to be. Rauschenbusch uses the term "a higher social order" where Harriet Beecher Stowe might have used the phrase "high moral and religious sensibility and principle," as she does in describing Mrs. Shelby (20), but the notion of religious "influence" is the same in both texts.

   Rauschenbusch also argues that the Christian socialist will find the sacred in the daily routine of manual labor, an attitude associated with female spirituality in domestic fiction such as Elizabeth Stuart Phelps's short story "The Angel Over the Right Shoulder" (1852).[6] In this tale, Mrs. James, an overworked mother of three small children, accepts her husband's challenge to set aside two hours a day to read, study, and generally improve her mind. After a month, she feels unsuccessful because the daily demands of housework and child care have frustrated her plan so much that "even her hours of religious duty had been encroached upon and disturbed" (161). Then she has a dream in which a woman is traveling with her small children toward a "region of light." Each time the woman stops to bathe the children's feet, to sing to them, or to set a wanderer gently back on the path, an angel peering over her right shoulder joyfully writes down her deed in a book. But each time "her eye was fixed so intently on [the] golden horizon, and she became so eager to make progress thither, that the little ones, missing her care, did languish or stray," a sorrowful angel over her left shoulder records her lapse (162–63). As the story ends, appropriately on New Year's Day, Mrs. James realizes that the interruptions she thought were restricting her spiritual development are the "duties and cares" that "[can] not be neglected without danger" to her spiritual development (164).

Rauschenbusch does not echo the veneration of domesticity that is obvious in Phelps's story, but he does appropriate the idea that daily physical tasks are an avenue to the sacred. He claims that the "older conception of religion viewed as religious only what ministered to the souls of men or what served the Church"; in this "older conception," "daily work" such as "ploughing, building, cobbling, or selling" was "secular." Rauschenbusch argues that it is now time to view the daily activities of living as sacred so that "a man making a shoe or arguing a law case or planting potatoes or teaching school, could feel that this was itself a contribution to the welfare of mankind, and indeed his main contribution to it" (*Christianity* 355–56). The socialist agenda in Rauschenbusch's argument seems to be the eradication of class boundaries that separated the ruling class of ministers and ordained church leaders from the masses of lay people. But to make these ideas Christian, he has to borrow some ideas about spirituality already endorsed by countless domestic fiction writers and viewed as a feminine approach to religion in the sense that the domestic sphere was the province of women. Rauschenbusch suggests that Christianity is a model for social relations rather than a religion, but he cannot escape altogether the religious structuring of reality that assumes a particular relationship between faith and behavior. He chooses to assume what Gilman would regard as a female approach to Christianity when he argues that action is the avenue to faith.

The Appropriation of Women's Spirituality

The social gospel appropriation of rhetoric associated with evangelical women suggests its power. It also suggests anxiety about allowing women control over powerful texts. Social gospel hymnists, predominantly male, pretended that notions of spirituality associated with women in domestic fiction and gospel hymns were male all along by setting them in the male world of war and work.[7] They also recast these ideas in what Thoreau termed the "father tongue" of written language instead of the "mother tongue" of language that simulated oral communication (70). These rhetorical devices suggest a need to control the growing power of women in evangelical churches. The hymns themselves preserve cultural traces of the war between traditionalists and modernists, which can, in fact, be analyzed as a conflict between what Rauschenbusch sees as the duality of masculine and feminine Christianity. However, social gospel hymns do not simply substitute what Rauschenbusch might call masculine Christianity for the feminized version on which he blames the social crisis. Instead, the masculine Christianity of social gospel hymns neutralizes by appropriation rather than by extinction and harnesses the power of the feminine as a way to redeem the secularism of social gospel theology.[8]

The one social gospel hymnal known to have been endorsed by Rauschenbusch was *Social Hymns of Brotherhood and Aspiration* (1914), edited by Mabel Hay Barrows Mussey (Spencer 22). The collection comprises III hymns collected explicitly to promote the social gospel movement. The six categories of texts in the hymnal indicate the major concerns of social gospelers: Aspiration and Faith; Liberty and Justice; Peace; Labor and Conflict; Brotherhood; and Patriotism. Most of the hymns have male lyricists, some of which are well-known poets such as John Greenleaf Whittier and Alfred Tennyson. Mussey describes the hymnal's purpose in her preface:

> Social aspiration is the dominant note in this book. The editor's first object was to find hymns that could be sung by all people in all places,—in churches, in halls, in schools, in the open. Many hymns, therefore, were chosen which Jew and Gentile, Protestant and Catholic may sing with equal fervor. . . . The line has been drawn to include hymns of cheer, courage and inspiration; other phases of religious life have been left to the church hymnals. Every year now leads us farther on the road to social living. May this collection mark a milestone on the way!

Mussey's description of the purpose for the hymn collection echoes the female model of spirituality described by mid-nineteenth-century hymnal editor Anna B. Warner. Like the introductory material to Warner's *Wayfarer's Hymns* (1869) and *Hymns of the Church Militant* (1859), this preface addresses itself to travelers "on the road to social living." Although Mussey hopes the collection will become "a milestone on the way" to "social living," the travel implied is the female walk rather than the male journey. The destination is, after all, the condition of mutually beneficial social relationships, not the Celestial City of eternal reward. Like Warner's wayfarers, Mussey's travelers are earthbound.

Mussey also endorses Warner's notion of a spirituality unbounded by historical concerns: she dissociates herself from organized religion and particularly from orthodox Christianity with its manifold historical associations. She implies that the hymns in her collection ignore theology and religious ritual—"phases of religious life [that] have been left to the church hymnals"—to focus instead on encouragement and inspiration of the travelers. The hymns also describe a religion of feeling whose practitioners require "cheer, courage and inspiration" rather than doctrinal instruction. In other words, Christian socialism is like the religion of Anna Warner because it is a religion of feeling and behavior rather than of intellectual activity. Finally, the phrase "social living" suggests a concern with material needs and the physical and emotional well-being of humanity, rather than an effort to lead people to a heavenly reward. Warner dedicates *Wayfaring Hymns* to "the Help of the Christian's life—the Joy and Comfort of the Sick Room—the Hope of the Doubting, and the Rest of the Weary in Heart" (n.p.); her emphasis on physical needs for health and rest as well as on emotional needs for hope and encouragement describes concerns implied by the phrase "social living." Although Mussey separates herself from nineteenth-century Protestantism by avoiding the allusions to the Bible and to *The Pilgrim's Progress* that characterize the introductions to *Wayfaring Hymns* and *Hymns of the Church Militant,* her construction of spiritual reality in female terms is very similar to Anna Warner's. The point is not that women wrote these introductions to hymnals and that Christian women should be essentialized by distinguishing their faith from the faith of Christian men. Rather, what I see here is the conscious use of faith models that, as Rauschenbusch states explicitly, have been identified in the faith community as masculine and feminine. Warner and Mussey both describe "feminine" uses for hymns, and Mussey's feminine model is especially intriguing as the introduction to hymns particularly concerned with a father God, the brotherhood of man, and the public sphere of work and war.

That Mussey is appropriating and adapting an older model of feminized Christianity is inherent in the way she envisions people using her hymns. Warner's texts are poems without music; they are obviously intended for private devotional use. Mussey's, on the other hand, are set to music so that they can be sung on public occasions. She imagines their use "in churches, in halls, in schools, in the open." Warner's hymns can remain the private property of women to be used, her domestic rhetoric implies, in the home, but Mussey's are public property available to both men and women. The social gospel hymns themselves are dominated by references to what Rauschenbusch would associate with the "outward world" of masculine Christianity: descriptions of cities and the problems of "the mill and the mart" (91) rather than of homes and domestic concerns. Nearly every hymn refers in some way to war, either to an allegorical battle "to crush the Wrong, uphold the Right" (43) or to a socialist "war of race and creed" (94). The evangelical vision of God as a lover, mother, or bosom companion is also missing; instead, the hymns describe a creator God "from [whom] all skill and science flow" (8)[9] or a God who engages in human activities such as sowing (14), if they make any reference to God at all. Many hymns focus entirely on humanity or "men," and the phrases "the Fatherhood of God" and "the brotherhood of man" are social gospel cliches. In fact, women are almost nonexistent in these hymns although one refers to America as the "Motherland" and another describes the church as a woman. The other occasional references to women make them victims, objects of pity, or people restricted to their proper sphere; examples of these references are phrases such as "save our mother-hood from need" (108), women turning their eyes "from their tragic shame" (6), and "mother's love makes happy home" (102).

The Kingdom of God[10]

While they glorify the world of men and trivialize the existence of women, however, the hymns in *Social Hymns of Brotherhood and Aspiration* rely very heavily on some aspects of the female model of spirituality popularized in domestic fiction and gospel hymns. The most obvious appropriation is of the version of millennialism articulated in the writing of influential nineteenth-century women rather than that promoted in male-authored sermons and theological treatises. That is, these hymns portray a golden age of social equality and spirituality grounded in the concrete details of everyday life rather than the triumph of American nationalism.

The word *millennium* in nineteenth-century literature is itself a commonplace expression that refers to a golden age or utopia. In 1852, newspaper columnist Fanny Fern, for example, used the word in this casual sense to describe the condition of women in a world without men:

> Women would keep *young* till the millennium; in fact, the millennium would be merely a nominal jubilee! because it would have *already come*. The world would be an universal garden of pretty, rosy, laughing women; no masculine mildew to mar their beauty or bow their sweet heads, the blessed year round!

Typically, Fern uses her slicing wit and ironic humor as social commentary in this passage. For her, a golden age requires social equality, which is clearly incompatible with the subjugation of women in marriage, the only thing Fern claims that teaches women "wickedness" (228–29).

Nineteenth-century millennialism could also be a religious concept. The followers of William Miller, for example, were premillennialists who believed that Christ's second advent would precede the thousand years of peace described in Revelation 20. Indeed, they predicted that the second coming would occur and the millennium would begin on October 22, 1844, and they prepared themselves for this event. The failure of their prediction dampened American enthusiasm for premillennialism until later in the century (Sandeen 54). Meanwhile, intellectuals such as the Beechers embraced a practical, optimistic postmillennialism, which anticipated the figurative reign of Christ ushered in by a millennial era of human improvement.

Harriet Beecher Stowe articulated the domestic version of postmillennialism in *Uncle Tom's Cabin* (1852), the most popular book of the nineteenth century. When African slaves George and Eliza are reunited at the breakfast table with their Quaker hosts, Stowe suggests the sacramental nature of time, as I describe more fully in chapter 3. Each meal in a kitchen run by a True Woman prefigures the scriptural feast at the end of time, when Christians forget differences in social station as they share a communal meal. More practically, mealtimes present recurring opportunities for believers to create a heaven of social equality on earth.[11] Stowe stresses the active involvement of believers in bringing in the kingdom, and she views technological achievement as a spiritual force.

A more explicit statement of Stowe's millennialism in *The Minister's Wooing* (1859) makes technological advancement a prerequisite of the golden age that will precede the second advent. Dr. Hopkins, the minister of the title, articulates this belief in conversation with Aunt Katy Scudder, just the sort of "Martha" whose housekeeping skills will most benefit from technological advancement that will free her and others to nurture the abstract spirituality of a Mary:[12]

"In the Millennium, I suppose, there will be such a fulness and plenty of all the necessaries and conveniences of life, that it will not be necessary for men and women to spend the greater part of their lives in labor in order to procure a living. It will not be necessary for each one to labor more than two or three hours a day,—not more than will conduce to health of body and vigor of mind; and the rest of their time they will spend in reading and conversation, and such exercises as are necessary and proper to improve their minds and make progress in knowledge." . . .

"But how will it be possible," inquired Mrs. Scudder, "that so much less work will suffice in those days to do all that is to be done?"

"Because of the great advance of arts and sciences which will take place before those days," said the Doctor, "whereby everything shall be performed with so much greater ease,—also the great increase of disinterested love, whereby the skill and talents of those who have much shall make up for the weakness of those who have less.

"Yes,"—he continued, after a pause,—"all the careful Marthas in those days will have no excuse for not sitting at the feet of Jesus; there will be no cumbering with much serving; the Church will have only Maries in those days." (609–10)

Dr. Hopkins puts his belief into practice after this conversation by visiting one of his parishioners and trying to convince him to free his slaves. He does his part to bring in the millennium by making society ready for it.

Catharine Beecher, Stowe's sister, also assigns to women the task of bringing in the millennium in *Treatise on Domestic Economy* (1841), an instruction manual for every possible domestic skill from doing laundry to lubricating carriage wheels. In chapter 1, "The Peculiar Responsibilities of American Women," Beecher claims that "the principles of democracy . . . are identical with the principles of Christianity," and she imagines a "day advancing, 'by seers predicted, and by poets sung,'" when America will lead all nations to "the beneficent influences of Christianity" (2). She claims for American women "the exalted privilege of extending over the world those blessed influences, that are to renovate degraded man" because women manage the domestic sphere and therefore determine "the intellectual and moral character of the mass of the people" (3). As Kathryn Kish Sklar observes, Catharine Beecher "agreed that the millennium seemed to be coming in a social rather than a strictly religious form" (159). In addition to stressing concrete action rather than piety in effecting this spiritual-social event, Beecher emphasizes the ennobling and equalizing effects of physical labor in establishing the new Jerusalem in America:

> It is the building of a glorious temple, whose base shall be coextensive with the bounds of the earth, whose summit shall pierce the skies, whose splendor shall beam on all lands, and those who hew the lowliest stone, as much as those who carve the highest capital, will be equally honored when its top-stone shall be laid, with new rejoicings of the morning stars, and shoutings of the sons of God. (14)

Beecher and Stowe's brother, Henry Ward Beecher, agreed with his sisters in an 1868 sermon called "The Family as an American Institution" that "in the new years that are coming, a nobler womanhood will give to us nobler households," and he praises intellectual achievement by women as a way to enhance the domestic sphere (430). However, he does not endorse the equalizing effect of marriage. Instead, marriage is a way of serving men, who need to be married to guard their moral purity. As he puts it,

> At no after period, perhaps, in their life, do young men need the inspiration of virtuous love, and the sympathy of a companion in their self-denying toil, as when they first enter the battle for their own support. Early marriages are permanent moralities, and deferred marriages are temptations to wickedness. (431)

In general, sermons by both Henry Ward Beecher and his father suggest their interest in a millennium of space (a new Zion) rather than a millennium of time. Their postmillennialism supports the American myth of progress, a convention of metanarratives of spiritual formation that excludes women. As George Marsden points out, American postmillennialism has sometimes merged with secular goals to support the American myth that "America has a special place in God's plans and will be the center for a great spiritual and moral reform that will lead to a golden age or 'millennium' of Christian civilization" (92, 112). Lyman Beecher, for example, predicted as early as 1835 that the millennium would come with the settlement of the West (*A Plea* 10–11). Thirty-four years later, Henry Ward Beecher—preaching on the text "Blessed are the meek; for they shall inherit the earth" (Matt. 5:5)—makes it clear that Americans are the "meek" of whom Jesus spoke and that what "some men call . . . the *millenium* [sic]" may be equated with "the ripeness of the race" as America comes to its inevitable triumph over other civilizations ("Inheritance" 260).

Beecher's emphasis on a millennium of space in his rather literal interpretation of "inherit[ing] the earth" confirms Sidney E. Mead's sense that those "who would understand America must understand that through all the formative years, space has overshadowed time . . . in the formation of all the ideals most cherished by the American mind and spirit." As Mead argues, for example, freedom for Americans inevitably meant moving to a free place rather than waiting for deliverance ("The American People" 11–12). So for social gospel proponents to adopt hymns that promoted a millennialism of time is ironic: it reclaims theological turf (space) by appropriating the emphasis on a golden age (time) articulated by women such as Fern, Stowe, and Catharine Beecher and counters fears about the growing power of New Women by adopting the older spiritual vision of True Women.

One hymn in *Social Hymns of Brotherhood and Aspiration* that pictures a utopian spiritual era breaking in from time to time is Edmund H. Sears's "It Came upon the Midnight Clear" (1850), a well-known Christmas carol and one of the four or five hymns included in this hymnal that people still sing. Like a number of hymns in the collection, this one was actually written before the gospel hymn era but was included in the hymnal as an expression of social gospel ideals. It expresses Stowe's sense of postmillennialism quite well and, in fact, was published only two years before *Uncle Tom's Cabin*. Sears's hymn describes the angels that sang to announce Christ's nativity. Their message of "Peace on the earth" is not something new; it is "that glorious song of old." The angel song still "floats / O'er all the weary world," and Sears implies that the advent can be recurrent if humanity will "hush the noise, ye men of strife / And hear the angels sing!"

The last verse of "It Came upon the Midnight Clear" describes time as cycles of years whose repetition is itself the cause for hope:

> For lo! the days are hastening on,
> By prophet-bards foretold,
> When with the ever-circling years

Comes round the age of gold;
When peace shall over all the earth
Its ancient splendors fling,
And the whole world send back the song
Which now the angels sing. (s h 46)[13]

Sears's God—who is incarnated again and again—is the immanent divinity breaking into history, the God of the social gospel.
Evangelical hymnists often image individual conversion in terms of
gaining a new song; Sears hears the "whole world" singing as the
race is saved from destruction. His view of time is not the modernist
vision of humanity evolving steadily toward ultimate perfection; by
1914, when Mussey's hymnal was published, the hymn represented
an antimodern evocation of the premodern model of time associated
with women and the domestic sphere.[14]

That Sears's hymn expresses a view of time specifically promoted
by the social gospel hymnists is evident not only from its inclusion
in the hymnal but from the way other social gospel hymnists imitate
it. Consider, for example, the first stanza of Ozora S. Davis's "At
Length There Dawns the Glorious Day," which was first published
in 1909 but reprinted five years later in *Social Hymns of Brotherhood
and Aspiration*:

At length there dawns the glorious day
By prophets long foretold,
At length the chorus clearer grows
That shepherds heard of old.
That day of growing brotherhood
Breaks on our eager eyes,
And human hatreds flee before
The radiant Eastern skies. (73)

Davis's hymn not only reproduces the meter and rhyme scheme
of "It Came Upon the Midnight Clear" and expresses the same general idea; it also virtually copies one of Sears's most resonant phrases:
"prophet-bards foretold" becomes "prophets long foretold" in
Davis's hymn. Other hymns in the hymnal also speak of the kingdom prophesied. Marion Dutton Savage, for example, calls it "thy
kingdom long foretold" in the 1913 "Teach Us, O Lord, True Brotherhood" (83), and Theodore C. Williams refers to "the coming,
golden time" (67), a rewording of Sears's "coming age of gold."

These later hymns borrow Sears's language to articulate their social gospel ideals. Davis emphasizes the fact that the "day of the Lord" is a "day of growing brotherhood," not simply a time of peace, as Sears puts it. And "brotherhood" is more than tolerance and good will among men. It is a kinship distinguished by equality of inheritance and lack of social hierarchy. A hymn by Sir Henry Wotton clarifies the notion of brotherhood as social equality:

> How happy is he born or taught,
> Who serveth not another's will;
> Whose armor is his honest thought,
> And simple truth his highest skill;
>
> Whose passions not his masters are;
> Whose soul is still prepared for death,
> Not tied unto the world with care
> Of prince's ear or vulgar breath;
>
> Who God doth late and early pray
> More of his grace than goods to lend;
> And walks with man, from day to day,
> As with a brother and a friend.
>
> This man is freed from servile bands
> Of hope to rise, or fear to fall;
> Lord of himself, though not of lands,
> And having nothing, yet has all. (s h 69)

This is a quintessential social gospel hymn in its emphasis on the corrupting nature of property, the eradication of social authority, and the good will initiated by "brotherhood." It describes the domestic version of the kingdom of God in its social relations, but it lacks the transcendent spirituality that makes Stowe's character George Harris lose his "pining, atheistic doubts" at the Halliday breakfast table (*Uncle Tom's Cabin* 170). It speaks of God as the author of both "grace" and "goods," but, ultimately, a man is "Lord of himself."

Even when social gospel hymns describe a holy war to bring in the day of the Lord, the battle is usually a way of unifying humanity in a common cause that knows no class lines. The battle, in other words, serves the same purpose as the "holy day" represented by breakfast in the Halliday kitchen. And, in Algernon C. Swinburne's "We Mix from Many Lands" (n.d.), the battle ends in a feast:

> Rise, ere the dawn be risen,
> Come, and be all souls fed;
> From field and streets and prison
> Come, for the feast is spread.
> Live! for the truth is living:
> Wake! for the night is dead. (s h 74)

Swinburne describes in these lines a utopia earned by those who bring in "all good things" "that no priests give nor kings." It is heavenly, but it is not an extraterrestrial heaven. Like Stowe, Swinburne envisions a heaven on earth defined by the eradication of social barriers. No human activity is so equalizing as eating at the same table.

However, hymns that promote "social living" neutralize the notion of the kingdom of God appropriated from domestic fiction by secularizing it. Social gospel hymns sometimes suggest that the coming of the kingdom is an inevitable feature of human progress, not the result of believers who employ technology to establish a kingdom of God in the kitchen of every home. Charles Kingsley's "From Thee All Skill and Science Flow" (1871), for example, suggests that once enough "skill and science" have come to earth, the kingdom will follow:

> And hasten, Lord, that perfect day
> When pain and death shall cease,
> And Thy just rule shall fill the earth
> With health and light and peace. (s h 8)

Kingsley places great faith in the working of natural law and the increase of knowledge on earth to end sickness, the darkness of ignorance, and war. His address to the God "of skill and science" implies faith in the natural progress of human technology. Frederick Hosmer also speaks of a time "when knowledge, hand in hand with peace / Shall walk the earth abroad" (s h 9). His hymn, though it does assume the presence of a deity, secularizes the kingdom by linking it to the rational idea of evolution rather than to the unfathomable behavior of God.

In another version of the Day of the Lord, abolitionist Thomas

Wentworth Higginson seems to credit the passing of time—"Time's wondrous will"—with the power to bring in the day of the Lord through a bloodless social revolution. Higginson led a slave regiment in the Union Army (Spencer 22); however, the inclusion of his hymn in the "Labor and Conflict" section of Mussey's collection recontextualizes what may have been his depiction of an army of poor slaves as a description of an army of poor laborers. I quote his hymn in its entirety because it captures so well the flavor of the hymns in this section titled "Labor and Conflict":

> From street and square, from hill and glen,
> Of this vast world beyond my door,
> I hear the tread of marching men,
> The patient armies of the poor.
>
> Not ermine-clad or clothed in state,
> Their title-deeds not yet made plain,
> But waking early, toiling late,
> The heirs of all the earth remain.
>
> The peasant brain shall yet be wise,
> The untamed pulse grow calm and still;
> The blind shall see, the lowly rise,
> And work in peace Time's wondrous will.
>
> Some day, without a trumpet's call
> This news will o'er the world be blown:
> "The heritage comes back to all!
> The myriad monarchs take their own!" (SH 59)

Higginson's description of "the patient armies of the poor" implies that a battle is at hand, although the eventual victory seems to be the triumph of work over tradition and privilege.

He specifically repudiates, however, the premillennialist view that would reward the poor and dispossessed either when they die or when Christ returns and begins his thousand-year reign on earth. In fact, Higginson leaves God and Christianity out of the picture altogether. The line "their title-deeds not yet made plain" could refer to Watts's "When I Can Read My Title Clear," the hymn Uncle Tom sings that infuriates Simon Legree because it reminds him "that his power over his bond thrall was somehow gone" (Stowe, *Uncle Tom's Cabin* 459). Tom's title is to a home in heaven at the end of human time. This passage provides an interesting contrast to Stowe's vision of the Halliday kitchen; it seems to say that making an extraterrestrial heaven the ultimate goal is necessary when Christians will not do what they must to create heaven on earth. One way or another, Stowe's kingdom is a spiritual event. Higginson, on the other hand, predicts that justice and an inversion of the social order will reward the patient suffering of the likes of Uncle Tom. His kingdom is totally secular. The true "monarchs" of the earth will not have to wait for the "trumpet's call" that Christians believe signals the end of recorded time because the power to change their lot is in their own hands. Ultimately, both Higginson and Stowe expect a millennium, but he predicts that justice will eventually prevail because the poor will work hard enough to earn it while she believes that the kingdom of God requires action that leads to faith.

Work Is Prayer

Besides the domestic version of the kingdom of God, then, social gospel hymnists also appropriate the element of feminine spirituality that assumes action leads to faith rather than that faith leads to action. Higginson believes the "patient armies of the poor" will work until they get a new gospel, the good "news" that "The heritage comes back to all!" Action and faith are also inextricably linked in domestic novels, but Higginson and Stowe would have had somewhat different interpretations of the social gospel cliche "work is prayer." For Higginson, work replaces prayer and affirms the value of humanity; for Stowe, work is a sacrament that makes spiritual reality observable and bolsters faith. The Halliday kitchen in *Uncle Tom's Cabin* bears out this relationship between work and faith. Rachel Halliday's domain is an efficient workshop in which labor is joy: "Even the knives and forks had a social clatter as they went on to the table; and the chicken and ham had a cheerful and joyous fizzle in the pan, as if they rather enjoyed being cooked than otherwise" (170). It is a place in which the worker is not alienated from the work because housework is both a service and an art. The kitchen itself reflects the triumph of loving craft. Stowe describes it as

a large, roomy, neatly-painted kitchen, its yellow floor glossy and
smooth, and without a particle of dust; a neat, well-blacked cooking-
stove; rows of shining tin, suggestive of unmentionable good things to
the appetite; glossy green wood chairs, old and firm; a small flag-bot-
tomed rocking-chair, with a patch-work cushion in it, neatly contrived
out of small pieces of different colored woollen goods, and a larger
sized one, motherly and old, whose wide arms breathed hospitable invitation. (162)

The attention to aesthetic detail in Rachel's domain transforms
what could be the sterile efficiency of a mid-nineteenth-century
kitchen with its advanced cooking stove replacing the older hearth
and the "row of shining tin" implements instead of cruder home-
made tools. The good housekeeping represented by the cleanliness
and neatness of the shining floor and chairs is a testimony to the human presence of the mother who creates a sanctuary in the home.
The "patch-work cushion" is an apt symbol of her art: it preserves
materials by creating what is both useful and attractive. The furniture itself takes on the personality of its mistress: the large rocking
chair, like Rachel herself, is "motherly and old"; its "arms breathed
hospitable invitation." The other chairs are also old, suggesting that
the art of the kitchen has tradition and history to give it richness
and substance.

The idea that work is holy is also characteristic of "traditional gospel hymns" such as Pollard's "Have Thine Own Way
Lord," which uses the biblical figure of pottery making to describe a
relationship between God and the believer. What distinguishes
work in the domestic setting from work in the marketplace is its
sacramental nature. It is "a visible sign of an inward grace," to quote
a dictionary definition, because it expresses the homemaker's
personality and creates spiritual reality, in some cases a heaven on
earth. Josephine Donovan describes work in the home in Marxist
terms as "creat[ing] objects for use rather than for exchange" and,
thus, as "relatively unalienated labor" (103). In other words, work
in the home invests the time and talent of the worker both in the
work itself and in the lives of those who benefit from it. While
this idealized picture of housework is probably far from the practical
reality of women who cooked and cleaned without electricity or
packaged laundry detergent, it represents a compelling idea that

Barbara Solomon argues empowered the nineteenth-century literary domestics and created the ideology that allowed them to publish housekeeping manuals, children's fiction, and domestic novels (16–18).

The connection between work and faith in social gospel hymns is summed up accurately in A. J. H. Duganne's phrase "work is prayer" (see SH 54 and 63). Three verses of one of his hymns articulate the idea that work is a sacred activity:

> Life is toil, and all that lives,
> Sacrifice of labor gives!
> Water, fire, and air, and earth,
> Rest not, pause not, from their birth,
> Sacred toil doth nature share—
> Love and labor—work is prayer.
>
> Patriot! toiling for thy kind!
> Thou shalt break the chains that bind!
> Shape thy thought and mold thy plan,
> Toil for freedom—toil for man!
> Sagely think and boldly dare—
> Labor! labor! work is prayer!
>
> Brother! round thee brothers stand—
> Pledge thy truth, and give thy hand—
> Raise the downcast—help the weak,
> Toil for good—for virtue speak;
> Let thy brethren be thy care—
> Labor! labor! work is prayer! (54)

What Duganne does here is to take the kind of work associated with the home, that is, work with sacramental value, and transfer it to the marketplace. Like housework, this is work that brings in the kingdom of God, in its secular sense, rather than work that brings in a salary. The constant references to "brothers" and the emphasis on relationships—"Let thy brother be thy care"—rather than on commerce appropriates what had been the property of women.[15]

Here also is an emphasis on cyclical time; the worker is like an element of nature, like "water, fire, and air, and earth" that ceaselessly sacrifice themselves and are remade. Water fuels machines and nurtures plants and animals, for example; it is changed but never used up. Like all natural elements, its individual identity is lost in the interdependent identity of Nature as a whole. Work is prayer because work is natural: "Sacred toil doth nature share." Prayer, then does not have to be a conscious act of piety or even a form of communication with the divine; it is a natural response to a world whose god is natural law. Prayer also does not require humility. In "Soul! Look Forth Where Shines the Future!" (n.d.), Duganne imagines a triumphant army of sacred laborers marching with "snow-white banners" that bear "glorious signs" symbolizing various occupations: the "press," the plow, the anvil, "the ponderous sledge."

Duganne manages to exclude women altogether from sacred labor in this second hymn. All the marchers are "stalwart men, with limbs of iron." Women are reduced to the role of cheerleaders and the status of children:

> Following close these conquering armies—
> Dancing on with happy feet—
> White-armed maids and flower-crowned children
> Haste those warrior men to greet—
> Hands are clasped in holiest union;
> Joy, like incense, soars above.
> Hail! thrice hail! th' industrial armies!
> Hail th' Immortal Strife of Love! (s h 63)

In the end, Duganne praises the "Immortal Strife of Love" rather than a "God of Love." A domestic novelist or an evangelical hymnist might see work as an avenue to faith or as a concrete expression of religious belief. Duganne makes work itself a god and men its high priests.

Some social gospel hymns are less misogynistic. Washington Gladden's "O, Master, Let Me Walk with Thee" (1879), which Spencer calls "the earliest piece written *for* the social gospel" (21), bears a striking resemblance to Mary B. C. Slade's gospel hymn "Footsteps of Jesus" (1871) and to Elizabeth Stuart Phelps's "The Angel Over the Right Shoulder." Gladden speaks in the first three verses of the walk of faith that characterizes many gospel hymns:

> O Master, let me walk with Thee
> In lowly paths of service free;
> Tell me Thy secret, help me bear
> The strain of toil, the fret of care.

Help me the slow of heart to move
By some clear winning word of love,
Teach me the wayward feet to stay,
And guide them in the homeward way.

Teach me Thy patience; still with Thee
In closer, dearer company,
In work that keeps faith sweet and strong,
In trust that triumphs over wrong. (SH 56)

Gladden's hymn could be a description of the mother's vision in "The Angel Over the Right Shoulder." Mrs. James dreams of a mother whose job is to teach her children "how to place their little feet." The sorrowful angel over her left shoulder records as a lapse the times "little children wandered away quite into forbidden paths" because she focused on a heavenly goal instead of on their welfare (Phelps 162–63). Her faith stays "sweet and strong," she learns from the dream, only when she does her appointed work of ministering to those entrusted to her care.

Gladden's hymn is characteristic of social gospel hymnody because it does not quote Scripture or allude to biblical stories. Slade's "Footsteps of Jesus," in contrast, has the believer follow Jesus to "Siloam's Fountain," where supernatural healings take place, and into the temple. In other words, "O Master, Let Me Walk with Thee" describes only Jesus' servant roles, the ones deemed appropriate for women in the nineteenth century. It appropriates women's roles to empower modern men skeptical of organized religion and of references to supernatural priestly activities. Slade's hymn, on the other hand, serves a different purpose as it makes both servant and priestly roles available to men and women. Another difference is that, despite the "Thee," Gladden's hymn has a contemporary sound because it lacks the language of the King James Bible that makes gospel hymns sound "old." It also lacks a chorus and a lively rhythm. Still, "O Master, Let Me Walk with Thee" is beloved among evangelicals; it is one of the five hymns in Mussey's collection I know from memory. (Of the five, one is a Christmas carol and two are patriotic hymns.) "O Master, Let Me Walk with Thee" is included in the Baptist *Broadman Hymnal,* the Methodist *Cokesbury Worship Hymnal,* and the Church of Christ *Great Songs of the Church.* Its survival can probably be attributed to the way it preserves elements of feminized Christianity: a concern with the material well-being of others, a depiction of a spiritual walk rather than a journey, a movement from action to faith, and the depiction of Christ as a bosom companion.

Not surprisingly, Walter Rauschenbusch did not find this hymn consonant with his social vision. According to him,

> The I.W.W. [Industrial Workers of the World] and many others cannot say that their work "keeps faith sweet and strong." It is often a bitter and weakening ingredient. Further, they don't want "a trust that triumphs over wrong," but a religion of action which will annihilate the wrong. (Qtd. in Spencer 21)

Today, despite what was surely an apt criticism, people outside universities and seminaries have largely forgotten Walter Rauschenbusch and most of the hymns in *Social Hymns of Brotherhood and Aspiration*, but ordinary people still sing "O Master, Let Me Walk with Thee." One reason is that hymns about "hero workers" and "armies of the poor" sound dated because they use the language of the labor movement, which evangelicals associate with a particular time in history and, worse, with socialism. More important, though, most social gospel hymns appropriate elements of the feminized Christianity that gospel hymns have made a tradition and then neutralize those same elements, usually by secularizing them. Duganne's hymns, for example, make labor an almost penitential act rather than an art. The toil he describes has relative value but not absolute value. Gladden's hymn, on the other hand, emphasizes unalienated labor and the "closer, dearer company" of God that leads to an immediate reward of sweet, strong faith. Because he does not neutralize the pleasure associated with feminized religion, his hymn has survived.

The Failure of Social Gospel Rhetoric

The secular qualities of social gospel hymns account in part for the fact that, with a few exceptions, they never caught on in evangelical churches—or in Protestant churches in general, for that matter. They just did not sound much like hymns. Three other rhetorical factors played a part as well. These characteristics challenged the feminized elements of evangelical Christianity that the invented tradition of gospel hymns preserved so well. First, social gospel hymns were misplaced. The "social" part of "Christian socialism" or the "social gospel" really meant something more like "public" or even "urban." Social gospel hymns were about cities, and evangelicals tend to be folks from the country or small towns. But more than that, they were hymns that ignored the female sphere of pure religion separated from the corruption of commerce. Second, hymns without a connection between spirituality and sexuality seem doomed to failure in the evangelical community. Among people who highly value mystical experience beyond the province of language, women's rhetoric of sexuality—perceived in the community as at once passionate and pure—is a way of articulating what cannot be stated. Finally, hymns that substituted the "father tongue" of literary rhetoric for the "mother tongue" of orality aroused the evangelical bias against printed texts. In short, hymns that reasserted masculinity at the expense of highly valued elements of feminized Christianity challenged something evangelicals could not lose without losing their identity as a textual community. Evangelicals distinguish themselves from other American Protestants by their feminine elements.

By setting their hymns primarily in cities, for example, social gospel hymnists made religion less personal than going home to a maternal deity and less mysterious than a romantic encounter in a garden. Another problem was that urban settings represented a world characterized by insincerity and deception for Christians whose religion had been shaped by sentimental fiction. Karen Halttunen argues that the city represented a "new world of strangers" for nineteenth-century Americans used to smaller communities where one seldom saw an unfamiliar face. In the city, outer appearances did not indicate inner reality, as they did in the country; both the con man and the painted woman projected signs of what they did not, in fact, possess. Halttunen concludes that "the central premise underlying all the sentimental fiction that poured off the American press in the nineteenth century was that private experience was morally superior to public life" (34, 37, 56–57).[16]

So, when social gospel hymnists began to write hymns that envisioned America as a great city (sh 43, 102) or described labor in terms of what people do in factories, where "lives are held / More cheap than merchandise" (sh 42), the evangelicals whose values had been shaped by sentimental fiction would have been suspicious. The "real" America, as they saw it, was the America of the country and the small town. Big cities were corrupt—that was obvious—but organizing the laborers was a secular solution for what an evangelical deemed a spiritual problem. Judging from current use, the only social gospel hymns that have survived the social gospel era are the ones that treat cities as mission opportunities—like foreign countries whose pagan culture must be overcome to convert heathens.

Frank Mason North's 1905 hymn, "Where Cross the Crowded Ways of Life," for example, is a hymn written specifically to advance the cause of city missions, and it is a hymn that still appears in late twentieth-century hymnals. North says that his inspiration for the hymn was watching the crowds in New York City:

> My life was for long years, both by personal choice and official duty, given to the people in all phases of their community life. New York was to me an open book. I spent days and weeks and years in close contact with every phase of the life of multitudes, and at the morning, noon, and evening hours was familiar with the tragedy, as it always seemed to me, of the jostling, moving crossings of the avenues; and I have watched them by the hour as they passed, by tens of thousands. (Qtd. in Reynolds 245)

The crowds of impersonal strangers North describes are exactly what made the big city suspect for evangelicals, and the pity and compassion that led North to write a missionary hymn are the correct responses. "Where Cross the Crowded Ways of Life" calls in verse 5 to the "Master, from the mountain side" to "tread the city's streets again" (SH 21), and what makes the hymn acceptable to evangelicals is this sense that Christ is not in the city and must be brought there to solve urban problems. Because North's hymn supports the evangelical understanding of the city, it could be included in the "Social Service Songs" of *Make Christ King*, a 1912 paperback gospel hymnal. The other hymns in this section are not social gospel hymns but missionary hymns with titles such as "Win Them One by One" and "Harvest Song!," which urges reapers to engage in a spiritual harvest of souls.

Fanny Crosby also lived in New York City and considered home missions her primary vocation after she reached sixty years of age (Ruffin 136). Hers is the evangelical strategy of evoking feeling in a setting that prompts emotional withdrawal. As I argue in chapter 3, rescuing a sinner lost in sin through motherly kindness is the domestic version of the evangelical missionary imperative. In "Rescue the Perishing," a hymn inspired by an experience in a rescue mission, Crosby advises bringing the private sphere into the public:

> Down in the human heart,
> Crushed by the tempter,
> Feelings lie buried that grace can restore;
> Touched by a loving heart,
> Wakened by kindness,
> Chords that are broken will vibrate once more. (BR 80)

Crosby's hymn and, to some extent, North's, work for evangelicals because they affirm a basic suspicion of the masculine sphere symbolized by the ethos of a large city. Hymns that lose the "feminine" perspective also lose their spiritual resonance. Temporal justice will not solve the problem of the city because it does not attend to the hearts of those who suffer there. Social harmony, the result of restoring those "broken" chords, will not occur until people "feel right," the solution Harriet Beecher Stowe offered to the social disharmony of slavery (*Uncle Tom's Cabin* 515).

When nineteenth-century evangelicals wanted to restore their feelings—that is, their connections to spiritual reality—they went to camp meetings or revivals, not to conferences in cities. Retreat to the wilderness also seemed to imply retreat to unrestrained emotionality with erotic overtones. In the early nineteenth century, these occasions allowed women to abandon the behavioral restrictions that normally restrained their sexual expression. Shirley Abbott interprets Frances Trollope's horror at the hysterical behavior of women at the revival meetings she observed on the American frontier in terms of her shock at the "sexuality" of the behavior. Women who writhed on the ground, prayed in ecstatic disregard of language conventions, and shouted with joy clearly simulated sexual abandon

(126–28). Carroll Smith-Rosenberg also describes these same "liminal women," that is, those on the threshold between separation from society and entry into a new order, in erotic terms:

> The liminal person is often removed from ordinary communal space, stripped of her normal clothing, and left naked or in rags. At the same time she is frequently encouraged or allowed to engage in unrestrained behavior and to experience new and heady spiritual powers. ("Women and Religious Revivals" 223)

Smith-Rosenberg's emphasis on removing clothing makes sexuality a metaphor for spirituality. The genuine experience removes or tears the public self—represented here by clothing—to free an instinctive response so private that it is associated with what civilized people do behind closed doors. In a religion that feminizes all believers, the male response to this behavior can be identification or voyeurism; one way or another, it necessarily unites male and female in a most basic human activity.

Even today, camping is an important component of the evangelical experience, especially for young people. At Falls Creek Baptist Assembly near Davis, Oklahoma, the largest religious youth camp in the world, adult sponsors know that the strongest spiritual response is likely to have sexual elements, especially among hormone-driven adolescents. It is no wonder that a new feature of the numerous weeklong sessions at this camp is a campaign called "True Love Waits," which encourages the teenagers during one worship service to sign cards pledging sexual abstinence before marriage. The hymns that stoke spiritual fires at such camps are not about "hero workers" (sh 61) or battles to establish a new city of God. "I Surrender All" and "Have Thine Own Way, Lord" are much more effective. Camp song leaders today also encourage the use of contemporary sounding gospel songs with a strong emphasis on rhythm; sometimes campers clap or sway in time to the music, and this rhythmic physical activity emphasizes the erotic overtones of the experience. The twentieth-century hymnal editor who changed Fanny Crosby's description in "To God Be the Glory" (1875) of "our wonder, our transport, when Jesus we see" to "our wonder, our victory, when Jesus we see" missed the point.[17] Transport is what the evangelical experience requires, and transport depends, finally, on the articulation of figures of speech that compare spirituality to sexuality, particularly to the sexual experience of women. As Amanda Porterfield puts it, "If American women have received pleasure by submitting to authority, they have also often received authority by submitting to pleasure" (5).

Transport also requires language that simulates orality. Gospel hymns are full of cliches, and these cliches serve the crucial function of rendering deeply internalized ideas in phrases such as "come to Jesus" and "washed in the blood of the lamb" that an evangelical might also use orally in a public prayer or sermon. The hymnist in an attitude of feminine submission to a divine Master receives such words—Fanny Crosby said on one occasion that she "memorized" them (*Memories* 180)—because they do not originate within the hymn writer. Crosby liked to work after midnight, when she "felt she could hear the unearthly harmonies of 'the Celestial Choirs'" and feel "the presence, not only of Christ and his saints and angels but also of her relatives and friends who had 'passed beyond the silent vale'" (Ruffin 140). The mystical experience that Crosby called "transport" is crucial to the authenticity of gospel hymns for evangelicals. Social gospel hymns, on the other hand, require "mastery" on the part of the writer. Some of the texts in *Social Hymns of Brotherhood and Aspiration* were authored by well-known writers such as Rudyard Kipling, Alfred Tennyson, Oliver Wendell Holmes, and John Greenleaf Whittier. Many of these hymns borrowed from earlier publications instead of being composed especially for the collection are distinguished by complex figures of speech and conscious attention to the interaction of sound and substance. A good example is Tennyson's "Ring Out, Wild Bells," which was probably chosen for its line "Ring in the thousand years of peace" (s H 44). For an evangelical, though, the very aspects of social gospel hymns that make them better literature than evangelical gospel hymns also make them suspect because they sound like the result of human craft.

Several of the hymns in Mussey's collection do allude to the evangelical distrust of print. A hymn by Edwin Markham, for example, predicts a postmillennial brotherhood that will come because "blind creeds and kings have had their day" (s H 89). But social

gospel hymns are difficult to sing because their language is complicated and because they tend to avoid the repetition that allows evangelicals to remember a gospel hymn after singing it once or twice. In
other words, social gospel hymns encourage singers to stay close to
the printed page, but gospel hymns allow singers to use the hymnal
only long enough to memorize a new arrangement of already familiar ideas and words. Singing words already imprinted in a wor-
shiper's mind feels spontaneous; reading as one sings is a constant
reminder that another person produced the words. Worse than that,
social gospel hymns describe lofty goals and ideals rather than personal experience—they are usually in the third person instead of the
first person of gospel hymns. So they give the appearance of doing
what evangelicals most fear about print: they give unalterable form
to creeds.

The account in Benjamin Franklin's autobiography of his encounter with "Dunker" (i.e., Baptist) Michael Welfare explains why
hymns that seem to freeze doctrine in print are anathema to conservative evangelicals. When Franklin explains to Welfare that his sect
would be better understood if they published "the Articles of their
Belief and the Rules of their Discipline," Welfare replies,

> "When we were first drawn together as a society," says he, "it had
> pleased God to enlighten our Minds so far as to see that some Doc-
> trines which we once esteemed Truths were Errors, and that others
> which we had esteemed Errors were real Truths. From time to time he
> has been pleased to afford us further Light, and our Principles have
> been improving and our Errors diminishing. Now we are not sure that
> we are arriv'd at the End of this Progression, and at the Perfection of
> Spiritual or Theological Knowledge; and we fear that if we should
> once print our Confession of Faith, we should feel ourselves as if
> bound and confin'd by it, and perhaps be unwilling to receive farther
> Improvement, and our Successors still more so, as conceiving what
> their Elders and Founders had done to be something sacred, never to
> be departed from." (Franklin 97)[18]

By endorsing orality over literacy as a way to be more receptive to
divine truth, Welfare also endorses language associated with women
and private communication over language associated with men and
public speaking. Thoreau describes these two forms of language in
Walden as the "mother tongue" and the "father tongue." What evan-

gelicals value about spoken language is exactly what Thoreau thinks makes it inferior:

> There is a memorable interval between the spoken and the written language, the language heard and the language read. The one is commonly transitory, a sound, a tongue, a dialect merely, almost brutish, and we learn it unconsciously, like the brutes, of our mothers. The other is the maturity and experience of that; if that is our mother tongue, this is our father tongue, a reserved and select expression, too significant to be heard by the ear, which we must be born again in order to speak. (101)

Thoreau's use of the biblical phrase "born again" here is striking.[19] He describes the move from spoken to written language in terms that an evangelical would use to describe a religious conversion. But an evangelical Christian is reborn to hear what God has to say, not to read what others have said about it. The transitory nature of spoken language illustrated by gospel hymns is exactly what an evangelical values because it allows for further revelation. As gospel hymnist Clara Scott put it:

> Open my ears that I may hear
> Voices of truth Thou sendest clear;
> And while the wavenotes fall on my ear,
> Ev'rything false will disappear. (BR 351)

Backlash in the Late Twentieth Century

Given evangelical assumptions about oral and written language, the most extraordinary aspect of the conflict between evangelicals and social gospel proponents was the publication between 1910 and 1915 of "*The Fundamentals,* twelve paperback volumes containing defenses of fundamentalist doctrines by a variety of American and British conservative writers." Fundamentalists, as they were called in 1920 by the editor of a Baptist paper, were evangelicals who promoted premillennialism, attention to evangelism, and a policy of excluding everyone who did not agree with their interpretation of Scripture (Marsden 57–60). Many conservative evangelicals agreed with fundamentalists' doctrine and with their repudiation of the social gospel, but what distinguished fundamentalists was their aggressive assault on theological modernism through promotion of public policies to make their beliefs the law of the land.[20] The publication of *The Fundamentals* also suggests that fundamentalists were as anxious to "masculinize" their churches as Walter Rauschenbusch was to masculinize his. Twelve volumes of printed language were a direct challenge to a religion that empowered women through veneration of oral language and the "mother tongue."

Fundamentalism still poses a threat to conservative evangelicals and it is still linked to masculine anxiety about the power of women and oral language. Like other ways of remasculinizing religion, fundamentalism attests to the strength of female authority expressed in feminized hymnody. In 1993, a group of young people led by a fundamentalist preacher from Claremore, Oklahoma, walked out of a session at a Youth Evangelism Conference in Oklahoma City when Jill Briscoe, a pastor's wife and the author of seventeen books, interpreted a passage of Scripture during a talk to the young people. The fundamentalist minister, Wayne Keely, "pointed his finger at her and announced that she was out of authority and contrary to the Word of God" (Williamson 3). The next day, the conference canceled a presentation by Anne Graham Lotz, daughter of evangelist Billy Graham, to avoid further disruptions. After this story was published in the state Baptist paper, *The Baptist Messenger,* conservative evangelical Baptists all over the state wrote letters to the editor, most of them protesting Keely's behavior. Some writers obviously struggled to reconcile their sense that women's use of language was crucial to their Christian experience with a literal interpretation of Scripture. One woman wrote that she had come to the conference feeling "very low" and that the woman's presentation provided spiritual encouragement:

> This isn't a women's lib or a male chauvinist issue. Keely is right, the Bible clearly states a woman's place, but God knew my needs as a woman and mother, and maybe He felt Mrs. Briscoe could help me, so He put her there as His witness. (Slate)

As this letter indicates, the conflict between written language and oral language created tension for the writer, but oral language took precedence because the writer perceived it as a direct message from

God directed personally to her; Briscoe's words were more immediate and, thus, more authentic even than the words of the Bible.

Another female writer responding in a letter to the editor perceived the issue more clearly as a conflict between men and women in the evangelical community. Her letter quoted Simone de Beauvoir: "When women begin to move in free response to the Spirit of God, men become nervous about their priestcraft" (Lewis). It is this tension between feminine Christianity—perceived as free, flexible, and responsive to the Spirit of God—and masculine Christianity—perceived as ordered, goal oriented, and stable—that has both threatened and energized the evangelical community. In evangelical churches that have not succumbed to fundamentalism, this creative tension has led congregations to incorporate elements of popular culture into their ethos, and these elements allow them to balance feminized religion with an overlay of masculine challenge.

One strategy for churches in the Bible Belt of the South and Midwest is to link Christianity and sports, particularly football with its all-male teams, scantily clad cheerleaders, and martial atmosphere. The Superbowl prompts some churches to have evening services early and bring in a big-screen television to keep men in the building during the game. The pastor of First Baptist Church in Norman, Oklahoma, preaches in a red suit to celebrate the OU school colors of crimson and cream on the Sunday after the Cotton Bowl when the Sooners beat Texas in the annual game. It is no accident that football spokesmen such as Terry Bradshaw, Barry Sanders, and Rosie Greer proudly claim membership in the Fellowship of Christian Athletes or that a joke about the Dallas Cowboys, America's team, goes like this: "Why is there a hole in the top of Texas Stadium? So God can watch his team play." The title of a country song perhaps inadvertently recognizes this move to appropriate female spirituality and clothe it in the language of sports when it begs, "Dropkick Me, Jesus, Through the Goal Posts of Life."

Many evangelical churches that have incorporated the ethos of sports into their communities still preserve the invented tradition of gospel hymns although the language of gospel hymnody is now the property of country song writers, who are making millions of dollars describing sexuality in terms of evangelical spirituality, a reversal of the gospel hymn formula.[21] Meanwhile, evangelical musicians who wish to distinguish themselves from fundamentalists often discuss the fact that fundamentalists seem to be rejecting the invented tradition and to have become enamored of simple choruses. The texts of these choruses are very simple, and some of them are very patriarchal. The chorus of Jack Hayford's "Majesty" (1981), for example, empowers men by envisioning a male God from whom "Majesty" and "kingdom authority flow . . . unto His own" (BH1991 215). "His own" are ostensibly Christians, but they can also be the believers most like "Him," in other words, the male Christians who receive power from the male God they represent on earth.

Anecdotal evidence suggests that the patriarchal doctrine inherent in such hymns shapes the worship practices of fundamentalists. A friend who teaches at Dallas Baptist University, a college with many fundamentalist students, tells me that the young people in her classes often use the phrase "Father God" as a form of address in public prayers. As another example of patriarchal power, fundamentalist pastors—all male, of course—commonly require a strict hierarchy of accountability within their staffs and a position of absolute authority over their congregations. Wayne Keely says in a letter to *The Baptist Messenger,* "Where do we go from here? I'm not sure, but as for me and the church in which I serve, we will follow the Word of God." His words imply that he feels justified to speak on behalf of his congregation and to dictate how they will interpret Scripture. His is an anti-evangelical stance in its insistence on the need of a mediator between believers and the Bible. It is also anti-evangelical in its insistence on the primacy of the written word, which Keely invoked literally to condemn a woman whom he perceived to be preaching. Perhaps he is making the same mistake social gospel proponents made more eloquently with their hymns when he associates patriarchal religion with printed Scripture: the loss of creative tension between masculine and feminine versions of Protestant Christianity can mean the loss of what energized it.

Gospel hymns themselves endure both inside and outside the evangelical community despite efforts to render them obsolete. No longer the exclusive property of the religious establishment, they appear in movies, contemporary novels, newspaper articles and obituaries, jokes, and cartoons as well as in country music. They shape notions—even for the unreligious—of God, of spiritual formation, of death and heaven: a God who is a bosom companion, the conflation of spirituality and sexuality, dying as the happy prospect of going home to perfect love.

Gospel hymn texts are accorded as much space as Scripture in the United States on tombstones in "garden" or "rural" cemeteries, those established, according to Ann Douglas, "on the outskirts of town or village" instead of in a churchyard. The first of these in the United States was Mount Auburn Cemetery in Cambridge, Massachusetts, established in 1831. Douglas claims that such cemeteries "functioned [for nineteenth-century visitors] not like experience but like literature; it was in several senses a sentimental reader's paradise" (208–10). It is also the place where texts prized for their disconnection from print are now, ironically, set in stone.

Consider the grave of eight-year-old Vernia Lee Hudson, who died on October 31, 1885, and was buried in Sunset Cemetery, Shelby, North Carolina. On her gravestone or "tomb rock," in the local idiom, is the chorus of Fanny Crosby's "Safe in the Arms of Jesus," with the last line changed to make it appropriate for a child's memorial:

> Safe in the arms of Jesus,
> Safe on His gentle breast,
> There by His love o'ershadowed,
> Sweetly our darling rests.[22]

This inscription appears on the face of a four-sided stone that includes the birth and death dates of Vernia's parents on the sides of the monument and her name on the side opposite Crosby's hymn. The hymn has been altered rather obviously to describe only the beloved child dead thirty years before her mother, Mary T. Lee Hudson, who is to be remembered by her family associations with

Tombstone from the grave of Vernia Lee Hudson in Sunset Cemetery, Shelby, North Carolina, with the chorus of Fanny Crosby's "Safe in the Arms of Jesus" (1869).

Tombstone from a family grave in Kenton, Oklahoma, with a line from Mariana B. Slade's "Gathering Home" (c. 1900).

the Lees of her birth and the Hudsons of her marriage. Vernia's father has a separate epitaph under his name and dates: like the biblical Enoch, the Rev. H. T. Hudson "walked with God."

Douglas believes that to the Hudsons' contemporaries Sunset Cemetery was a sort of "Disney World for the mortuary imagination," that they would have visited it as a "twentieth-century descendant goes to the movies: with the hopefulness attendant upon the prospect of borrowed emotions" (210). I would say that hymns on tombstones both then and now serve a very different function for the evangelical. They are engraved in stone not because they elicit a cheap thrill for the unimaginative but because their appeal to imagination and memory is so immediate and so rich. "Safe in the Arms of Jesus" would have invoked for Vernia Lee Hudson's parents an entire theological system centered on a Savior whose power lies in bonds of relationship that not only continue, but are refined and strengthened after death. Each of the formulas in the text—"safe in the arms," "on His tender breast," "sweetly," "rest"—connects the evangelical reader's imagination to feminized texts and personal experiences alive with rapturous possibilities.

From time to time, I visit the cemetery on the hill overlooking tiny Kenton, Oklahoma, now officially a ghost town although the valley is still peopled by a few sturdy families. Here is the grave of my paternal grandparents, who homesteaded on the Black Mesa just north of the graveyard. On their tombstone is a line from a hymn: "God's children are gathering home." My imagination has been so shaped by hymns that this line immediately calls up a memory of going home from college for my grandmother's funeral. Upon receiving news of her death, I traveled with two cousins, who were also students at Oklahoma Baptist University in central Oklahoma, to the panhandle of the state (and the only Oklahoma town on Mountain Standard Time). As we drove down the long dirt road to the ranch house of the family matriarch, all was dark except for a porch light illuminating the yard on the side of the house. Other cars ahead of us were pulling up, and as each motor was silenced, we saw the weary passengers met by small groups of family members who ran from the house to pull them out of the darkness and into the pool of light. It was exactly as I had always imagined God's children "gathering home" in heaven. Mariana B. Slade's hymn was not a cliche but a resonant spiritual insight depicted typologically in the gathering of my own family. Today, one line from the hymn summons that moment in its complexity. If anything, the formulaic character of the line enhances its power because it shapes but does not dictate a specific response grounded in the rhetorical tradition of a textual community. The experience testifies to the power of women's hymns as living texts and to the textuality of our lives.

ℕotes

Abbreviations

BH1956   *Baptist Hymnal.* Ed. Walter Hines Sims. Nashville: Convention Press, 1956.

BH1975   *Baptist Hymnal.* Nashville: Convention Press, 1975.

BH1991   *The Baptist Hymnal.* Nashville: Convention Press, 1991.

BR   *The Broadman Hymnal.* Ed. B. B. McKinney. Nashville: Broadman Press, 1940.

CWH   *The Cokesbury Worship Hymnal.* Ed. C. A. Bowen. Baltimore: The Methodist Publishing House, 1938.

GS   *The New Alphabetical Hymnal: Great Songs of the Church, Number Two: A Treasury of Six Hundred Sacred Songs Suitable for All Services of the Church.* Comp. E. L. Jorgenson. Louisville: Great Songs Press, 1937.

BH1926   *New Baptist Hymnal.* Nashville: Broadman Press, 1926.

RP   *Revival Praises.* Comp. George R. Stuart et al. Nashville: Methodist Publishing House, 1907.

SH   *Social Hymns of Brotherhood and Aspiration.* Comp. Mabel Hay Barrows Mussey. New York: A. S. Barnes, 1914.

Chapter 1.
Words and Women in the Evangelical Community

1. This much-reprinted hymn appears in several different forms in hymnals intended for use in revivals and camp meetings. The version I quote here appears with no author's name although some hymnals name Charlie D. Tillman as the arranger and owner of the 1891 copyright.

2. Of course, Welty was correct in saying that popular hymn tunes were often originally secular. Martin Luther was fond of using German folk songs for his hymns, Charles Wesley sometimes borrowed melodies from operas, and Ira Sankey copied the style of Stephen Foster (Hustad 35). General Booth, founder of the Salvation Army, defended singing his hymns to popular tunes by saying, "I rather enjoy robbing the Devil of his choice tunes" (Tamke 5).

3. See Reynolds for the publication history of these hymns (27–29). Reynolds speculates that Hudson adapted a refrain already in use with other hymns for "At the Cross."

4. Brian Stock points out that stories work not because their arguments persuade but because they produce verisimilitude (11).

5. Sandra Sizer argues that gospel hymns changed eighteenth-century hymn rhetoric by referring to people as "wanderers," not "worms." She claims that the purpose of this change is to "portray the human condition as that of a passive victim" (27–30). Reynolds asserts that the change is simply a "literary consideration" that implies no "theological compromise" (27–28). His defensiveness on this point suggests his awareness that people were shocked by the change.

6. The gospel hymn tradition did not, of course, spring full-grown onto the American scene in 1870. Folk songs of the early nineteenth-century camp meetings, which began in Kentucky in 1800 and were followed by urban revivals, were the first examples of what came to be known as gospel hymns or songs (Reynolds 15; Hitchcock n.p.). Most of these, if they were published at all, appeared in ephemeral, paperbacked social hymnals. After the Civil War, however, denominational hymnals began to publish gospel hymns, thus giving them the authority of church approval. Gospel hymns have now become associated with African-American churches and with Southern evangelicals (Hitchcock n.p.).

7. As Lears explains, "What critics call modernism and what I call anti-modernism share common roots in the *fin-de-siècle* yearning for authentic experience—physical, emotional, or spiritual" (xix).

8. As Marsden notes, evangelicalism is "a style as well as a set of Protestant beliefs," especially the notions that the Bible, not the church, is the only basis for a true theology and the belief that salvation comes from a personal response to God. Both of these assumptions require a belief that human beings can interpret Scripture for themselves. Marsden's use of the term *style* refers to the worship practices of evangelicals, which are characterized, at least in theory, by spontaneous responses to fervent Bible preaching (2). Because these beliefs and practices are not confined to any one Protestant group, the term *evangelical* can be applied, Marsden states, to "holiness churches, pentecostals, traditionalist Methodists, all sorts of Baptists, Presbyterians, black churches in all these traditions, fundamentalists, pietist groups, Reformed and Lutheran confessionalists, Anabaptists such as Mennonites, Churches of Christ, Christians, and some Episcopalians" (5).

9. For similar definitions, see Marsden, 4–5, and Tamke, 32.

10. In his writing, Richard Foster uses "Word" to refer to written Scripture, to the divine message it represents, and to Jesus as the incarnate Word. He explicates this complicated meaning of "Word" in *Celebration of Discipline:*

> As we submit ourselves to the Word of God living (Jesus), so we submit ourselves to the Word of God written (Scripture). We yield ourselves first to hear the Word, second to receive the Word and third to obey the Word. We look to the Spirit who inspired the Scriptures to interpret and apply them to our condition. The word of Scripture, animated by the Holy Spirit, lives with us throughout the day. (107)

11. For discussions of the defining characteristics of modernism or turn-of-the-century liberalism, see Szasz 69–70, Marsden 32–36, Hordern 73–110, and Marty and Appleby 11–13.

12. Marty and Appleby point out that the evangelical concept of biblical interpretation is based on the tenets of Scottish Common-Sense Realism, which posits that "the mind [is] a kind of mediator between actual things as they are, and ideas, which [have] a separate reality." In other words, a loving God gave human beings "common sense," which enables them to interpret the words of the Bible without complicated theoretical or rhetorical analyses (59–60). I would add, though, that Common-Sense Realism was altered by a romantic view of reality in which, as James Berlin sees it, language is a metaphoric representation of reality (9–11, 47). To put it another way, for an evangelical, the words of Scripture themselves express spiritual reality and truth and can be used to bypass rational processes. Sometimes, for example, evangelicals use the Bible as a sort of spiritual Ouija board by opening it at random to a Scripture that they then assume is a personal and prophetic message from God.

13. George Marsden presents a similar argument (37).

14. Since Crosby was blind, she speaks of memorizing the words to be transcribed by others. Reynolds reports that she also transcribed hymns on a Braille writer (291).

15. This hymn is also known by its first line, "There's a Land That Is Fairer Than Day." Hymnal editors often label and index hymns by their first lines. However, many have become popularly known by a phrase in the refrain, an understandable phenomenon since the same refrain is sung with each verse and thus becomes the best-known part of the hymn. When the first-line title does not accord with the familiar title stored in my own memory, I have used the popular title.

16. For an excellent discussion of the effect of the higher criticism of the Bible on American Protestantism, see Szasz 15–41. Szasz observes that higher criticism was enormously controversial for evangelicals who, unlike Episcopalians, could not "rely on the church as having equal authority to Scripture" (23).

17. As Susan Tamke argues, evangelical Christianity is essentially conservative, and "to a conservative the disruption of established patterns and rituals is often viewed as a threat to . . . security." Tamke uses her argument to explain that hymnal changes are major events among evangelicals because they disrupt secure patterns (9).

18. Most evangelicals use the terms *Jesus, Christ,* and *God* interchangeably except when speaking of a specific biblical incident in which, say, Jesus or God would be an actor in the drama.

19. One should take care not to equate evangelicals with fundamentalists although the terms are frequently used interchangeably. All fundamentalists are evangelicals, but not all evangelicals are fundamentalists. A fundamentalist is, to borrow George Marsden's apt description, "an evangelical who is angry about something" (1). In other words, fundamentalists are militant in their reaction to a world from which they are displaced. Martin Marty and Scott Appleby offer another well-articulated statement of this distinction: "When agents of secular modernity threaten *conservatives* like old-time Baptists, the conservatives simply try to keep it at bay. . . . *Fundamentalists,* however, *fight back.* That is their mark" (17). A conservative evangelical and a fundamentalist might agree, for example,

that abortion is a sin. But the conservative evangelical would respond by praying for the abortionist, and the fundamentalist would block the entrance to the abortion clinic.

20. From C. Austin Miles's "I Come to the Garden Alone" (1912).

21. Ruth Y. Jenkins makes this same claim for Victorian English women in *Reclaiming Myths of Power: Women Writers and the Victorian Spiritual Crisis* (1995): "The Victorian period . . . experienced an increase in the number of women writing hymns—one of the few remaining opportunities for women to find a voice in religion." Jenkins also asserts, as I do, that "many of the hymns written by women present an alternative vision of God and an individual's relationship to the divine, reflecting differences present in male and female spirituality" (151). However, she is speaking of women outside the evangelical tradition in England. She notes, in fact, "the similar emphasis on experience found in both hymns written by women [in the established church] and those by Evangelicals reveals an interesting correlative in their respective positions in organized Christianity" (152).

22. I do not mean to imply that no hymnals were published until the 1870s. Millions of paperback hymnals were published between 1840 and 1870 for use in camp meetings, Sunday schools (which were not necessarily associated with churches), and revivals. However, these hymnals were not sponsored by particular denominations (Hustad 248). Many of them contained gospel hymns that are now "lost" except in archives or personal collections. The hymns that have become an enduring part of the evangelical invented tradition owe their longevity in part to being preserved in hardback books.

23. Croly was herself a "literary domestic," i.e., an author of domestic fiction, who used the pen name Jennie June.

24. For this description of the True Woman, see Welter, esp. 151–52.

25. For helpful discussions of women's missionary societies, in addition to Hill, see Beaver, Allen, Brumberg, Hageman, and Garrett. Hardesty offers general information on evangelical women in the nineteenth century.

26. See Hill, 93–122, for a fascinating account of the "science of missions" within women's missionary support groups.

27. One rationale for allowing women to leave home and serve as foreign missionaries was that only women could enter the enclosures where foreign women were confined.

Chapter 2. Hymns as the Cultural Property of Nineteenth-Century Women

1. Henry Wilder Foote explains that in the English Protestant tradition metrical psalms were "for more than two hundred years . . . commonly bound up with copies of the Bible and the Book of Common Prayer" (26); their "primary use" was "in private devotions or at social gatherings, and their use in church was secondary" (28). Even in 1760, Mather Byles's introduction of a hymnal containing both psalms and hymns into his New England church was an event of some note, indicating that hymn singing had continued to be frowned upon in many Protestant churches (Ninde 51).

2. As Amanda Porterfield argues, "The American idealization of femininity was more than a polite convention; it became interwoven into the defense and promulgation of Christian religion" (52).

3. The home in Taylor's poem is significant as the site of production rather than an escape from the "real" world. And, although Taylor's God is engaged in "huswifery," the divine attributes are skill and creativity, characteristics that could belong to either sex. However, the believer's status is that of Puritan women, whom Lyle Kohler describes as "malleable inferiors in the hands of a higher being" (56).

4. See, for example, the bridal mysticism represented by Edward Taylor's "Upon Wedlock, & Death of Children" (c. 1632). Hymns also used this theme (see Marshall and Todd 22; De Jong 464–65).

5. This special duty of mothers is inherent in the title of a hymnal published in 1834 by Thomas Hastings. *The Mother's Hymn Book* was composed of hymns that "bore on the dedication of children to God and kindred topics" (Ninde 165).

6. See Josephine Donovan's discussion of these concepts from Sara Ruddick's "Maternal Thinking" in her description of a "woman-centered epistemology" (Donovan, "Toward a Woman's Poetics" 104).

7. To the modern reader the language of physical affection is the language of sexual expression, and the intimacy between Alice and Ellen has erotic overtones that may seem disturbing in a narrative about a young woman and a child. Indeed, the novel as a whole, like many nineteenth-century sentimental novels, describes intimacy between women in graphic detail. For example, a few years after this scene between Alice and Ellen, Ellen, now a young teenager, first meets her grandmother in Scotland. Giving her no chance to get acquainted, the older woman insists that Ellen sit on her lap, where "she overwhelmed her with caresses," and later forces Ellen to lie down and take a nap on her bed with her (502). All of this occurs within an hour or two of the pair's introduction to each other.

To avoid an anachronistic reading of such scenes, one must consider not only the nineteenth century's idealization of motherhood but the complex social interaction possible between women in a homosocial culture. Carroll Smith-Rosenberg describes this female world deftly in "The Female World of Love and Ritual: Relations Between Women in Nineteenth-Century America." Also see Lillian Faderman's *Surpassing the Love of Men: Romantic Friendship and Love Between Women from the Renaissance to the Present* (1981), which supplements Smith-Rosenberg's argument by explaining that a modern definition naming lesbianism and classifying it as a sexual perversion did not emerge from the studies of sexologists until the 1890s (239–40, 291).

8. Carroll Smith-Rosenberg argues that women's status is difficult to determine within the spiritual hierarchy of nineteenth-century evangelicalism because a religious woman may be elevated to two different positions. As the Woman on the Pedestal, she is spiritually superior to men, an "affirmation of order" that places women above men in terms of religious sensibility but gives them no social power. As the Woman on Top, on the other hand, she has real social power, but her spiritual position is lower than that of religious men because of her power to create disorder ("Women and Religious Revivals" 231). I argue a more complicat-

ed view that religious female characters in domestic novels maintain an appearance of Woman on the Pedestal as a way of promoting true (i.e., woman's) spirituality that challenges androcentric values. Thus, women who use hymns to influence men act on the assumption that, while they must not enter the corrupt public sphere, they are required to use their power to change individual men within it.

9. This date is somewhat arbitrary. Most experts on hymnody (e.g., Ninde and Foote) describe a renewed interest in church music that coincides with the rise of the gospel hymn movement in the late nineteenth century. There was also a proliferation of hymnals with both texts and tunes published during the last third of the century. Reynolds cites an 1871 hymnal as the first collection of Sunday school hymns with music published by the Baptist Sunday School Board. The denominational publication of a gospel hymn collection constitutes a public endorsement of gospel hymns, an important fact since Reynolds indicates that Sunday school music revitalized a church music tradition that "had declined into a meaningless experience, lacking in vitality and warmth" (20). According to Robert Guy McCutchan, the official *Hymn Book of the Methodist Episcopal Church, South* was published in 1889 in two versions, one with music and one without (11), so complete acceptance of hymns in public worship may have been a vexed issue throughout the end of the century.

Gospel hymns were most enthusiastically received, of course, in the South among Baptists and Methodists. However, the early 1870s seem to have been a time of shifting views in the North as well. Beecher, a Congregationalist, indicates in his Yale lectures (published in 1873) the controversial nature of granting importance to hymns as an aid to worship. His piece is as much an argument that ministers should take an interest in music as an analysis of how to use hymns and other music to the best advantage. The fact that he devoted an entire lecture to the subject indicates that many ministers were not entirely happy about supporting hymn use and that opinions were in a state of flux.

10. Harvey Green notes that "the 'Rock of Ages' motif was common in both the commercially produced and the home-crafted arts of the era. Women more frequently than men were depicted clinging to the cross" (175).

11. Most of the texts are, in fact, reproduced in the novel.

Chapter 3. His Religion and Hers

1. An earlier version of this chapter was published in *Nineteenth-Century Women Learn to Write,* ed. Catherine Hobbs. It is reprinted with the kind permission of the University Press of Virginia.

2. I refer to female hymnists by the name under which their hymns were usually published. Thus, Leila Naylor Morris will be Mrs. C. H. Morris, but Fanny J. Crosby, who was also Mrs. Alexander Van Alstyne, will retain her birth name.

3. Tompkins goes on to point out that "the tradition of Perry Miller, F. O. Mathiessen, . . . Henry Nash Smith," and others dismisses sentimental novels "in a struggle to supplant" the values of nineteenth-century evangelical women: "In reaction against their world view, and perhaps even more against their success,

twentieth-century critics have taught generations of students to equate popularity with debasement, emotionality with ineffectiveness, religiosity with fakery, domesticity with triviality, and all of these, implicitly with womanly inferiority" (*Sensational Designs* 123). See also Nina Baym's comments on the purpose of the nineteenth-century female Bildungsroman in her introduction (1988) to Maria Susanna Cummins's *The Lamplighter* (1854). She points out that this genre, another way to classify the domestic novels, "intends to be useful" (xi), particularly by promoting "a particular kind of Protestantism" to aid a young girl's development. Baym argues, however, that the Protestantism of *The Lamplighter* is not evangelicalism but a religion of progressive "enlightenment" (xix).

4. Sizer explains that lyrics for gospel hymns often came from "other songbooks or . . . devotional poems published in religious periodicals" (22). Eskew and McElrath also cite the influence of popular songs on hymnody. They claim, for example, that Fanny Crosby "incorporated in her hymns such words of sentiment found in the popular songs of her day as *gentle, precious,* and *tenderly*" (177). I argue that all these sources drew upon the language of the domestic/sentimental novel, which created the most fully articulated narratives or scripts using the notions of female spirituality.

5. In "I Want to Be Like Jesus": The Self-Defining Power of Evangelical Hymnody," Mary G. De Jong examines four figures of speech used to describe Christ in evangelical hymns: "the Lover, Companion, Savior, and Captain" (464). She argues that these four figures allow the singers of hymns to define themselves in comparison or contrast to "gender-linked qualities" of Christ that "interacted with contemporary social norms" (463). While I agree with her assessment that hymns present roles considered gender specific and her assumption that hymns provide scripts for believers, I diverge by claiming that evangelical hymnody of the period is based in a female epistemology that had to be altered to provide male roles. De Jong also does not consider the influence of domestic novels on hymnody.

6. Both of these hymns as well as Crosby's "Jesus Is Tenderly Calling Thee Home," discussed later in the section, are in current use in evangelical churches as "invitation hymns," hymns sung during the altar call when people are urged to come to the front of the church and make professions of faith or other spiritual decisions.

7. For the classic description of the True Woman, who is pious, pure, submissive, and domestic, see Barbara Welter's "The Cult of True Womanhood, 1820–1860."

8. The feminine character of God to a nineteenth-century evangelical is particularly apparent if one compares a hymn such as "Softly and Tenderly" to an eighteenth-century hymn such as Charles Wesley's "Jesus, Lover of My Soul." Wesley's sinner calls to Jesus, who is described as a large bird, capable of flight through the air as well as of sheltering the sinner under his wing. God is a "refuge" for Wesley, but he is also a fountain of life, the source of "healing streams." God's power to move ("Spring Thou up within my heart / Rise to all eternity"), his separation from the sinner, and his complex personality are sharply different from the qualities of Thompson's God. I use masculine pronouns here to

refer to God, in keeping with the tradition of Wesley's time; however, the eighteenth-century God seems to combine masculine and feminine traits.

9. God in Thompson's hymn fits the guidelines in Nancy M. Theriot's *The Biosocial Construction of Femininity: Mothers and Daughters in Nineteenth-Century America* (1988) for the "imperial mother." She centers her identity in her child; stays rooted in her home; does not assert herself by showing anger and, in fact, suffers on behalf of her child instead of for herself; and achieves "adult status" through maternity (26–29, 31). Her trade-off for "child-centeredness" is an "empire" based on her power to form souls (30).

10. For an excellent discussion of the Victorian construction of femininity as a way to restore order in a rapidly changing world, see Carroll Smith-Rosenberg's *Disorderly Conduct: Visions of Gender in Victorian America* (New York: Knopf, 1985), esp. the first essay, "Hearing Women's Words" (11–52).

11. Nancy Theriot also asserts that "the sentimentalization of the home and the woman in the home was an expression of new male needs stemming from the separation of work and home" (44). And see Baym's argument that Cummins's *The Lamplighter* is "conversing" with Charles Dickens's critique of urban society (xvii–xix). She claims that *The Lamplighter* and, by implication, other domestic novels support the values of the middle-class home "as antidote to social turmoil in nineteenth-century America" (xx). Her argument may be extended to hymns in which going home corrects the damage inflicted by a materialistic society.

12. For a discussion of dualism in gospel hymns, see Sizer, 24–25. Hélène Cixous argues that dichotomous thinking is characteristic of androcentric rhetoric (see "Sorties: Out and Out: Attacks/Ways Out/Forays").

13. See Julia Kristeva's "Women's Time" for a discussion of time as a feminist issue. Kristeva asserts that "female subjectivity would seem to provide a specific measure that essentially retains *repetition* and *eternity* from among the multiple modalities of time known through the history of civilizations" (34).

14. An interesting parallel to this hymn occurs in Cummins's *The Lamplighter* (1854). Before she dies, Willie Sullivan's mother dreams that she "was rapidly sailing through the air" to her son, who is abroad. There she is able to assess his companions and activities intuitively and to provide guidance against associating with worldly people. Upon awakening, she observes that

> Willie's living mother might be powerless to turn him from temptation and evil; but the spirit of that mother will be mighty still, and in the thought that she, in her home beyond the skies, is ever watching around his path and striving to lead him in the straight and narrow way, he may find a truer shield from danger, a firmer rest to his tempted soul, than she could have been while yet on earth. (170–73)

Later, Willie recounts the story of his many temptations abroad and attributes his salvation from them to the "recollection of my pure-minded and watchful mother" (356). Many hymns reenact the narrative of a dead mother who guards and guides her wandering son from her home in heaven. J. H. Weber's "Can a Boy Forget His Mother?" (1889) is a good example (RP 114).

15. See Tompkins's *Sensational Designs: The Cultural Works of American Fiction*

1790–1860 for a discussion linking women with God in the Halliday home. Tompkins calls the meal in the Halliday home "the redeemed form of the Last Supper" (142), but she does not describe it specifically as an allusion to the marriage feast of the Lamb.

16. "Gathering Home" was sung at my paternal grandparents' funerals, and the phrase "God's children are gathering home" is inscribed on their tombstone. I have discovered at least two other hymns from the period titled "Gathering Home" and several more with altered versions of that title.

17. Mary Gray Phelps Ward used the name of her mother, Elizabeth Stuart Phelps, as a pseudonym.

In *The Feminization of American Culture* (1977), Ann Douglas compares the concept of home in a different Crosby hymn to that developed in Phelps's series of novels about heaven. Her point is that nineteenth-century hymns about heaven are examples of consolation literature in which "the subject . . . is not simply heaven, but its accessibility" (220). Douglas argues that novelists like Phelps are "committed to the denial of death as a separate state" achieved by "the confusion of heavenly and earthly spheres" (224).

While Douglas's book is crucial to any understanding of the feminized culture of nineteenth-century America, I take issue with her use of examples such as those above to prove the "loss of theology" that went along with the feminization of culture. Speaking of the doctrine of the Atonement, she writes:

> The difficulty for modern thinkers in the newer, "softer" theory is not that it opposes the older, male-dominated concept of the Atonement, but rather that its opposition is incomplete and finally unimaginative; patriarchy is denied, but truly matriarchal values are not espoused. Strength, as essential to genuinely feminine as to genuinely masculine social and intellectual structures, is absent; weakness itself, no matter how unintentionally, is finally extolled. (124)

In contrast, I argue that nineteenth-century evangelical literature develops an enormously powerful, imaginative, and complex model of female spirituality. As Jane Tompkins points out, it is ironic to label such writing "escapist" since it is aimed at those who cannot escape from an enclosed space (*Sensational Designs* 175–76).

18. Amanda Porterfield reports that *The Gates Ajar* sold 180,000 copies in thirty years and that its popularity inspired "'a gates ajar' collar and tippet, cigar, funeral wreath, and patent medicine, the last dispensed with a free copy of the book" (76).

19. Josephine Donovan makes this same point (105).

20. Douglas applies similar androcentric standards, particularly the valorization of linear time to her subjects. Writing about nineteenth-century female biographers, she complains that these women focus on "organic markers" such as "birth, conversion, marriage, aging, and above all, illness and death" rather than on dates. She concludes: "Biography is merged with something close to a vegetation myth" (195).

21. For an example of a hymn that addresses surrender in purely military terms, see "Make Me a Captive Lord" (1896) by the Scottish hymnist George

Matheson. This hymn and Matheson's "O Love That Will Not Let Me Go" (1882) have been widely sung in America.

22. Reynolds theorizes that Pollard wrote this hymn in the 1890s, although it was not published until 1907.

23. For a feminist model of spirituality as a dance with the divine, see Maria Harris's *Dance of the Spirit: The Seven Steps of Women's Spirituality* (New York: Bantam, 1989). Harris contends "that women's spirituality is a rhythmic series of movements, which, unlike the steps of a *ladder* or a *staircase,* do not go up and down. Instead the steps of *our* lives are much better imagined as steps in a dance" (xii).

24. For an excellent discussion of the concept of "usefulness" as applied to late-nineteenth-century women, see Ruether and Keller's *Women and Religion in America,* esp. Carolyn De Swarte Gifford's essay, "Women in Social Reform Movements," (1:294–303) and Rosemary Skinner Keller's "Lay Women in the Protestant Tradition" (1:242–53). Gifford argues that charitable work became the religion of many pious women, "a position of faith as much as a cause espoused" (1:296). Keller points out that some male church leaders saw benevolence as a way to keep women out of the "real" business of the church, that is, the preaching ministry (1:252).

25. Donovan argues that an oppressed woman must either deny spirituality, identify with her body, and risk being objectified by men or that she must deny her body and retreat into her mind, presumably the center of spiritual consciousness (101). Adelaide A. Pollard suggests that form is a matter of function or action. Thus, spirituality and actions performed by the body (including the expression of sexuality) are no longer separate.

26. Scott sometimes used the pseudonym Charles H. Scott.

27. Also see Susan S. Tamke's discussion of a similar phenomenon in Toplady's "Rock of Ages" (1776), a hymn much loved in America for the last three centuries. Tamke quotes a stanza in which Toplady expresses a wish to be lost in Christ's "precious Side-hole's cavity" (38). Apparently, this verse did not enjoy long popularity in America; Reynolds reports that the version of the hymn now popular is a compilation of verses from an 1815 version, none of which mention side holes (186).

28. Douglas points out that "the garden was the chosen and consecrated terrain of the feminine sensibility in mid-nineteenth-century American culture" (369–70 n. 104). Also, see her discussion of the importance of flower names for women writers (186).

29. Popular songs of the period in which women and courtship are associated with flowers and gardens confirm Freud's conclusion. William Jerome's "I'll Make a Ring Around Rosie" (1910) and Harry H. Williams's "In the Shade of the Old Apple Tree" (1905) are good examples.

30. In point of fact, Genesis does not describe God walking in the garden until just after Adam and Eve eat the forbidden fruit. However, the passage implies that walking there was a habit since Adam and Eve are concerned about their nakedness rather than about God's presence. Reynolds reports that Miles wrote the hymn after a vision in which he witnessed the meeting between the newly

risen Christ and Mary Magdalene described in John 20 (96). In this passage, Mary mistakes Jesus for a gardener (v. 15). Once she realizes his true identity, Jesus specifically warns her not to touch him (v. 17). The complexity of references to innocence and experience, spiritual intimacy and sexuality make "In the Garden" a particularly rich and interesting text.

31. Chodorow argues that "the attainment of masculine gender identity" requires both "denial of attachment or relationship" and "the repression and devaluation of femininity on both psychological and cultural levels" (51).

32. The idea that women save men is standard in religious domestic novels. In *Uncle Tom's Cabin*, several men see their wives as agents of their conversion. Mr. Shelby, for example, "seemed . . . to indulge a shadowy expectation of getting into heaven through [Mrs. Shelby's] superabundance of qualities to which he made no particular pretension" (21).

33. For a fascinating description of the female world as an enclosed garden, see American naturalist Gene Stratton-Porter's novel *The Magic Garden*, in which a rich young girl devotes her childhood and young womanhood to creating a beautiful garden at the home of a young violinist while he is abroad studying. At the end of the story, the girl, appropriately named Amaryllis, waits in the garden for her beloved to return and marry her.

34. See Ortner's description of women on the periphery (85).

35. Matthew 16:25, Mark 8:35, Luke 9:24.

36. *Fanny Crosby's Life Story* (1903) claims that the hymn is "now sung wherever Christian music is known" (128), and its inclusion in early twentieth-century hymnals seems to be almost automatic. Crosby's *Memories of Eighty Years* (1906) records a number of anecdotes that illustrate the widespread popularity of the hymn (175–76). Current Baptist and Methodist hymnals, however, do not include "Safe in the Arms of Jesus" although I recently heard it at an Assembly of God funeral and have been told by a Free Will Baptist music minister that it is still a standard in that tradition. These facts suggest that mainstream evangelicals are rejecting the feminized Christianity so amply illustrated in the hymn.

37. See De Jong for a discussion of Christ as a "bosom companion" (469–71).

38. Crosby's stories about this hymn indicate that "safe in the arms of Jesus" was a figure describing both the security of salvation during a believer's life on earth and the security of eternal life (*Memories* 175–76).

39. Ortner, a twentieth-century anthropologist, argues that hunting and warfare are valued because of "the transcendental (social, cultural) nature of these activities, as opposed to the naturalness of the process of birth" (75). Her analysis is an interpretation of Simone de Beauvoir's view of male and female creativity: woman creates life and man transcends it.

Chapter 4. Women's Hymns as Narrative Models

1. Crosby herself does not indicate what she needed the money for. Also, Ruffin says she needed $10, but she says the amount was $5.

2. As autobiographical statements, hymns achieve a particular resonance for

Christians who feel compelled to give a public testimony of their faith as a witness to the unsaved. Sandra Sizer argues that gospel hymns are usually not "creedal affirmations" so much as eyewitness accounts, as if Jesus were on trial and the believer must testify on his behalf (45–48). Jane Tompkins comments in *Sensational Designs* that the rhetoric of such testimony does not require "independent verification . . . because supernatural events, by definition, cannot be repeated experimentally" (155). As public testimony, then, these hymns locate truth and ultimate reality in the experience of the individual believer.

Also, see the preface to Hezekiah Butterworth's *The Story of the Hymns; or Hymns That Have a History: An Account of the Origin of Hymns of Personal Religious Experience* (1875). Butterworth argues that knowing the story of a hymn's composition gives the reader or singer "confidence" because the words are grounded in human experience.

3. A charge of excessive sentimentality is a common way to devalue gospel hymns in general and those by women in particular. Foote criticizes gospel hymns for "overwrought sentimentality" (270) and notes that Fanny Crosby's hymns are "superficial in thought and weak in form." He attributes Crosby's astonishing popularity to the value of the hymn tunes associated with her hymns, to her childlike qualities of character, and to "public sympathy for her blindness" (268). Ninde criticizes Crosby's sentimentality and argues, "None would claim that she was a poetess in any large sense" (344). Nicholas Smith includes only two Crosby hymns in his collection, neither of them a gospel hymn and both of them in current disuse. He argues that the hymns included are her finest because they do not "run on the plane of 'gospel songs'" (148–52).

4. Elizabeth Say also makes this point (130). She argues that "all theologies presuppose a narrative . . . against which individual persons examine their lives" (110). Say explains that men have assumed their experience of reality is universal and normative and that, in contrast, women's narratives are individual and idiosyncratic (130).

5. Allegorical narrative has the effect of creating an inflexible pattern that imposes meaning on concrete experience. As Bunyan makes clear, going off the path is always fraught with dangers. In its constant use by nineteenth-century female authors of domestic fiction and hymns, however, *The Pilgrim's Progress* becomes less allegorical. Gwenn Davis points out to me that the occasional nature of women's writing means their own experiences of "doubt or personal crisis or demands" represent the "bumps on the road" of a personal pilgrimage. Thus, women can use autobiographical narrative to offer advice to other pilgrims in a flexible way that undermines the very nature of allegory. Also, see Jane Tompkins's related observation in *Sensational Designs* that domestic novels turn narratives such as *The Pilgrim's Progress* into "spiritual 'training' narratives" that emphasize the "toils and sorrows of the 'way'" instead of the end result of redemption (183).

6. See Psalm 46:4, Rev. 22:1, Gen. 2:10.

7. Sidonie Smith argues that a trip into the wilderness is really a trip into the self that celebrates the agency of the subject and the teleological significance of the journey: "Launched on a romantic journey, the 'self' streams into the interior

of itself, through lake after lake, layer after layer of circumstance to an unencumbered center of quiet water, pure being or essence" ("Resisting" 78).

8. Spengemann and Lundquist argue that only a certain kind of self can play a
role in the "American myth" of progress. It must be

> an integrated, continuing personality which transcends the limitations and ir-
> regularities of time and space and unites all of one's apparently contradictory
> experiences into an identifiable whole. This notion of individual identity, in
> fact, may well be the central belief of our culture. (516)

9. See also Sidonie Smith, *A Poetics* 22; Peterson 2; Swaim 37; and Culley,
"What a Piece of Work" 10.

10. Linda Peterson's analysis of the proscription on women preaching in England is illuminating. She cites an instance in which John Wesley advised a de-
vout woman to testify but not to explicate Scripture: "For Wesley, the crucial issue
is not public speaking but taking a biblical text—and, worse yet, expounding
upon the text in 'continued discourse'" (131). Peterson argues that denying women
the right to use autobiography meant denying them the tool that gave "coherence
to experience" (137).

11. Constructing the self through a spiritual journey is, according to Spengemann and Lundquist, a "cultural act" (500) that makes movement and change
necessary to self-definition. They argue that autobiography is a way of supporting
"the belief in America as a moral idea":

> The American myth, in its most general form, describes human history as a
> pilgrimage from imperfection to perfection; from a dimly remembered union
> with the Divine to a re-establishment of that union. Within these very broad
> outlines, Americans have continually reinterpreted the several terms of the
> myth. (503)

12. As Lois Rudnick observes, a True Woman could not by definition be like a
"self-made man" who was "able to transcend the impediments of class, past, and
family in order to seize the opportunities that brought fame, fortune, and public
recognition" (145). See also Estelle Jelinek's contention that literary critics have
perceived a man's autobiography as "representative of his times, a mirror of his
era" and a woman's autobiography as individual and devoid of allegorical significance (7–8).

13. Sidonie Smith argues that the "'I' of autobiography" is not a neutral designation: "that 'I' is gendered and it is male" ("Resisting" 79).

14. I thank an anonymous reader for the University of Pittsburgh Press for this
insight.

15. Sidonie Smith's interpretation is that Stanton's autobiography both uses
her embodiment as a woman to legitimize her life and rejects that same embodiment to take on a male identity. Thus, her perception of her own subjectivity may
not be as simple as "The Solitude of Self" would lead one to believe. Smith also
observes that Stanton herself discusses *The Woman's Bible* as an act of "rewriting"
Scripture ("Resisting" 85–90).

16. In her biography of Elizabeth Cady Stanton, Elisabeth Griffith describes

this conflict as a strong influence on Stanton's involvement with reform movements. Stanton's conversion at an 1831 revival led by Charles Grandison Finney influenced her rejection of organized religion. Griffith explains that, while "ministers demanded that female activities be modest, unobtrusive, and 'appropriate,'" they created a climate in which women "could not keep silent" and could not in good conscience reject reform activities (22). Unlike female hymnists, Stanton simplified the issue by rejecting evangelicalism as a religion while keeping its social conscience.

17. Spengemann and Lundquist offer a more secular explanation of this difficulty. They argue that the term *autobiography* refers only to the fact that an author makes himself or herself the subject of the writing, not that the text represents "factual truth." In addition,

> autobiography does not communicate raw experience, for that is uncommunicable. It presents, rather, a metaphor for the raw experience. The language of autobiography stands in symbolic relation to both author and subject. As an author translates his life into language he creates for himself a symbolic identity and sees himself through the focusing glass of language. (501–02)

In Crosby's case, translating raw experience into language at all creates an identity conflict. She is both a disorderly woman and an obedient believer.

18. My use of the term *disorder* here is informed by Carroll Smith-Rosenberg's "Women and Religious Revivals: Anti-Ritualism, Liminality, and the Emergence of the American Bourgeoisie." Smith-Rosenberg describes the "liminal disorderliness" of women during revivals as a "rite of passage" into new social roles "that accompanied the rise of the bourgeoisie" (226). She argues that the unrestrained behavior of newly converted women had to be constrained outside the revival setting because "the powerful woman" is an "almost universal symbol of disorder" (231).

19. See also Matt. 16:25; Mark 8:35; Luke 9:24, 17:33.

20. Here Smith paraphrases Philippians 2:13. The Quaker doctrine of inner light allows her to interpret Scripture for her audience. A similar belief in what came to be known as "the priesthood of the believer" allows evangelical women to trust their own experience of the divine and of holy texts.

21. H. Leon McBeth describes specifically the proscription of singing by men and women together among early General Baptists. However, he uses the term "promiscuous singing" more generally to describe singing by "a multitude" (93).

22. The first instances in the OED of *promiscuous* and *promiscuity* being used in any country specifically to refer to sexual impurity are from the nineteenth century.

23. Elizabeth Say argues that "all theologies presuppose a narrative . . . against which individual persons examine their lives"; thus, alternative narratives create new "theological ground" (110). Since narrative presupposes a narrator, telling stories instead of framing an argument allows women to challenge who may speak as well as "*how* we ground issues of truth" (116).

24. Ninde observes that Chautauqua started as a Methodist movement but "soon lost its sectarian character" (309).

25. For example, the introduction to Isaiah in *The New Oxford Annotated Bible* suggests that Isaiah could actually have been three different men (Metzger and Murphy 866). The evangelical view that Lathbury adopts, though, assumes that the Bible is literally true and that the book has one author because it begins by identifying a singular narrative "I."

26. This narrative also appears in Mark 6:30–44, Luke 9:10–17, and John 6:1–13.

27. The account of the feeding of the five thousand in John 6:1–14 is followed by the story of Jesus walking on water and then, in vv. 25–58, by the passage in which Jesus identifies himself as the bread of life.

28. I am indebted to Catherine Hobbs [Peaden] for pointing out this connection between "breadgiver" and the lady of the house. Hobbs associates these terms with the Christian discourse of True Womanhood; she points out in "Jane Addams and the Social Rhetoric of Democracy" that Addams's class at Rockford Female Seminary, many of whose members became missionaries, "named themselves 'breadgivers' after the ideal of the 'Saxon lady' whose mission it was to give bread unto her household" (194). The virtuous woman of Proverbs 31 is also described as distributing food (see v. 15).

29. This is not to say, however, that nineteenth-century evangelical women did not believe suffering could be imposed as beneficent discipline to remove obstacles to their total devotion to God. In *The Wide, Wide World*, for example, Ellen is told that she has been separated from her mother so that she will learn to love no one better than God (73).

30. In her discussion of western selfhood in the late eighteenth and nineteenth centuries, Sidonie Smith argues that "the consolidation of Protestant ideology with its emphasis on the accessibility of God to individual prayer and intercession" is one of the historical developments of the period that privileged "the self-determining individuality of desire and destiny" (*Subjectivity* 9).

31. Zion is the hill on which the temple stood in Jerusalem; it is used metonymically to refer to the Jewish people and typologically to mean Christians, those chosen like the Jews to be a blessing to all nations (see Gen. 12:2–3 and Gal. 3:7–9, 14). "Zion" can also refer to heaven, as it does in Isaac Watts's hymn "Come We That Love the Lord," also known as "Marching to Zion" (1707). Thomson's use of the term suggests both her wish to stress the scriptural basis for missions—and thus to authorize herself as a woman giving advice—and her millenarian fervor.

32. See, for example, the reproduction of this hymn in the 1956 and 1975 *Baptist Hymnal*.

33. Significantly, literature produced by women's missionary support groups often uses the plural *missions* instead of the singular *mission*. This word choice reflects the sense that opportunities for service are suited to the various individual callings of the women involved. Rhetorically, then, the word affirms the value of subjective religious experience while the notion that "missions" itself is a woman's special religious domain reinforces the collective identity of evangelical women.

34. Reynolds states that this hymn was written in 1856 though not published until 1869 (142).

35. This idea is a major theme in Prentiss's novel *Stepping Heavenward*. Toward the end of the story, Katy, the heroine, prays this prayer:

> Bring into captivity every thought to the obedience of Christ. Take what I cannot give—my heart, body, thoughts, time, abilities, money, health, strength, nights, days, youth, age, and spend them in Thy service. . . . My heart is athirst for God, for the living God. (348)

36. Reynolds says that Russell's hymn was written several years before this publication date (221).

37. I have been unable to find a publication date for this hymn.

38. The presidency of the organization has traditionally been an unsalaried position; for the early presidents, however, it was a full-time job.

39. Among other things, WMU created a church calendar for Southern Baptist churches by establishing "seasons of prayer" for missionary concerns, made tithing (giving a tenth of one's income to the church) the norm, and developed powerful youth organizations that trained several generations of children and young women to view service to others as a higher priority than doctrinal purity.

40. Most hymnals attribute this hymn to "Colin Sterne," Nichol's pseudonym. "We've a Story to Tell" was published in 1896.

41. Although Adams's hymn was written in 1840, it expresses ideas very similar to those in Hawks's "I Need Thee Every Hour" and of American female gospel hymnists in general: the awareness of a divine consciousness, the sense that singing a song can express identity, and an appropriation of a biblical story that allows the hymnist's identification with a biblical hero.

Chapter 5. The Patriarchal Backlash

1. For a fuller description of the use of hymns in Sunday revivals, see McLoughlin, 81–90, 94–95.

2. These are Henry Sloane Coffin and Ambrose White Vernon's *Hymns of the Kingdom of God* (1911), Mornay Williams's *Hymns of the Kingdom of God* (n.d.), and Mabel Mussey's *Social Hymns of Brotherhood and Aspiration* (1914) (Spencer 19).

3. Catherine B. Allen notes that in Baptist circles, "Women were the majority of that 'small minority' who practiced social Christianity. Christian benevolence had always been women's work among Southern Baptists" (212).

4. Also see Rosemary Skinner Keller's "Patterns of Laywomen's Leadership in Twentieth-Century Protestantism" for information about practical Christianity and Protestant women of the social gospel period (in Ruether and Keller, *Women and Religion in America*).

5. Some proponents of the social gospel favored a much more active political agenda. For example, Josiah Strong, head of the Congregational Home Mission Society and author of the best-selling novel *Our Country* (1885), was a Social Darwinist who believed that immigrants were the root of American social problems and that Christians should vigorously proselytize these elements of society as a way of Americanizing them. George Marsden believes that views such as Strong's

influenced foreign policy. He quotes President William McKinley, who, in 1898, was "faced with the question of what to do with the Philippines" and decided after a late-night prayer session that the only solution was "to take them all and to educate the Filipinos and uplift and civilize and Christianize them" (19–20).

6. This Elizabeth Stuart Phelps (1815–1852) is the mother of the Elizabeth Stuart Phelps (1844–1911) who wrote *The Gates Ajar, Beyond the Gates,* and the other popular heaven books. The younger Phelps was born Mary Gray Phelps and later married Herbert Dickinson Ward, so she is sometimes identified as Elizabeth Stuart Phelps Ward (Solomon 340–41). Most of the younger Phelps's work is published under her mother's name.

7. Robert H. Walker and Dewey D. Wallace Jr., comment that the sheer number of sermons, hymns, novels, and other texts produced to support Christian socialism "suggests something of its popularity—not every religious movement gave rise to such a wealth of song and story" (xv).

8. This last point is informed by T. J. Jackson Lears's discussion of Protestant appropriation of Catholic aesthetics in the late Victorian period. Lears argues that "both ministers and laymen thought art and ritual [associated with Catholicism] might provide a 'lyrical lift' to the faltering claims of urban Protestantism" (194). Lears describes the antimodern association of Mother Church with women and a cult of inner experience in general (see esp. 192–97), and he argues that "if culture had been 'feminized,' it was possible to redefine femininity as a source of strength" (223).

9. These words are an obvious reworking of Thomas Ken's doxology (c. 1673), which begins "Praise God, from whom all blessings flow." Reynolds identifies it as "the most widely used [doxology] throughout the English-speaking world" (179).

10. All of the synoptic gospels speak of a spiritual kingdom. The book of Matthew refers to this concept as the "kingdom of heaven" while the other gospels use the phrase "kingdom of God." Because these phrases are virtually interchangeable in the Bible, hymnists sometimes use them interchangeably as well. In the Bible as well as in hymns, neither phrase refers exclusively to a place of eternal reward, i.e., the popular nineteenth-century vision of heaven. The idea of the kingdom of God or the kingdom of heaven that influences hymnists and other religious writers seems to be a matter of perception rather than of geography.

11. Scriptural descriptions of the great feast are in Luke 14:15–24, Matt. 22:1–10, and Rev. 19:9. Jane Tompkins also notes the millenarian focus in Stowe's description of the Halliday kitchen (*Sensational Designs* 142).

12. For the story of Mary and Martha, see Luke 10:38–42.

13. Numerical references for hymns from *Social Hymns of Brotherhood and Aspiration* are to hymn numbers rather than to page numbers.

14. T. J. Jackson Lears explains the connection between premodern attitudes and femininity during the era of gospel and social gospel hymns in this way:

> Merged with antimodern vitalism, the "feminine" ideal of dependence acquired a new cultural resonance. In the *fin-de-siecle* imagination, many of the "childlike" qualities associated with premodern character, and with the uncon-

scious, were also linked with femininity: fantasy, spontaneity, aesthetic creativity. The premodern unconscious generated androgynous alternatives to bourgeois masculinity. Those options especially appealed to the men and women who were most restive under bourgeois definitions of gender identity, and who suffered most acutely from the fragmenting sense of selfhood. (223)

15. Thoreau also made work an element of spirituality. Sherman Paul even labels *Walden* a "social gospel" (xxvii). However, Thoreau represents the spirituality of a John the Baptist, who leaves society for the wilderness, where he works to prepare the way of the Lord. In Paul's words, Thoreau's "economy, like his withdrawal to Nature, was not an ultimate abdication from social life; it was only the means of . . . self-emancipation" that allowed him to return eventually and help reform society (xxvi–xxvii). Harriet Beecher Stowe, on the other hand, sees work within the social setting of the home as a means of self-emancipation. The plots of many of her novels move from kitchen to kitchen, where women prepare the way of the Lord by being immersed in a community.

16. See also George Marsden's argument that the urban influx of immigrants, many of whom were poor Catholics, was disturbing to Protestants in general: "In a nation with a large Catholic (and other non-Protestant) population, [Protestants] could not simultaneously claim to believe in democracy and also claim that Protestant ideals and values should always rule" (14).

17. Compare, for example, the version of this line in the 1991 *Baptist Hymnal* (p. 4) to the one in the 1956 *Baptist Hymnal* (p. 41).

18. My thanks to Dan Hobbs, who pointed out this passage to me.

19. Jesus tells the Pharisee Nicodemus that he must be "born again" to "see the kingdom of God" in John 3:3. The evangelical interpretation of this narrative usually centers on Nicodemus's role as a Pharisee who promoted strict adherence to the law of Moses. Evangelical Christians view Nicodemus as overconcerned with legality, especially as it is expressed in a sanctimonious expectation that true religion requires scrupulous attention to written religious laws, behavior that the Pharisee exemplifies. In other words, Nicodemus needs to be "born again" to free him from the bondage of print.

20. Teaching evolution in public schools, prayer in schools, and anti-abortion laws are examples of fundamentalist issues.

21. Phrases such as *washed in the blood of the Lamb, redemption, shelter in the storm,* and *I see the light,* for example, are standard in country songs. A Martina McBride song, "Safe in the Arms of Love," echoes the title of Fanny Crosby's "Safe in the Arms of Jesus."

22. The original uses "o'ershaded" instead of "o'ershadowed" and ends with "Sweetly my soul shall rest."

Works Cited

Hymnals

Baptist Hymnal. Ed. Walter Hines Sims. Nashville: Convention Press, 1956.

The Baptist Hymnal. Nashville: Convention Press, 1975.

The Baptist Hymnal. Nashville: Convention Press, 1991.

The Broadman Hymnal. Ed. B. B. McKinney. Nashville: Broadman Press, 1940.

The Cokesbury Worship Hymnal. Ed. C. A. Bowen. Baltimore: The Methodist Publishing House, 1938.

Gospel Hymns No. 2. Ed. P. P. Bliss and Ira D. Sankey. New York: Biglow & Main and John Church, 1876.

Great Revival Hymns for the Church, Sunday School and Evangelistic Services. Ed. and comp. Homer Rodeheaver and B. D. Ackley. Chicago: Rodeheaver, 1911.

Hymns of the Church Militant. Ed. Anna B. Warner. New York, 1859.

Make Christ King: A Selection of High Class Gospel Music for Use in General Worship and Special Evangelistic Meetings. Ed. E. O. Excell and William Edward Biederwolf. Chicago: Glad Tidings, 1912.

The New Alphabetical Hymnal: Great Songs of the Church, Number Two: A Treasury of Six Hundred Sacred Songs Suitable for All Services of the Church. Comp. E. L. Jorgenson. Louisville: Great Songs Press, 1937.

New Baptist Hymnal. Nashville: Broadman Press, 1926.

Revival Praises. Comp. George R. Stuart et al. Nashville: Methodist Publishing House, 1907.

Social Hymns of Brotherhood and Aspiration. Comp. Mabel Hay Barrows Mussey. New York: A. S. Barnes, 1914.

Songs of the Bible for the Sunday School. Ed. W. A. Ogden and A. J. Abbey. Toledo: W. W. Whitney, 1873.

Wayfaring Hymns, Original and Translated. Ed. Anna B. Warner. New York, 1869.

Books, Articles, and Lectures

Abbott, Shirley. *Womenfolks: Growing Up Down South*. New York: Ticknor and Fields, 1983.

Addams, Jane. *Twenty Years at Hull House*. New York: Macmillan, 1910.

Alcott, Louisa May. *Little Women*. 1868. New York: Signet Classic-Penguin, 1983.

———. *Work: A Story of Experience*. 1872–73. New York: Schocken, 1977.

Allen, Catherine B. *A Century to Celebrate: History of Woman's Missionary Union*. Birmingham, Ala.: Woman's Missionary Union, 1987.

Ames, Mary Clemmer. *A Memorial of Alice and Phoebe Cary, with Some of Their Later Poems*. New York: Hurd and Houghton, 1873.

Baum, L. Frank. *The Wizard of Oz.* 1900. New York: Del Rey–Ballantine, 1956.

Baym, Nina. Introduction to *The Lamplighter,* by Maria Susanna Cummins, ix–xxxi. 1854. New Brunswick, N.J.: Rutgers University Press, 1988.

Beaver, R. Pierce. *American Protestant Women in World Mission: History of the First Feminist Movement in North America.* Rev. ed. Grand Rapids, Mich.: Eerdmans, 1980.

Beecher, Catharine. *A Treatise on Domestic Economy.* Boston: Marsh, Capen, Lyon, and Webb: 1841.

Beecher, Henry Ward. "The Family as an American Institution." *The Sermons of Henry Ward Beecher, in Plymouth Church, Brooklyn.* First Series: September 1868–March 1869. New York: J. B. Ford, 1869. 423–38.

———. "Inheritance of the Meek." *The Sermons of Henry Ward Beecher, in Plymouth Church, Brooklyn.* Third Series: September 1869–March 1870. New York: J. B. Ford, 1870. 247–62.

———. "Relations of Music to Worship." *Yale Lectures on Preaching 2.* New York: J. B. Ford, 1873. 114–45.

Beecher, Lyman. *A Plea for the West.* 2d ed. Cincinnati: Truman & Smith, 1835.

Bennett, Paula. "Critical Clitoridectomy: Female Sexual Imagery and Feminist Psychoanalytic Theory." *Signs* 18 (winter 1993): 235–59.

Bercovitch, Sacvan. *The Puritan Origins of the American Self.* New Haven: Yale University Press, 1975.

Berlin, James A. *Writing Instruction in Nineteenth-Century American Colleges.* Carbondale: Southern Illinois University Press, 1984.

Bradford, Amory H. *Heredity and Christian Problems.* New York: Macmillan, 1895.

Brumberg, Joan Jacobs. "The Ethnological Mirror: American Evangelical Women and Their Heathen Sisters, 1870–1910." In *Women and the Structure of Society: Selected Research from the Fifth Berkshire Conference on the History of Women,* ed. Barbara J. Harris and JoAnn K. McNamara, 108–28. Durham: Duke University Press, 1984.

Bunyan, John. *Grace Abounding to the Chief of Sinners* and *The Pilgrim's Progress from this World to that which is to Come.* 1666, 1678, and 1684. Ed. Roger Sharrock. Oxford Standard Authors ed. London: Oxford University Press, 1966.

Butterworth, Hezekiah. *The Story of the Hymns; or Hymns That Have a History: An Account of the Origin of Hymns of Personal Religious Experience.* New York: American Tract Society, 1875.

Campbell, Duncan. *Hymns and Hymn Makers.* 5th ed. London: A & C Black, 1912.

Carnegie, Andrew. *The Gospel of Wealth and Other Timely Essays.* 1901. Belknap Press of Harvard University Press, 1962.

Child, Lydia Maria. *The Mother's Book.* 1831. Cambridge: Applewood, 1989.

Chodorow, Nancy. "Family Structure and Feminine Personality." In *Woman, Culture, and Society,* ed. Michelle Zimbalist Rosaldo and Louise Lamphere, 43–66. Stanford: Stanford University Press, 1974.

Cixous, Hélène. "Sorties: Out and Out: Attacks/Ways Out/Forays." *The Newly Born Woman.* Trans. Betsy Wing. Minneapolis: University of Minnesota Press, 1986. 558–78.

Croly, Mrs. J. C. [Jennie June]. *The History of the Woman's Club Movement in America*. New York: Henry G. Allen, 1898.

Crosby, Fanny J. *Fanny Crosby's Life-Story*. New York: Every Where, 1903.

———. *Memories of Eighty Years*. Boston: James H. Earle, 1906.

Culley, Margo, ed. *American Women's Autobiography: Fea(s)ts of Memory*. Madison: University of Wisconsin Press, 1992.

Culley, Margo, ed. "What a Piece of Work Is 'Woman'!: An Introduction." In *American Women's Autobiography*, ed. Culley, 3–31.

Cummins, Maria Susanna. *The Lamplighter*. 1854. New Brunswick, N.J.: Rutgers University Press, 1988.

Davidson, Cathy N. *Revolution and the Word: The Rise of the Novel in America*. New York: Oxford University Press, 1986.

Davis, Natalie Zemon. *Fiction in the Archives: Pardon Tales and Their Tellers in Sixteenth-Century France*. Stanford: Stanford University Press, 1987.

Davis, Thomas M. "The Traditions of Puritan Typology." *Typology and Early American Literature*. Ed. Sacvan Bercovitch. Amherst: University of Massachusetts Press, 1972.

De Jong, Mary G. "'I Want to Be Like Jesus': The Self-Defining Power of Evangelical Hymnody." *Journal of the American Academy of Religion* 54 (fall 1986): 461–93.

Donaldson, Scott. Introduction to *The Damnation of Theron Ware* or *Illumination*, by Harold Frederic. 1896. New York: Penguin, 1986.

Donne, John. "Batter My Heart, Three-Personed God." *John Donne: The Complete English Poems*. Ed. A. J. Smith. London: Penguin, 1971, 314–15.

Donovan, Josephine. "Toward a Women's Poetics." *Tulsa Studies in Women's Literature* 3 (spring/fall 1984): 99–110.

Douglas, Ann. *The Feminization of American Culture*. 1977. New York: Anchor-Doubleday, 1988.

Elbert, Sarah. Introduction to *Work: A Story of Experience*, by Louisa May Alcott. New York: Schocken, 1977. ix–xliv.

Emerson, Ralph Waldo. *Nature*. 1841. *Ralph Waldo Emerson*. Ed. Richard Poirier. New York: Oxford University Press, 1990. [2]–36.

Eskew, Harry, and Hugh T. McElrath. *Sing with Understanding: An Introduction to Christian Hymnology*. Nashville: Broadman Press, 1980.

Faderman, Lillian. *Surpassing the Love of Men: Romantic Friendship and Love Between Women from the Renaissance to the Present*. New York: William Morrow, 1981.

Fern, Fanny. "Woman's Wickedness." 1852. In *Ruth Hall and Other Writings*, ed. Joyce W. Warren, 228–29. New Brunswick, N.J.: Rutgers University Press, 1994.

Fletcher, Angus. *Allegory: The Theory of a Symbolic Mode*. Ithaca: Cornell University Press, 1964.

Foote, Henry Wilder. *Three Centuries of American Hymnody*. Cambridge: Harvard University Press, 1940.

Foster, Edward Halsey. *Susan and Anna Warner*. Twayne's United States Authors Series. Boston: Twayne, n.d.

Foster, Richard J. *Celebration of Discipline: The Path to Spiritual Growth*. San Francisco: Harper and Row, 1978.

————. Sermon. McFarlin Memorial Methodist Church, Norman, Oklahoma, 7 November 1993.

Franklin, Benjamin. *Benjamin Franklin's Autobiography: An Authoritative Text*. Ed. J. A. Leo Lemay and P. M. Zall. New York: Norton, 1986.

Frederic, Harold. *The Damnation of Theron Ware* or *Illumination*. 1896. New York: Penguin, 1986.

Friedman, Susan Stanford. "Women's Autobiographical Selves: Theory and Practice." In *The Private Self: Theory and Practice of Women's Autobiographical Writings*, ed. Shari Benstock. Chapel Hill: University of North Carolina Press, 1988.

Garrett, Shirley S. "Sisters All: Feminism and the American Women's Missionary Movement." In *Missionary Ideologies in the Imperialist Era: 1880–1920*, ed. Torben Christensen and William R. Hutchison, 221–30. [Århus], Den.: Aros, 1982.

Gaskin, J. M. "Baptist Education in Oklahoma." *The Oklahoma Baptist Chronicle* 32.1 (spring 1989): 49–69.

Gilligan, Carol. *In a Different Voice: Psychological Theory and Woman's Development*. Cambridge: Harvard University Press, 1982.

Gilman, Charlotte Perkins. *His Religion and Hers: A Study of the Faith of Our Fathers and the Work of Our Mothers*. 1923. Pioneers of the Woman's Movement Series. Westport, Conn.: Hyperion Press, 1976.

Ginzburg, Carlo. *The Cheese and the Worms: The Cosmos of a Sixteenth-Century Miller*. Trans. John and Anne Tedeschi. Baltimore: Johns Hopkins University Press, 1980.

Green, Harvey. *The Light of the Home: An Intimate View of the Lives of Women in Victorian America*. New York: Pantheon, 1983.

Griffith, Elisabeth. *In Her Own Right: The Life of Elizabeth Cady Stanton*. New York: Oxford University Press, 1984.

Hageman, Alice L. *Sexist Religion and Women in the Church: No More Silence*. New York: Association Press, 1974.

"Hall of Fame." *Royal Service*, May 1988: 20–22.

Halttunen, Karen. *Confidence Men and Painted Women: A Study of Middle Class Culture in America, 1830–1870*. New Haven: Yale University Press, 1982.

Hammons, Paul. Address. First Baptist Church, Norman, Oklahoma, 18 October 1992.

Harris, Maria. *Dance of the Spirit: The Seven Steps of Women's Spirituality*. New York: Bantam, 1989.

Heck, Fannie E. S. *In Royal Service: The Mission Work of Southern Baptist Women*. Richmond: Foreign Mission Board, Southern Baptist Convention, 1913.

Heilbrun, Carolyn G. *Writing a Woman's Life*. New York: Ballantine, 1988.

Hill, Patricia Ruth. *The World Their Household: The American Woman's Foreign Mission Movement and Cultural Transformation, 1870–1920*. Ann Arbor: University of Michigan Press, 1985.

Hitchcock, H. Wiley. Introduction to *Gospel Hymns Nos. 1 to 6 Complete*, by Ira D. Sankey et al. 1895. New York: Da Capo Press, 1972.

Hobbs, Dan S. "Baptists and the Run of '89." *Oklahoma Baptist Chronicle* 32.1 (spring 1989): 7–24.

Hobbs, June Hadden. "His Religion and Hers in Nineteenth-Century Hymnody." In *Nineteenth-Century Women Learn to Write*, ed. Catherine Hobbs, 120–44. Charlottesville: University Press of Virginia, 1995.

———. "Who Are We Baptist Women?" *Royal Service*, April 1985: 4–7.

Hobsbawm, Eric. "Introduction: Inventing Traditions." In *The Invention of Tradition*, ed. Eric Hobsbawm and Terence Ranger, 1–14. Cambridge: Cambridge University Press, 1983.

Hofstadter, Richard. "The Meaning of the Progressive Movement." In *The Progressive Movement 1900–1915*. Englewood Cliffs: Prentice-Hall, 1963. 1–15.

Hordern, William E. *A Layman's Guide to Protestant Theology*. Rev. ed. London: MacMillan, 1968.

Howard, David. "Baptist Music." *Baptist Messenger*, 23 September 1993: 10.

Howells, William D. *Indian Summer*. 1886. New York: Dutton, 1951.

Hustad, Donald. *Jubilate!: Church Music in the Evangelical Tradition*. Carol Stream, Ill.: Hope, 1981.

Hyde, William DeWitt. *Outlines of Social Theology*. New York: Macmillan, 1895.

Jelinek, Estelle C. "Introduction: Women's Autobiography and the Male Tradition." In *Women's Autobiography: Essays in Criticism*, ed. Estelle C. Jelinek, 1–20. Bloomington: Indiana University Press, 1980.

Jenkins, Ruth Y. *Reclaiming Myths of Power: Women Writers and the Victorian Spiritual Crisis*. Lewisburg: Bucknell University Press, 1995.

Keely, Wayne. "Claremore Pastor Responds to Critical Letters." *Baptist Messenger*, 4 February 1993: 7.

Keller, Rosemary Skinner. "Patterns of Laywomen's Leadership in Twentieth-Century Protestantism." In *Women and Religion in America*, ed. Rosemary Radford Ruether and Rosemary Skinner Keller, *3:266–77*. San Francisco: Harper and Row, 1981–86.

Kelley, Mary. *Private Woman, Public Stage: Literary Domesticity in Nineteenth-Century America*. New York: Oxford University Press, 1984.

Kerber, Linda K. "Separate Spheres, Female Worlds, Woman's Place: The Rhetoric of Women's History." *The Journal of American History* 75 (June 1988): 9–39.

Kohler, Lyle. "The Case of the American Jezebels: Anne Hutchinson and Female Agitation During the Years of Antinomian Turmoil, 1636–1640." In *Women's America: Refocusing the Past*, 2d ed., ed. Linda K. Kerber and Jane DeHart Mathews, 52–65. New York: Oxford University Press, 1987.

Kristeva, Julia. "Women's Time." Trans. Alice Jardine and Harry Blake. *The Kristeva Reader*. Ed. Toril Moi. New York: Columbia University Press, 1986. 188–213.

Larcom, Lucy. *A New England Girlhood*. 1889. Boston: Northeastern University Press, 1986.

Lears, T. J. Jackson. *No Place of Grace: Antimodernism and the Transformation of American Culture, 1880–1920*. New York: Pantheon, 1981.

Lewis, Gladys. "Quotations." *Baptist Messenger*, 28 January 1993: 12.

Littlefield, Henry M. "The Wizard of Oz: Parable on Populism." *American Quarterly* 16 (spring 1964): 47–58.

McBeth, H. Leon. *The Baptist Heritage*. Nashville: Broadman, 1987.

McCutchan, Robert Guy. *Our Hymnody: A Manual of the Methodist Hymnal*. 2d ed. New York: Abingdon, 1937.

McLoughlin, William G., Jr. *Billy Sunday Was His Real Name*. Chicago: University of Chicago Press, 1955.

Marsden, George M. *Understanding Fundamentalism and Evangelicalism*. Grand Rapids, Mich.: Eerdmans, 1991.

Marshall, Madeleine Forell, and Janet Todd. *English Congregational Hymns in the Eighteenth Century*. Lexington: University Press of Kentucky, 1982.

Marty, Martin E., and R. Scott Appleby. *The Glory and the Power: The Fundamentalist Challenge to the Modern World*. Boston: Beacon, 1992.

Mason, Mary G. "The Other Voice: Autobiographies of Women Writers." In *Autobiography: Essays Theoretical and Critical*, ed. James Olney, 207–35. Princeton: Princeton University Press, 1980.

Mead, Sidney E. "The American People: Their Space, Time, and Religion." In *The Lively Experiment: The Shaping of Christianity in America*, 1–15. New York: Harper, 1963.

Metzger, Bruce M., and Roland E. Murphy, eds. Introduction to Isaiah, *The New Oxford Annotated Bible*. New York: Oxford University Press, 1991.

Montgomery, Helen Barrett. *Western Women in Eastern Lands: An Outline Study of Fifty Years of Woman's Work in Foreign Missions*. New York: Macmillan, 1911.

Mussey, Mabel Hay Barrows. Preface to *Social Hymns of Brotherhood and Aspiration*. New York: A. S. Barnes, 1914.

Newton, R. Heber. *The Right and Wrong Uses of the Bible*. New York: John W. Lovell, 1883.

Ninde, Edward S. *The Story of the American Hymn*. New York: Abingdon, 1921.

Ochs, Carol. *Women and Spirituality*. New Feminist Perspectives Series. Totowa, N.J.: Rowman and Allanheld, 1983.

Ong, Walter J. *Orality and Literacy: The Technologizing of the Word*. London: Routledge, 1982.

Ortner, Sherry B. "Is Female to Male as Nature Is to Culture?" In *Woman, Culture, and Society*, ed. Michelle Zimbalist Rosaldo and Louise Lamphere, 67–87. Stanford: Stanford University Press, 1974.

Parry, Ellwood C., III. *The Art of Thomas Cole: Ambition and Imagination*. Newark: University of Delaware Press, 1988.

Paul, Sherman. Introduction to *Walden and Civil Disobedience*, by Henry David Thoreau, vii–xxxix. Boston: Riverside-Houghton Mifflin, 1957.

Peaden, Catherine [Catherine Hobbs]. "Jane Addams and the Social Rhetoric of Democracy." In *Oratorical Culture in Nineteenth Century America: Transformations in the Theory and Practice of Rhetoric*, ed. Gregory Clark and S. Michael Halloran, 184–207. Carbondale: Southern Illinois University Press, 1993.

Peterson, Linda H. *Victorian Autobiography: The Tradition of Self Interpretation*. New Haven: Yale University Press, 1986.

Phelps, Elizabeth Stuart. "The Angel Over the Right Shoulder." In *Rediscoveries: American Short Stories by Women, 1832–1916*, ed. Barbara H. Solomon. New York: Mentor-Penguin, 1994.

Phelps, Elizabeth Stuart [Mary Gray Phelps Ward]. *Beyond the Gates.* Boston, 1883.
———. *A Singular Life.* Boston: Houghton Mifflin, 1894.
Plett, James Wendall. "The Poetic Language of Isaac Watts' Hymns." Ph.D. diss., University of California, 1986.
Porter, Gene Stratton. *The Magic Garden.* Garden City, N.Y.: Doubleday-Page, c. 1927.
Porterfield, Amanda. *Feminine Spirituality in America: From Sarah Edwards to Martha Graham.* Philadelphia: Temple University Press, 1980.
Powell, Earl A. *Thomas Cole.* New York: Abrams, 1990.
Prentiss, Elizabeth. *Stepping Heavenward.* New York, 1869.
Rauschenbusch, Walter. *Christianity and the Social Crisis.* Boston: Pilgrim Press, 1907.
———. *Prayers of the Social Awakening.* Boston: Pilgrim Press, 1909.
Reynolds, William J. *Companion to the Baptist Hymnal.* Nashville: Broadman Press, 1976.
Roe, Edward P. *Barriers Burned Away.* New York: Dodd and Mead, 1873.
Rosaldo, Michelle Zimbalist. "Woman, Culture, and Society: A Theoretical Overview." In *Woman, Culture, and Society,* ed. Michelle Zimbalist Rosaldo and Louise Lamphere, 17–42. Stanford: Stanford University Press, 1974.
Rothenbusch, Esther. "The Joyful Sound: Women in the Nineteenth-Century United States Hymnody Tradition." In *Women and Music in Cross-Cultural Perspective,* ed. Ellen Koskoff, 177–94. Contributions in Women's Studies 79. New York: Greenwood Press, 1987.
Rudin, Cecilia Margaret. *Stories of Hymns We Love.* Chicago: John Rudin, 1934.
Rudnick, Lois. "A Feminist American Success Myth: Jane Addams' *Twenty Years at Hull House.*" In *Tradition and the Talents of Women,* ed. Florence Howe, 145–67. Urbana: University of Illinois Press, 1991.
Ruether, Rosemary Radford, and Rosemary Skinner Keller, eds. *Women and Religion in America.* 3 vols. San Francisco: Harper and Row, 1981–86.
Ruffin, Bernard. *Fanny Crosby.* Philadelphia: United Church Press, 1976.
Sandeen, Ernest R. *The Roots of Fundamentalism: British and American Millenarianism 1800–1930.* Chicago: University of Chicago Press, 1970.
Sanville, George. *Forty Gospel Hymn Stories.* Winona Lake, Ind.: Rodeheaver-Hall Mack, 1943.
Say, Elizabeth A. *Evidence on Her Own Behalf: Women's Narrative as Theological Voice.* Savage, Md.: Rowman and Littlefield, 1990.
Sehested, Nancy Hastings. "Smiling Through a Sunday Morning." *Christianity and Crisis,* 20 July 1992: 244–45.
Sheldon, Charles. *In His Steps: "What Would Jesus Do?"* 1896. N.p.: David McKay, 1958.
Showalter, Elaine. "Feminist Criticism in the Wilderness." *Critical Inquiry* 8 (winter 1981): 179–205.
Sizer, Sandra S. *Gospel Hymns and Social Religion.* American Civilization Series. Philadelphia: Temple University Press, 1978.
Sklar, Kathryn Kish. *Catharine Beecher: A Study in American Domesticity.* New Haven: Yale University Press, 1973.

Slate, Trena. "She Witnessed to Me." *Baptist Messenger,* 28 January 1993: 12.

Smith, Hannah Whitall. *The Christian's Secret of a Happy Life.* 1870. Old Tappen, N.J.: Spire-Revell, 1942.

Smith, Nicholas. *Songs from the Hearts of Women: One Hundred Famous Hymns and Their Writers.* Chicago: A. C. McClurg, 1903.

Smith, Sidonie. *A Poetics of Women's Autobiography: Marginality and the Fictions of Self Representation.* Bloomington: Indiana University Press, 1987.

———. "Resisting the Gaze of Embodiment: Women's Autobiography in the Nineteenth Century." In *American Women's Autobiography: Fea(s)ts of Memory,* ed. Margo Culley, 75–110. Madison: University of Wisconsin Press, 1992.

———. *Subjectivity, Identity, and the Body.* Bloomington: Indiana University Press, 1993.

Smith-Rosenberg, Carroll. "The Female World of Love and Ritual: Relations Between Women in Nineteenth-Century America." *Signs: Journal of Women in Culture and Society* 1 (1975): 1–30.

———. "The New Woman as Androgyne." In *Disorderly Conduct: Visions of Gender in Victorian America,* 245–96. New York: Knopf, 1985.

———. "Women and Religious Revivals: Anti-Ritualism, Liminality, and the Emergence of the American Bourgeoisie." In *The Evangelical Tradition in America,* ed. Leonard I. Sweet, 199–231. Macon: Mercer University Press, 1984.

Solomon, Barbara H. Introduction to *Rediscoveries: American Short Stories by Women, 1832–1916,* ed. Solomon. New York: Mentor-Penguin, 1994.

Spacks, Patricia Meyer. *Imagining a Self: Autobiography and the Novel in Eighteenth-Century England.* Cambridge: Harvard University Press, 1976.

"Speaker Says Hymns Vital to Worship." *The Tie,* January–February 1985: 8.

Spencer, Jon Michael. "Hymns of the Social Awakening: Walter Rauschenbusch and Social Gospel Hymnody." *The Hymn* 40 (April 1989): 18–24.

Spengemann, William C., and L. R. Lundquist. "Autobiography and the American Myth." *American Quarterly* 17.3 (fall 1965): 501–19.

Stanton, Elizabeth Cady. "The Solitude of Self." 1892. In *The Search for Self-Sovereignty: The Oratory of Elizabeth Cady Stanton,* ed. Beth M. Waggenspack, 159–67. Great American Orators 4. New York: Greenwood, 1989.

Stock, Brian. *Listening for the Text: On the Uses of the Past.* Baltimore: Johns Hopkins University Press, 1990.

Stowe, Harriet Beecher. *The Minister's Wooing.* 1859. In *Three Novels: Uncle Tom's Cabin or, Life Among the Lowly; The Minister's Wooing; Oldtown Folks,* ed. Kathryn Kish Sklar, 521–876. New York: Library of America–Literary Classics of the United States, 1982.

———. *Uncle Tom's Cabin; or, Life Among the Lowly.* 1852. In *Three Novels: Uncle Tom's Cabin or, Life Among the Lowly; The Minister's Wooing; Oldtown Folks,* ed. Kathryn Kish Sklar, 11–519. New York: Library of America–Literary Classics of the United States, 1982.

Swaim, Kathleen M. "'Come and Hear': Women's Puritan Evidences." In *American Women's Autobiography: Fea(s)ts of Memory,* ed. Margo Culley, 32–56. Madison: University of Wisconsin Press, 1992.

Szasz, Ferenc Morton. *The Divided Mind of Protestant America, 1880–1930.* University: University of Alabama Press, 1982.

Tamke, Susan S. *Make a Joyful Noise Unto the Lord: Hymns as a Reflection of Victorian Social Attitudes.* Athens: Ohio University Press, 1978.

Taves, Ann. "Self and God in the Early Published Memoirs of New England Women." In *American Women's Autobiography: Fea(s)ts of Memory,* ed. Margo Culley, 57–74. Madison: University of Wisconsin Press, 1992.

Taylor, Edward. "Huswifery." *The Poems of Edward Taylor.* Ed. Donald E. Stanford, 467. New Haven: Yale University Press, 1960.

Taylor, William. *The Model Preacher: Comprised in a Series of Letters Illustrating the Best Mode of Preaching the Gospel.* Cincinnati, 1860.

Theriot, Nancy M. *The Biosocial Construction of Femininity: Mothers and Daughters in Nineteenth-Century America.* Contributions in Women's Studies 93. New York: Greenwood Press, 1988.

Thoreau, Henry David. *Walden.* 1854. Ed. J. Lyndon Shanley. *The Writings of Henry D. Thoreau.* Princeton: Princeton University Press, 1971.

Tillett, Wilbur F., and Charles S. Nutter. *The Hymns and Hymn Writers of the Church: An Annotated Edition of "The Methodist Hymnal."* Nashville: Smith and Lamar, 1913.

Tompkins, Jane. Afterword to *The Wide, Wide World,* by Susan Warner, 584–608. New York: Feminist Press, 1987.

———. *Sensational Designs: The Cultural Work of American Fiction 1790–1860.* New York: Oxford University Press, 1985.

Walker, Robert H., and Dewey D. Wallace, Jr. Introduction to *The Social Christian Novel,* by Robert Glenn Wright, xi–xviii. Contributions in American Studies 93. New York: Greenwood, 1989.

Warner, Susan. *The Wide, Wide World.* 1850. New York: Feminist Press, 1987.

Warner, Susan, and Anna B. Warner. *Say and Seal.* 2 vols. Philadelphia: Lippincott, 1860.

Welter, Barbara. "The Cult of True Womanhood: 1820–1860." *American Quarterly* 18 (1966): 151–74.

Welty, Eudora. *One Writer's Beginnings.* New York: Warner–Harvard University Press, 1983.

Whittle, D. W., ed. *Memoirs of Philip D. Bliss.* New York: A. S. Barnes, 1897.

Wilder, Laura Ingalls. *On the Banks of Plum Creek.* 1937. New York: Harper Trophy–HarperCollins, 1971.

Williamson, Dana. "East/West Youth Evangelism Conferences Draw 5,600." *Baptist Messenger,* 14 January 1993: 3–4.

Index